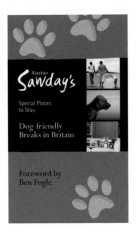

Alastair
Sawday's

Special Places
to Stay

Dog-friendly
Breaks in Britain

Foreword by
Ben Fogle

Alastair
Sawday's

Special Places
to Stay

British
Bed & Breakfast

"The B&B bible."
The Times

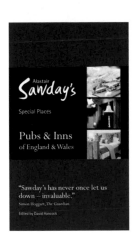

Alastair
Sawday's

Special Places

Pubs & Inns
of England & Wales

"Sawday's has never once let us
down – invaluable."
Simon Hoggart, The Guardian

Edited by David Hancock

Alastair
Sawday's

Special Places
to Stay

Italy

"A great resource to find that
extra-special place to stay."
The Times

Alastair
Sawday's

Special Places to Stay

Fourteenth edition
Copyright © 2012
Alastair Sawday Publishing Co. Ltd
Published in October 2012
ISBN-13: 978-1-906136-59-8

Alastair Sawday Publishing Co. Ltd,
The Old Farmyard, Yanley Lane,
Long Ashton, Bristol BS41 9LR, UK
Tel: +44 (0)1275 395430
Email: info@sawdays.co.uk
Web: www.sawdays.co.uk

The Globe Pequot Press,
P. O. Box 480, Guilford,
Connecticut 06437, USA
Tel: +1 203 458 4500
Email: info@globepequot.com
Web: www.globepequot.com

Series Editor Alastair Sawday
Editor Tom Bell
Assistant to Editor Joanne Hayers
Editorial Director Annie Shillito
Senior Editor Jo Boissevain
Production Coordinator Helen Burke
Photo Editor Alec Studerus
Inspections Tom Bell
Writing Tom Bell
Sales & Marketing & PR 01275 395433
*And thanks to those who did an inspection
or write-up or two.*

*We have made every effort to ensure the accuracy
of the information in this book at the time of
going to press. However, we cannot accept
any responsibility for any loss, injury or
inconvenience resulting from the use of
information contained therein.*

Alastair Sawday has asserted his right to be identified
as the author of this work.

Maps: Maidenhead Cartographic Services
Printing: Butler, Tanner & Dennis, Frome
UK distribution: The Travel Alliance, Bath
Production: The Content Works

Alastair Sawday's

Special Places to Stay

British
Hotels & Inns

4 Contents

I write at a time of great uncertainty for the country's small hotels. This is worrying, because the finest of them are beacons of civilisation in a finance-obsessed world. The lovely small hotels that we celebrate in this book are the very antithesis of the monolithic chains, the investor-driven 'hospitality' centres, the fashionable outposts of privilege. They need us, and deserve our support.

Apparently it is now common to treat the motorway drive to, say, the Lake District as an opportunity to negotiate, to pit one small hotel against another. Husband steers as wife wields the mobile phone, driving bargains ever lower. Discount sites offer silly rates into which hotels are trapped, and the final cost will be the loss of some of our finest. Compare how we seek bargains in supermarkets, only to weep when the last butcher closes. Is it too much to ask that we become

Photo: Tom Germain

conscious of our own roles in the losses around us?

So let us take our best beloveds away for those wonderful old-fashioned weeks and weekends that we can still read about in books. In these hotels, run with old-fashioned commitment and spanking new ideas, you can find picnic hampers, rugs, cocktails, comfort, kindness and a G&T at your elbow when you enter, back from some wet, windy afternoon walk. You will sink into sofas in front of fires, tease the ears of the resident dog, idle through languorous breakfasts, slip back into an older slowness. More than ever do we need these moments. Let us throw off the shackles of the 'information age' and settle into gentle hotel oblivion. I love the quote by Fran Lebowitz: "I am not the sort who wants to go back to the land; I am the sort who wants to go back to the hotel."

I should not, however, mislead you. Hundreds of Britain's best small hotels are as up-to-the-minute as an iPad, and as exquisitely connected. They are agile and imaginative, keen to explore new ideas. They, too, are having a hard time.

May I exhort you, dear reader, to ramp up your plans to escape to a small hotel, to bring forward your small extravagances? Put aside the new lawnmower and the decking, and take off to a small hotel. You won't regret it.

Alastair Sawday

It's simple. There are no rules, no boxes to tick. We choose places that we like and are fiercely subjective in our choices. We also recognise that one person's idea of special is not necessarily someone else's so there is a huge variety of places, and prices, in this book.

Those who are familiar with our Special Places series know that we look for comfort, originality, authenticity, and reject the anonymous and the banal. The way guests are treated comes as high on our list as the setting, the architecture, the atmosphere and the food.

Inspections

We visit every place in the guide to get a feel for how both hotel and owner tick. We don't take a clipboard and we don't have a list of what is acceptable and what is not. Instead, we chat for an hour or so with the owner or manager and look round. It's all very informal, but it gives us an excellent idea of who would enjoy staying there. If the visit happens to be the last of the day, we may stay the night. Once in the book, properties are re-inspected regularly, so that we can keep things fresh and accurate.

Feedback

In between inspections we rely on feedback from our army of readers, as well as from staff members who are encouraged to visit properties across the series. This feedback is invaluable to us and we always follow up on comments.

So do tell us whether your stay has been a joy or not, if the atmosphere was great or stuffy, the owners and staff cheery or bored. The accuracy of the book depends on what you, and our inspectors, tell us. A lot of the new entries in each edition are recommended by our readers, so

Photo: Drunken Duck Inn, entry 60

keep telling us about new places you've discovered too. Please use the forms on our website at www.sawdays.co.uk.

However, please do not tell us if your starter was cold, or the bedside light broken. Tell the owner, immediately, and get them to do something about it. Most owners, or staff, are more than happy to correct problems and will bend over backwards to help. Far better than bottling it up and then writing to us a week later!

Subscriptions

Owners pay to appear in this guide. Their fee goes towards the high costs of inspecting, of producing an illustrated book and of developing our website. We only include places that we find special: it is not possible for anyone to buy their way onto these pages. Nor is it possible for the owner to write their own description. We will say if the bedrooms

are small, or if a main road is near. We do our best to avoid misleading people.

Disclaimer

We make no claims to pure objectivity in choosing these places. They are here simply because we like them. Our opinions and tastes are ours alone and this book is a statement of them; we hope you will share them. We have done our utmost to get our facts right but apologise unreservedly for any mistakes that may have crept in.

You should know that we don't check such things as fire alarms, swimming pool security or any other regulation with which owners of properties receiving paying guests should comply. This is the responsibility of the owners. At some of our smaller places – particularly our inns - you should request a contact number for emergencies if staff are not present overnight.

Photo: Penbontbren, entry 310

Finding the right place for you

All these places are special in one way or another. All have been visited and then written about honestly so that you can take what you want and leave the rest. Those of you who swear by Sawday's trust our write-ups precisely because we don't have a blanket standard; we include places simply because we like them. But we all have different priorities, so do read the descriptions carefully and pick out the places where you will be comfortable.

Maps

Each property is flagged with its entry number on the maps at the front. These maps are a great starting point for planning your trip, but please don't use them as anything other than a general guide – use a decent road map for real navigation. Most places will send you detailed instructions once you have booked your stay.

Symbols

These are explained at the very back of the book. They are based on the information given to us by the owners. However, things do change: bikes may be under repair or a new pool may have been put in. Please use the symbols as a guide rather than an absolute statement of fact and double-check anything that is important to you – owners occasionally bend their own rules, so it's worth asking if you may take your child or dog even if they don't have the symbol.

Wheelchair access ɢ – Some hotels are keen to accept wheelchair users into their hotels and have made provision for them. However, this does not mean that wheelchair users will always be met with a perfect landscape. You may encounter ramps, a shallow step, gravelled paths, alternative routes into some rooms, a

Photo: Lords of the Manor, entry 120

bathroom (not a wet room), perhaps even a lift. In short, there may be the odd hindrance and we urge you to call and make sure you will get what you need.

Limited mobility – The limited mobility symbol 🏃 shows those places where at least one bedroom and bathroom is accessible without using stairs. The symbol is designed to satisfy those who walk slowly, with difficulty, or with the aid of a stick. A wheelchair may be able to navigate some areas, but in our opinion these places are not fully wheelchair friendly. If you use a chair for longer distances, but are not too bad over shorter distances, you'll probably be OK; again, please ring and ask. There may be a step or two, a bath or a shower with a tray in a cubicle, a good distance between the car park and your room, slippery flagstones or a tight turn.

Children – The 🌱 symbol shows places which are happy to accept children of all ages. This does not mean that they will necessarily have cots, high chairs, etc. If an owner welcomes children but only those above a certain age, we have put these details at the end of their write-up. These houses do not have the child symbol, but even these folk may accept your younger child at quiet times. If you want to get out and about in the evenings, check when you book whether there are any babysitting services. Even very small places can sometimes organise this for you.

Pets – Our 🐕 symbol shows places which are happy to accept pets. It means they can sleep in the bedroom with you, but not on the bed. It's really important to get this one right before you arrive, as many places make you keep dogs in the car. Check carefully: Prince's emotional wellbeing may depend on it.

Owners' pets – The 🐈 symbol is given when the owners have their own pet on the premises. It may not be a cat! But it is there to warn you that you may be greeted by a dog, serenaded by a parrot, or indeed sat upon by a cat.

Photo: The Wheatsheaf Inn, entry 121

Types of places

Hotels can vary from huge, humming and slick to those with only a few rooms that are run by owners at their own pace. In some you may not get room service or have your bags carried in and out. In smaller hotels there may be a fixed menu for dinner with very little choice, so if you have dishes that leave you cold, it's important to say so when you book your meal. If you decide to stay at an inn remember that they can be noisy, especially at weekends. If these things are important to you, then do check when you book.

Rooms

Bedrooms – These are described as double, twin, single, family or suite. A double may contain a bed which is anything from 135cm wide to 180cm wide. A twin will contain two single beds (usually 90cm wide). A suite will have a separate sitting area, but it may not be in a different room. Family rooms can vary in size, as can the number of beds they hold, so do ask. And do not assume that every bedroom has a TV.

Bathrooms – All bedrooms have their own bathrooms unless we say that they don't. If you have your own bathroom but you have to leave the room to get to it we describe it as 'separate'. There are very few places in the book that have shared bathrooms and they are usually reserved for members of the same party. Again, we state this clearly.

Photo: The Royal Oak Inn, entry 222

Meals

Breakfast is included in the room price unless otherwise stated. If only a continental breakfast is offered, we let you know.

Some places serve lunch, most do Sunday lunch (often very well-priced), the vast majority offer dinner. In some places you can content yourself with bar meals, in others you can feast on five courses. Most offer three courses for £25-£35, either table d'hôte or à la carte. Some have tasting menus, very occasionally you eat communally. Some large hotels (and some posh private houses) will bring dinner to your room if you prefer, or let you eat in the garden by candlelight. Always ask for what you want and sometimes, magically, it happens.

Prices and minimum stays

We quote the lowest price per night for two people in low season to the highest price in high season. Only a few places have designated single rooms; if no single rooms are listed, the price we quote refers to single occupancy of a double room. In many places prices rise even higher when local events bring people flooding to the area, a point worth remembering when heading to Cheltenham for the racing or Glyndebourne for the opera.

The half-board price quoted is per person per night and includes dinner, usually three courses. Mostly you're offered a table d'hôte menu. Occasionally you eat à la carte and may find some dishes carry a small supplement. There are often great deals to be had, mostly mid-week in low season.

Most hotels do not accept one-night bookings at weekends. Small country hotels are rarely full during the week and the weekend trade keeps them going. If you ring in March for a Saturday night in July, you won't get it. If you ring at the last moment you may. Some places insist on three-night stays on bank holidays.

Photo: Y Meirionnydd, entry 318

Booking and cancellation

Most places ask for a deposit at the time of booking, either by cheque or credit/debit card. If you cancel – depending on how much notice you give – you can lose all or part of this deposit unless your room is re-let.

It is reasonable for hotels to take a deposit to secure a booking; they have learnt that if they don't, the commitment of the guest wanes and they may fail to turn up.

Some cancellation policies are more stringent than others. It is also worth noting that some owners will take the money directly from your credit/debit card without contacting you to discuss it. So ask them to explain their cancellation policy clearly before booking so you understand exactly where you stand; it may well avoid a nasty surprise. And consider taking out travel insurance (with a cancellation clause) if you're concerned.

Arrivals and departures

Housekeeping is usually done by 2pm, and your room will usually be available by mid-afternoon. Normally you will have to wave goodbye to it between 10am and 11am. Sometimes one can pay to linger. Some inns are closed between 3pm and 6pm, so do try and agree an arrival time in advance or you may find nobody there.

Closed

When given in months this means for the whole of the month stated. So, 'Closed: November–March' means closed from 1 November to 31 March.

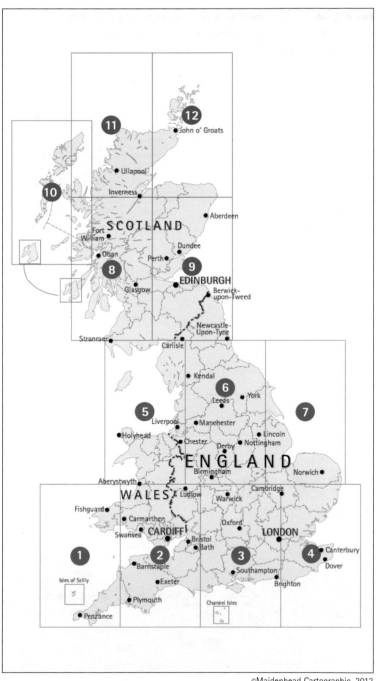

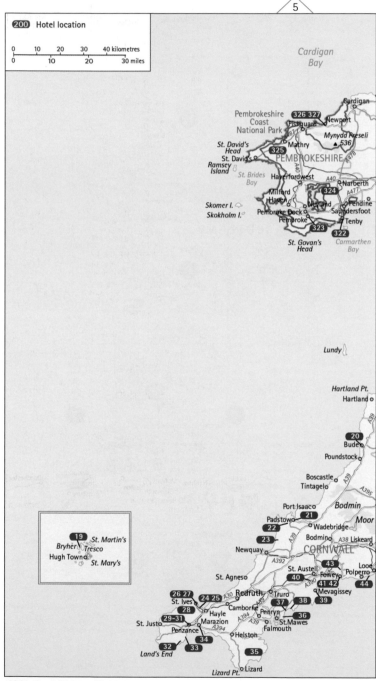

Map 2   15

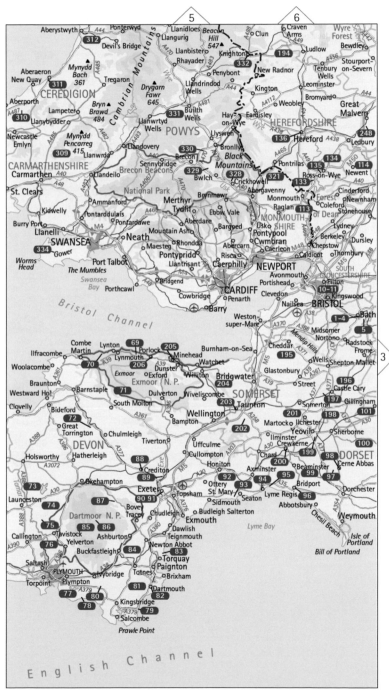

Halesowen · Bedworth · Desborough · Sawtry · Ramsey
Kidderminster · Solihull · COVENTRY · Rugby · Naseby · Rothwell · Thrapston · Kettering · Huntingdon · CAMBRIDGESHIRE
Bromsgrove · Kenilworth · Irthlingborough · Raunds · St. Ive
Redditch · Henley- · Warwick · Royal · Wellingborough · Rushden · Kimbolton
Droitwich · in-Arden · Leamington Spa · NORTHANTS
Alcester · Southam · Daventry · Northampton · St. Neots
Worcester · Stratford-upon-Avon · Byfield · Olney · Bedford · Potton
Pershore · Ettington · Towcester · Newport · Kempston · Biggleswade
Evesham · 127 128 · Banbury · Silverstone · Pagnell · BEDFORDSHIRE · Royston
126 · Chipping Campden · Brackley · Wolverton · Ampthill · Baldock
Broadway · 125 · Moreton- · Buckingham · Milton · Bletchley · Letchworth
Tewkesbury · 119 · 124 · in-Marsh · Adderbury · Keynes · Leighton · Hitchin · Stevenage
Stow-on- · Chipping · Deddington · Buzzard · Dunstable · Luton · HERTS
115 · 116-118 · the-Wold · Norton · Winslow · BUCKS · Harpenden · Ware
120 · Charlbury · Bicester · Aylesbury · Hemel · Hertford
Cheltenham · 177 · 178 · 180 181 · 12 · Tring · Hempstead · St. Albans
Gloucester · 122 · 179 · Woodstock · Kidlington · Princes · Chesham · Amersham · Watford · Cheshunt
Painswick · 121 · Northleach · 183 · 182 · Burford · Oxford · 186 · Thame · Risborough · High · Bushey
GLOUCESTERSHIRE · Witney · 187 · Wheatley · Wycombe · Beaconsfield
Stroud · Cirencester · 123 · 184 · Fairford · 185 · Cowley · Abingdon · Marlow · LONDON
Nailsworth · Lechlade · Dorchester · Henley- · 158-164
Tetbury · Cricklade · Highworth · Didcot · Wallingford · on-Thames · Slough
Malmesbury · Swindon · Wantage · Goring · Maidenhead · 6 · Heathrow
240 · 241 · Wootton · Lambourn · Pangbourne · Reading · Windsor · Staines
Chippenham · Bassett · Hungerford · Newbury · Ascot · Esher · Epsom
Corsham · Calne · Avebury · Thatcham · Bracknell · Sandhurst · Woking · Caterham
243 · 242 · Marlborough · Aldermaston · Camberley · Farnborough · SURREY · Reigate
Melksham · Burbage · Kingsclere · Basingstoke · Aldershot · Guildford · Dorking · Horley
Devizes · Whitchurch · Farnham · Godalming · Gatwick
Trowbridge · Vale of Pewsey · Andover · HAMPSHIRE · Alton · Liphook · Haslemere · Horsham · 226
Westbury · WILTSHIRE · North Tidworth · 132 · Petersfield · WEST SUSSEX · Hayward
Warminster · Salisbury · Amesbury · Stockbridge · Midhurst · Billingshurst · Heath
244 · 245 · Plain · Winchester · South · Pulborough · Burgess Hill
246 · Wilton · Salisbury · Romsey · Eastleigh · Downs · Arundel · 227
247 · Shaftesbury · Bishop's Waltham · 221 · 222 · 224 · BRIGHTON
102 · 103 · Fordingbridge · SOUTHAMPTON · Horndean · 225 · & HOVE
Blandford · Lyndhurst · Fareham · Havant · Chichester · Bognor · 7-9
Forum · 104 · Ringwood · New Forest · Gosport · South · 223 · Regis · Worthing
Wimborne · Brockenhurst · Fawley · Hayling · PORTSMOUTH · Selsey · Littlehampton
Minster · 129 · 130 · Lymington · Cowes · Ryde · 139 140 · Selsey Bill
Poole · 107 · 131 · Yarmouth · Newport · Seaview
106 · Christchurch · ISLE OF · Sandown
Wareham · BOURNEMOUTH · 138 · WIGHT · Shanklin
Wool · 105 · Isle of · The Needles · St. Catherine's · Ventnor
Purbeck · Point
Swanage
Durlston
Head

CHANNEL · 264
ISLANDS · Alderney
Guernsey · Herm
Sark
265

Jersey

©Maidenhead Cartographic, 2012

Map 4   17

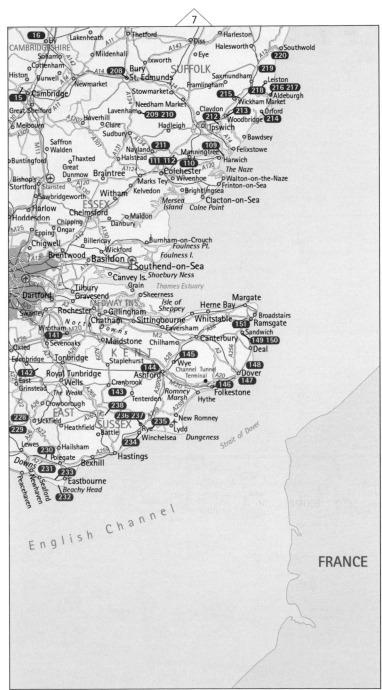

8   9

Stranraer
Portpatrick Glenluce Wigtown
276 The Rhins Luce Bay The Machars
Port William Whithorn
Drummore Wigtown Bay
Mull of Galloway Burrow Head

Gatehouse of Fleet Dalbeattie
277
Kirkcudbright
Solway Firth Wigton Carlisle
Aspatria A596
Maryport A595
Cockermouth 65 CUMBRIA
Workington 64 Penrith
Keswick A66
Whitehaven 63 Helvellyn Ullswater
Cleator 62 949
St. Bees Head Moor Scafell Cumbrian Mountains Lake District
St. Bees Egremont Pike Grasmere
978 61 National Park
59 Ambleside
60 54-58
Windermere District
A595 53
Broughton- 51 Newby
in-Furness 52 Bridge
Millom Milnthorpe
Dalton-in-Furness A590 50 49
Barrow- Carnforth
in-Furness Morecambe
Isle of Morecambe Heysham
Walney Bay 152

Point of Ayre

A3 Ramsey
Isle of Man A2
Peel A4 Laxey A1
A3 A5 Douglas
Port Erin Castletown

Irish   Sea

Fleetwood
Cleveleys Garstang
Poulton-le-Fylde Thornton
BLACKPOOL 153 M55
Lytham St. Anne's Kirkham
A59
Southport
Ormskirk
Formby Skelmersdale
Liverpool Crosby Kirkby
Bay Wallasey St. Helens
Amlwch Hoylake LIVERPOOL
ANGLESEY Great Birkenhead Widnes
Holyhead Ormes Prestatyn Heswall Runcorn
Valley ISLE Head Colwyn Rhyl A548 Neston
Holy Benllech 313 Bay Rhuddlan Helsby
Island Llandudno Abergele Holywell Flint
Rhosneigr 308 Beaumaris Llanfairfechan St. Asaph Chester
Llangefni Bangor Conwy Denbigh FLINTSHIRE
Menai Bethesda CONWY 314 Mold Buckley
Caernarfon Bridge Llanrwst Bylchau A525 Llay Holt
Caernarfon 316 Capel Curig Betws-y-Coed Clwydian Range Ruthin A51
Bay Snowdon Pentrefoelas DENBIGHSHIRE Wrexham Malpas
1085 A5 Dee Llangollen Ruabon
Nefyn Blaenau Corwen A5 Chirk Overton
Lleyn Peninsula Criccieth Ffestiniog Ellesmere
Pwllheli Ffestiniog Snowdonia 191 Whittington Wem
317 Abersoch Porthmadog Trawsfynydd Bala A499 A5
Aberdaron Harlech National Bala 315 Oswestry 192
Tremadog 318-320 Park Lake 333 Llanfyllin Shrewsbury
Bardsey Bay GWYNEDD Vyrnwy A458
Island Doigellau A483 Welshpool Minsterley
Barmouth A470 Llanfair SHROPSHIRE
Barmouth Bay Cader Mallwyd Caereinion Church
Idris A487 Montgomery Stretton
892 A493 Cambrian Mountains A489 A49
Tywyn Machynlleth Caersws Bishop's
Aberdovey Moelfre Severn 193 Castle
Borth Talybont 468 Newtown

Map 6   19

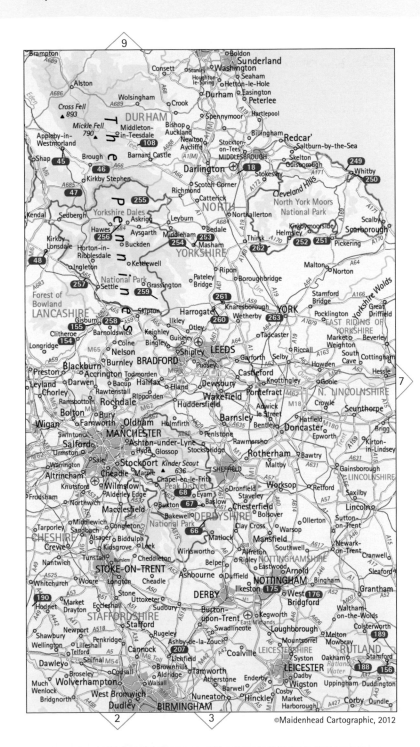

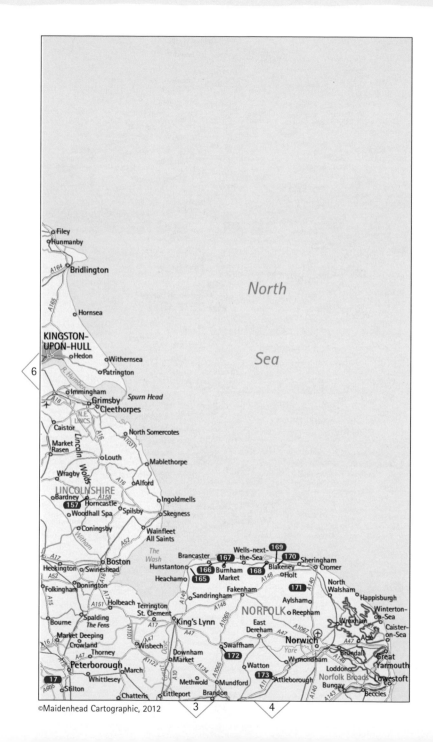

North

Sea

Filey
Hunmanby
A164 Bridlington
A165
Hornsea
KINGSTON-
UPON-HULL
R. Humber
Hedon   Withernsea
Patrington
6
Immingham   Spurn Head
A18   Grimsby
N.E.   Cleethorpes
LINCS.
Caistor   North Somercotes
A16
Market
Rasen
Lincoln   Louth   Mablethorpe
Wragby   A16   Alford
Wolds
LINCOLNSHIRE
Bardney   A158
157 Horncastle   Ingoldmells
Woodhall Spa   Spilsby   Skegness
Coningsby
Witham   Wainfleet
All Saints
A52   Wells-next- 169
The   Brancaster 167 the-Sea 170
A17   Wash   168 Sheringham
Boston   Hunstanton   Burnham Blakeney Cromer
Heckington Swineshead   166 Market 168 Holt
A52   Heacham 165 A148
Folkingham   Donington   Fakenham   North
A15   A17   Walsham Happisburgh
Holbeach   Sandringham 171
A151   Terrington Aylsham Winterton-
Bourne   Spalding St. Clement   A148 on-Sea
The Fens   NORFOLK Reepham Caister-
A17 King's Lynn A1065 East Wroxham on-Sea
Market Deeping   Dereham A47 Acle
A16 Crowland A47   Swaffham Norwich A47 Great
Thorney Wisbech   Yare Brundall Yarmouth
Peterborough A1122 Downham 172 Watton Wymondham Loddon
March   Market A134 173 Norfolk Broads Lowestoft
17 Whittlesey A10 Methwold Mundford Attleborough Bungay
A605 Stilton Chatteris Littleport Brandon A11 A140 A143 Beccles

Map 8

21

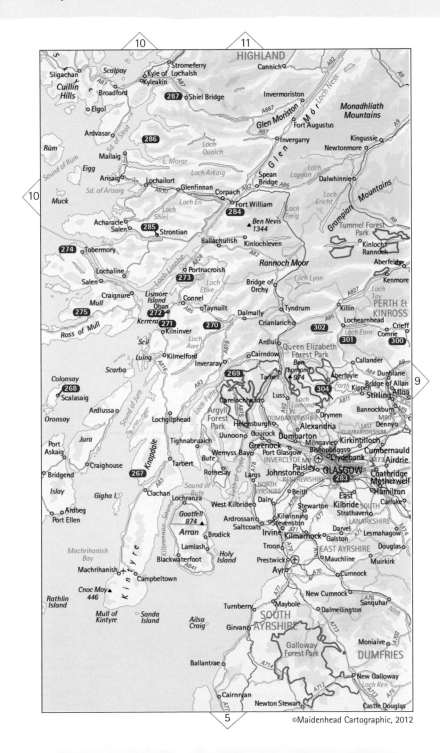

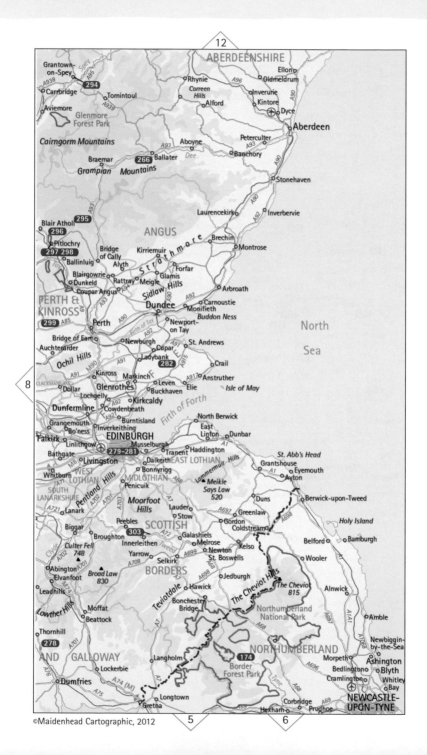

Map 10   23

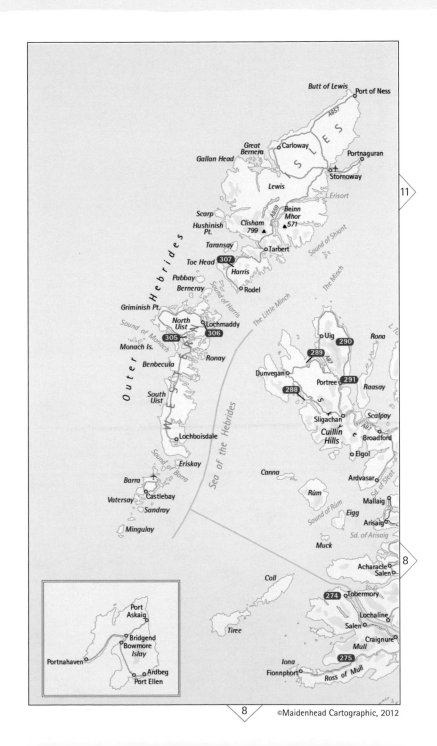

Butt of Lewis Port of Ness

A857

L E S

Great
Bernera Carloway
Gallan Head   Portnaguran

S   Stornoway

Lewis   L.Erisort

11

Scarp   Beinn
Mhor
Hushinish   Clisham ▲571
Pt.   799 ▲

Taransay
Toe Head 307   ▲ Tarbert
Harris   Sound of Shiant

Pabbay
Berneray   ○ Rodel   The Minch

H
e
b
r
i
d
e
s

Griminish Pt.   The Little Minch

Sound of Monach   North
Uist ○ Lochmaddy
305   ○ Uig 290   Rona
Monach Is.   306   289
Benbecula   Ronay   Dunvegan ○   291   Raasay
O   Portree ○
u   288
t   South   Sligachan ○   Scalpay
e   Uist   Cuillin   e   Broadford
r   Hills   ○ Elgol
Lochboisdale ○

Sound of Harris

Sea of the Hebrides

Eriskay   Canna   Ardvasar ○

Barra   Rùm   Mallaig ○
Vatersay Castlebay ○   Eigg
Sandray ○   Arisaig ○
Sound of Barra   Sound of Rùm Sd. of Arisaig
Mingulay ○
Muck   8

Acharacle ○
Salen

Coll   274 ○ Tobermory

Lochaline
Port   Salen ○
Askaig ○   Tiree   Craignure ○
Bridgend ○   Mull
Bowmore ○
Islay   Iona   275
Portnahaven ○   Ardbeg ○   Fionnphort ○ Ross of Mull
Port Ellen

©Maidenhead Cartographic, 2012

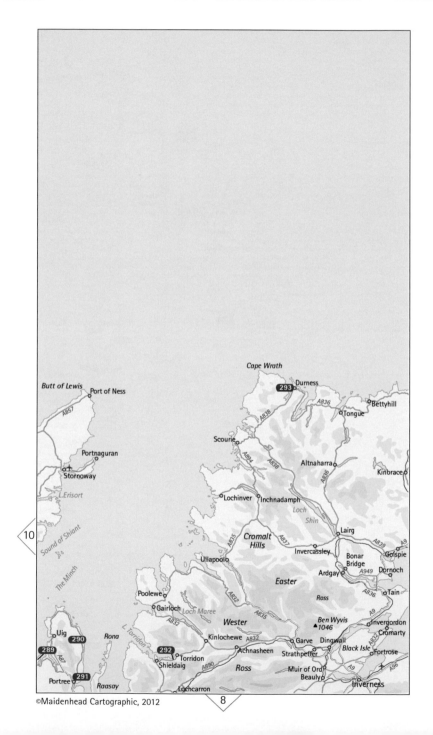

Cape Wrath

Butt of Lewis   Port of Ness   **293** Durness

A857   A836   Bettyhill

A838   Tongue

Scourie

Portnaguran   A894   A838   Altnaharra   Kinbrace

Stornoway   A836

L Erisort   Lochinver   Inchnadamph

Loch Shin

Sound of Shiant   Cromalt Hills   A837   Lairg   A839   A9

10   A835   Invercassley   Golspie

The Minch   Ullapool   Bonar Bridge   Dornoch

Ardgay   A949

Easter   A836   Tain

Poolewe   A832   Ross   A9

Gairloch   Loch Maree   A835   Ben Wyvis   Invergordon

Uig   **290**   Rona   Wester   ▲1046   Cromarty

L Torridon   A832   Kinlochewe   A832   Garve   Dingwall   Black Isle   Fortrose

289   A87   **292**   Torridon   Achnasheen   Strathpeffer

Shieldaig   A890   Ross   Muir of Ord   A9   A96

291   Beauly

Portree   Raasay   Lochcarron   Inverness

Map 12

25

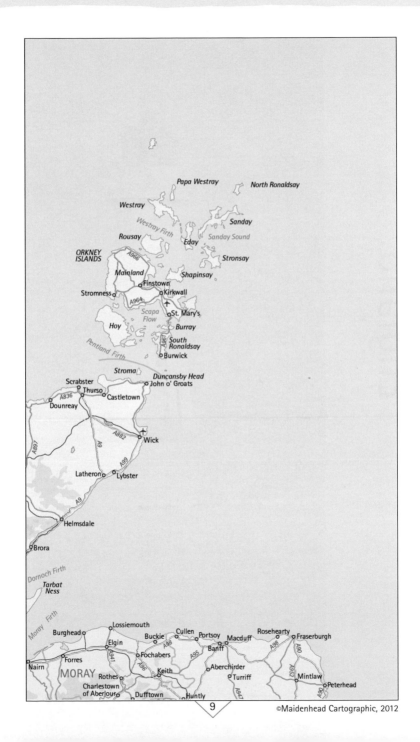

©Maidenhead Cartographic, 2012

England

SACO Bath Serviced Apartments

Fabulous Bath is England's loveliest city, Georgian to its bone. It's built of mellow golden stone, so wander its streets for elegant squares, beautiful gardens, pavement cafés, delicious delis and the imperious Roman Baths (there's a spa if you want to take a dip). Close to the river, bang in the middle of town, these serviced apartments bask behind a beautifully restored Regency façade – look out for the pillared entrances. Inside you find a collection of airy studios and apartments, all of which come with sparkling kitchens fully stocked with ovens, dishwashers, washer/dryers, microwaves, fridges, and freezers. Some are small, some are big. If you need a bolthole for a night, a base for a fun-filled weekend or a cool pad for a week, you'll find one here. You get white walls, Italian designer furniture, flat-screen TVs, CD players and good-sized bathrooms. There's a lift to whisk you up and away, 24-hour reception, and high-speed broadband connection throughout. Supermarkets are close, but there are masses of great restaurants on your doorstep, too. *Minimum two nights at weekends.*

Price	Studios £108–£126. Apt for 2, £150–£174. Apt for 4, £204–£240.
Rooms	43: 9 studios, 29 apartments for 2, 5 apartments for 4.
Meals	Self-catered. Restaurants within 0.5 miles.
Closed	Never.
Directions	In centre of town, 5-minute walk from station. Full directions on booking.

Karen Sheppard
37 St James's Parade,
Bath BA1 1UH

Tel	+44 (0)1225 486540
Email	bath@sacoapartments.com
Web	bath.sacoapartments.com

Entry 1   Map 2

Brooks Guesthouse Bath

Owners and staff go out of their way to make your stay here special. Add to this comfy rooms, excellent breakfasts and a central position and you have a great base from which to explore Bath. The house is close to Victoria Park (hot-air balloon rides, children's playground, botanical gardens) and just below the stupendous Royal Crescent, a three-minute walk. Inside, an easy style flows. There's a sitting room in vibrant yellow, an honesty bar if you fancy a drink and a breakfast room for smoked salmon and scrambled eggs or the full cooked works; there are daily specials, free-range eggs, while the meat is reared in Somerset. Bedrooms are split between two Victorian townhouses. A couple are small, a couple are big, most are somewhere in between. All have a similar style: big colours, good beds, crisp white linen, excellent shower rooms; two have baths. A map of town, compiled by guests, shows the top ten sights: don't miss the Roman Baths or the Thermae Spa. One of the best pubs in Bath is around the corner and serves great food. Expect a little noise from the road.

Price	£75–£150. Family rooms £120–£160. Singles from £70.
Rooms	21: 10 twins/doubles, 7 doubles, 2 singles, 2 family rooms.
Meals	Restaurants close by.
Closed	Christmas Day.
Directions	Head west on A4 from centre of town. On right before Victoria Park, below Royal Avenue.

Carla & Andrew Brooks
1 Crescent Gardens,
Bath BA1 2NA

Tel	+44 (0)1225 425543
Email	info@brooksguesthouse.com
Web	www.brooksguesthouse.com

Bath Paradise House Hotel

You'll be hard pressed to find better views in Bath. They draw you out as soon as you enter these cosy, intimate, Georgian interiors, while the 180-degree panorama from the garden is a dazzling advertisement for this World Heritage city. The Royal Crescent and the Abbey are floodlit at night; in summer, hot-air balloons float by low enough for you to hear the roar of the burners. Nearly all the rooms make full use of the view – the best have bay windows – and all have a soft, luxurious, country feel with contemporary fabrics and white waffle robes in fabulous bathrooms. There are also two garden rooms in a smart extension that planners took years to approve; it's quite an achievement, and in keeping with the original Bath stone house. The whole place has glass in all the right places, especially the sitting room, with its lovely stone-arched French windows that pull in the light. Don't miss afternoon tea in summer in the half-acre garden, a perfect place to lose yourself in the view. The occasional peal of bells comes for a nearby church. The Thermae Spa with its rooftop pool is a must. *7-minute walk down to centre.*

Price	£120-£175. Singles £75-£120.
Rooms	11: 3 doubles, 3 twins, 1 family room, 4 four-posters.
Meals	Restaurants in Bath 0.5 miles.
Closed	24 & 25 December.
Directions	From train station one-way system to Churchill Bridge. A367 exit from r'bout up hill; 0.75 miles, left at Andrews estate agents. Left down hill into cul-de-sac; on left.

David & Annie Lanz
86-88 Holloway,
Bath BA2 4PX

Tel	+44 (0)1225 317723
Email	info@paradise-house.co.uk
Web	www.paradise-house.co.uk

Villa Magdala

Villa Magdala is one of those lovely places that scores top marks across the board. You're pretty much in the middle of town, but nicely hidden away on a side street opposite a park. Then, there's a batch of lovely bedrooms, all recently refurbished in great style. Add to this staff on hand to book restaurants, balloon flights or day trips to Stonehenge and you have a perfect base. You're a five-minute stroll from magnificent Pulteney Bridge; the station isn't much further, so leave your car at home and come by train; you can hire bikes in town, then follow a towpath along the river and into the country. Back home, there's tea and cake on arrival, buck's fizz for breakfast, even bats and balls for children who want to go to the park. Breakfast is served in an airy dining room: smoked salmon and free-range scrambled eggs, buttermilk pancakes, the full cooked works. Smart rooms have big beds, pretty wallpaper, small armchairs and lovely sparkling bathrooms. Excellent restaurants wait close by. Don't miss the Christmas market or the magnificent Thermae Spa. *Minimum stay two nights at weekends.*

Price	£120-£170. Singles from £110.
Rooms	20: 9 doubles, 11 twins/doubles.
Meals	Restaurant within 500m.
Closed	24-29 December.
Directions	West into Bath on A4. Left into Cleveland Place (signed Through Traffic & University). Over bridge, 2nd right and on right opposite park.

Amanda & John Willmott
Henrietta Street,
Bath BA2 6LX

Tel	+44 (0)1225 466329
Email	enquiries@villamagdala.co.uk
Web	www.villamagdala.co.uk

Wheelwrights Arms

In winter grab the table in front of the ancient fire where the wheelwright worked his magic; in summer, skip outside for a pint on the terrace. You're in the country, two miles south of Bath, so drop down to the nearby Kennet & Avon canal and cycle or walk through glorious country into the city. The Wheelwrights dates to 1750. Inside, contemporary colours mix with soft stone walls and exposed timber frames. Logs are piled high in the alcoves, the daily papers are left on the bar and the food is delicious, perhaps seafood tempura, grilled lemon sole, warm treacle tart with stem ginger ice cream; in summer you can eat in the garden illuminated by lights in the trees. Airy bedrooms in the wheelwright's erstwhile annexe come in fresh, original style. Expect dark wood floors, shuttered windows, old-style radiators, flat-screen TVs. Wooden beds are covered in immaculate linen, white bathrooms come with robes and L'Occitane potions. The inn holds two season tickets for Bath Rugby Club. Guests can take them at cost price, so book early. Walkers are very welcome. *Minimum two nights at weekends.*

Price	£100–£150. Singles from £80.
Rooms	7: 5 doubles, 1 twin, 1 single.
Meals	Lunch, 2 courses, £11. Sunday lunch from £11.90. Dinner, 3 courses, about £25.
Closed	Never.
Directions	A36 south from Bath for 3 miles, then right, signed Monkton Combe. Over x-roads, into village, on left.

David Munn
Church Lane, Monkton Combe,
Bath BA2 7HB

Tel	+44 (0)1225 722287
Email	bookings@wheelwrightsarms.co.uk
Web	www.wheelwrightsarms.co.uk

The Christopher Hotel

The Christopher, an old coaching inn, sits quietly on Eton High Street, with the school running away to the north and Windsor Castle a stroll across the river. Many years ago the hotel stood opposite the school, but was politely asked to move as too many boys were popping in for refreshments; remarkably, it obliged. These days colour and comfort come in equal measure. A brasserie-style restaurant and a half-panelled bar stand either side of the coach arch and both come in similar vein with warm colours, stripped floors and big windows that look onto the street. In the restaurant you can stop for a bite, perhaps crispy duck salad, fillet of sea bass, classic Eton Mess (what else?); in the bar you'll find sofas, armchairs and champagne by the glass. Bedrooms – some in the main house, others stretching out at the back in motel-style – have comfy beds, padded heads, top linen, a sofa if there's room, trouser presses and all the rest. Those in the main house have the character, three are in the old magistrate's court, all have internet access and adequate bathrooms. Windsor, the castle and the Great Park wait.

Price	£158–£200. Suites £216–£260. Singles from £114.
Rooms	34: 21 twins/doubles, 4 suites, 9 singles.
Meals	Breakfast £5–£14. Lunch & dinner from £8.
Closed	Never.
Directions	M4 junc. 5, into Datchet, through to Eton & left onto High Street. On right. Free parking (limited spaces).

Janet Tregurtha
110 High Street, Eton,
Windsor SL4 6AN

Tel	+44 (0)1753 852359
Email	reservations@thechristopher.co.uk
Web	www.thechristopher.co.uk

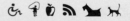

Drakes

Drakes has the lot: cool rooms, a funky bar, big sea views, the best food in town. It's stands across the road from Brighton beach with the famous pier a three-minute stroll. Inside, you find one of the chicest boutique hotels in the land. Bedrooms are exemplary. Eleven have free-standing baths in the room, while the list of must-haves is as long as your arm, from waffle bathrobes to White Company lotions. Yet what impresses most is the detail and workmanship. Handmade beds rest on carpets that are changed every year, contemporary plaster mouldings curl around ceilings like mountain terraces, Vi-Spring mattresses, wrapped in the crispest linen, are piled high with pillows. Don't worry if you can't afford the best rooms; others may be smaller and those at the back have city views, but all are fantastic and the attic rooms are as cute as could be; Kylie loved hers. As for the food, expect the best, perhaps half a dozen oysters, roast lamb with grilled kidney and pommes Anna, banana parfait with bitter chocolate sauce. The Lanes are close and packed with hip shops. *Minimum stay two nights at weekends.*

Price	£115–£275. Suite £295–£345.
Rooms	20: 16 doubles, 1 twin/double, 2 singles, 1 suite.
Meals	Breakfast £5–£12.50. Lunch from £29.95. Dinner from £39.95.
Closed	Never.
Directions	M23 & A23 into Brighton. At seafront, with pier in front, turn left up the hill. Drakes on left after 300 yds.

Richard Hayes
43-44 Marine Parade,
Brighton BN2 1PE

Tel   +44 (0)1273 696934
Email   info@drakesofbrighton.com
Web   www.drakesofbrighton.com

Kemp Townhouse

The sun rises over the sea – just at the end of the street. A big wheel spins on the beach, Brighton Pier is a breezy stroll and the cool restaurants and bars of Kemptown are around the corner; the rest of Brighton's colourful cornucopia is not much further away. This is a beautifully renovated Regency townhouse. Suave, spotless interiors comes as standard, filling the place with cool comfort. Walls shine in period colours, charcoal carpets run throughout, an Art Deco-style chandelier hangs in the dining room/bar. Bedrooms come in different shapes and sizes but all have the same graceful restraint: gorgeous bijou wet rooms, lovely linen, padded headboards, incredibly comfortable beds. You glimpse the sea from front-facing rooms (one has a free-standing bath). Spin down to the dining room for an excellent breakfast (proper orange juice, baskets of pâtisserie, American pancakes, the full cooked works) or drop in for a glass of wine 'on the house' before heading out for the evening. Impeccable service, stylish comfort, great breakfasts – and Brighton; all to be relished.

Price	£95–£185. Four-poster £195–£215. Singles from £75. Min. 2 nights at weekends.
Rooms	9: 6 doubles, 2 four-posters, 1 single.
Meals	Pubs/restaurants nearby.
Closed	Never.
Directions	South to seafront, then left at r'bout in front of pier. Uphill, past New Steine, then left at lights into Lower Rock Gardens. Right at lights; 1st right into Atlingworth. On left.

Paul Lantsbury & Robert Philpot
21 Atlingworth Street,
Brighton BN2 1PL
Tel   +44 (0)1273 681400
Email   reservations@kemptownhouse.com
Web   www.kemptownhousebrighton.com

brightonwave

A small, friendly, boutique B&B hotel in the epicentre of trendy Brighton. The beach and the pier are a two-minute walk, the bars and restaurants of St James Street are around the corner. An open-plan sitting room/dining room comes in cool colours with big suede sofas, fairy lights in the fireplace and ever-changing art on the walls. Bedrooms at the front are big and fancy, with huge padded headboards that fill the wall and deluge showers in sandstone bathrooms. Those at the back have been recently renovated in great style; they may be smaller, but so is their price and they come with spotless compact showers; if you're out more than in, why worry? All rooms have fat duvets, lush linen, flat-screen TVs and DVD/CD players; the lower-ground king-size has its own garden. Richard and Simon are easy-going and happy for guests to chill drinks in the kitchen (there are corkscrews in all the rooms). Breakfast, served late at weekends, offers pancakes, the full English or sautéed tarragon mushrooms on toast. Fabulous Brighton waits. *Minimum two nights at weekends.*

Price	£95–£185. Singles from £65.
Rooms	8: 4 twins/doubles, 3 doubles, 1 four-poster.
Meals	Restaurants nearby.
Closed	Rarely.
Directions	A23 to Brighton Pier roundabout at seafront; left towards Marina; 5th street on left. On-street parking vouchers £9 for 24 hours.

Richard Adams & Simon Throp
10 Madeira Place,
Brighton BN2 1TN

Tel	+44 (0)1273 676794
Email	info@brightonwave.co.uk
Web	www.brightonwave.co.uk

Brooks Guesthouse Bristol

Super rooms, irresistible prices and a great position in the middle of the old town make this funky hotel a great launch pad for England's loveliest city. You're close to the floating harbour, St Nicholas market stands directly outside, and there's a fabulous sun-trapping courtyard for inner-city peace. Inside: airy interiors, leather sofas, and walls of glass that open onto the courtyard. Free WiFi runs throughout, a computer is on hand for guests to use, and you can help yourself to drinks at the honesty bar. Breakfast is served leisurely – though if you're in a hurry you can take it with you – and you eat at pretty tables while watching the chef whisk up your scrambled eggs. Stylish bedrooms aren't huge, but nor is their price. You get super comfy beds, crisp white linen, Cole & Son wallpaper and iPod docks. Excellent travertine shower rooms have underfloor heating and White Company oils. Rooms at the back get noise from nearby bars, so ask for a room at the front if that matters. Bristol waits: the water, the Downs, Clifton's 'camera obscura', Brunel's spectacular suspension bridge.

Price	£79–£99. Triples £99–£149. Singles from £69.
Rooms	23: 17 doubles, 4 twins, 2 triples.
Meals	Restaurants on your doorstep.
Closed	Christmas Day.
Directions	Hotel entrance on St Nicholas Court, an alleyway marking the western flank of the covered market; it runs between St Nicholas St & Corn St.

Carla & Andrew Brooks
St Nicholas Court, Exchange Avenue,
Bristol BS1 1UB

Tel	+44 (0)117 930 0066
Email	info@brooksguesthousebristol.com
Web	www.brooksguesthousebristol.com

SACO Bristol Serviced Apartments – Broad Quay

SACO and their wonderful serviced apartments are going from strength to strength and here's the evidence: a fantastic new property down by the water in the middle of Bristol. So what do you get? Think cool hotel suites with sparkly kitchens thrown in for good measure. Walls of glass bring in the view, those at the front overlook the water, several have balconies that make the most of good weather. Prices are attractive too – good for business in the week (WiFi and parking) and great for weekends away (you breakfast whenever you want). You're in one of Britain's loveliest cities: stroll around the floating harbour, spin up the hill to Clifton, check out St Nicholas' market, or head off to the posh shops at Cabot Circus. Come back to stylish interiors: smartly tiled bathrooms, fully loaded kitchens, chic sofas in front of flat-screen TVs, comfy beds for a good night's sleep; studios are smaller, but nice and snug, perfect for weekends. There are local shops if you want to cook and restaurants everywhere if you don't. Don't miss Brunel's magnificent suspension bridge. The train from London is fast.

Price	Studios £118. Apartments £124–£230.
Rooms	70: 12 studios, 58 apartments for 2-6.
Meals	Self-catered. Restaurants within 0.5 miles.
Closed	Never.
Directions	Sent on booking.

Emma Granado
Central Quay South, Broad Quay,
Bristol BS1 4AW

Tel	+44 (0)117 927 6722
Email	bristol@sacoapartments.com
Web	bristol.sacoapartments.com

Five Arrows Hotel

Baron Ferdinand de Rothschild began building Waddesdon Manor in 1874. Modelled on the grand châteaux of the Dordogne, it was built in Renaissance style, then filled with the baron's enormous art collection. As for the Five Arrows (the Rothschild coat of arms), it stands by the main gate and was built to accommodate the architects and artisans who built the house. It's not as vast as you might expect, but few inns have mullioned windows and gilded ironwork, or a lawned garden tended by the gardeners from the manor. You enter through a cobbled courtyard to the rear, where wicker chairs flourish in summer, then step into the house for high ceilings, green leather armchairs by reception, pictures from the big house, warm reds and yellows. Bedrooms upstairs have period colours, one has a half tester, others are simpler with padded headboards, perhaps a chandelier; ask for one away from the road. The bridal suite, in the old stables, has high ceilings and a four-poster bed. Delicious dinner is an English affair: tea-smoked salmon, venison pie, treacle tart with clotted cream. The inn is owned by the National Trust.

Price	£105–£135. Suites £185. Singles from £75.
Rooms	11: 8 twins/doubles, 2 suites, 1 single.
Meals	Lunch & dinner £5–£30.
Closed	Never.
Directions	In village on A41, 6 miles west of Aylesbury.

Alex McEwen
High Street, Waddesdon,
Aylesbury HP18 0JE

Tel	+44 (0)1296 651727
Email	five.arrows@nationaltrust.org.uk
Web	www.thefivearrows.co.uk

Three Horseshoes Inn

London may be only an hour's drive, but you'll think you've washed up in the 1960s. Red kites circle a bowl of deep countryside, smoke curls from cottages that hug the hill. As for the Three Horseshoes, you find flagstones and an open fire in the tiny locals' bar, exposed timbers and country views in the airy restaurant. If the setting is exquisite, the food is delicious. Simon, chef/patron, has cooked in The Connaught, Chez Nico, Le Gavroche – all the best places – and dinner is a treat, the homemade piccalilli worth the trip alone. Come for lunch and dig into baked camembert with garlic and rosemary, stay for dinner and try tiger prawns, boeuf bourguignon, then poached pear with chocolate mousse. Guests have a private entrance, stairs lead up to super-smart rooms with silky quilts, goose down pillows, funky furniture, Farrow & Ball paints. Also: views of the Chilterns and two garden rooms (nice and quiet). Breakfast indulgently, hike in the hills, walk by the Thames, hop over to Windsor. In summer you can eat on the terrace while ducks circle a sunken phone box in the pond. Only in England.

Price	£90–£150.
Rooms	6: 2 doubles, 2 garden rooms, 2 suites.
Meals	Lunch from £6.50. Bar meals from £7.50. Dinner from £15. Sun lunch £27.50. Not Sun eve or Mon lunch.
Closed	Rarely.
Directions	M40 junc. 5, A40 south thro' Stokenchurch, left for Radnage. After 2 miles left to Bennett End. Sharp right, up hill, on left.

	Simon Crawshaw
	Horseshoe Road, Radnage,
	High Wycombe HP14 4EB
Tel	+44 (0)1494 483273
Email	threehorseshoe@btconnect.com
Web	www.thethreehorseshoes.net

The Old Bridge Hotel

A smart hotel, the best in town, one which inspired the founders of Hotel du Vin. A battalion of devoted locals come for the food (delicious), the wines (exceptional) and the hugely comfortable interiors. Ladies lunch, business men chatter, kind staff weave through the throng. You can eat wherever you want: in the muralled restaurant; from a sofa in the lounge; or sitting in a winged armchair in front of the fire in the bar. You feast on anything from homemade soups to rack of lamb (starters are available all day), while breakfast is served in a panelled morning room with Buddha in the fireplace. Beautiful bedrooms are scattered about. Expect warm colours, fine fabrics, padded bedheads, crisp linen. One has a mirrored four-poster, several have vast bathrooms, others overlook the river Ouse, all have spoiling extras: Bose iPod docks, Bang & Olufsen TVs, power showers and bathrobes. Finally, John, a Master of Wine, has an irresistible wine shop opposite reception, so expect to take something home with you. The A14 may pass to the back, but it doesn't matter a jot.

Price	£140–£230. Singles from £89. Half-board £95–£125 p.p.
Rooms	24: 13 doubles, 1 twin, 7 singles, 3 four-posters.
Meals	Lunch & dinner £5–£35.
Closed	Never.
Directions	A1, then A14 into Huntingdon. Hotel on southwest flank of one-way system that circles town.

Nina Beamond
1 High Street,
Huntingdon PE29 3TQ
Tel   +44 (0)1480 424300
Email   oldbridge@huntsbridge.co.uk
Web   www.huntsbridge.com

Hotel Felix

Propel your punt along the Cam, duck your head to avoid stone bridges, stop to explore riverside colleges or head to King's for evensong. Beautiful Cambridge is a great place to while away a weekend and if you prefer to escape the city at night, then potter up to Hotel Felix. It stands in peaceful gardens two miles north, a metaphor for this resurgent city – a grand old villa reborn in contemporary style. Two new wings run off at right angles, creating a courtyard with parterre garden. Bedrooms have a smart simplicity and mix corporate necessities (this is Silicon Fen, after all) with comfort and style: dark wood furniture, crisp white linen, silky curtains, a sofa if there's room. Some are big, others smaller, all have excellent bathrooms with robes and White Company lotions. There's a peaceful sitting room for the daily papers, an attractive terrace for afternoon tea, an airy bar for pre-dinner drinks. As for the restaurant, you eat surrounded by contemporary art, perhaps seared scallops, Gressingham duck, pineapple tarte tatin; a bar menu runs at night, too. Very dog friendly.

Price	£200–£250. Suites £300–£320. Singles from £165.
Rooms	52: 28 doubles, 19 twins/doubles, 5 suites.
Meals	Continental breakfast included; cooked dishes from £3.75. Lunch & dinner £5–£45.
Closed	Never.
Directions	M11, junc. 13, then A1303 into Cambridge. Left at T-junction, 2nd left into Castle Street/Huntingdon Road, signed right after a mile.

Shara Ross
Huntingdon Road, Girton,
Cambridge CB3 0LX
Tel   +44 (0)1223 277977
Email   help@hotelfelix.co.uk
Web   www.hotelfelix.co.uk

The Anchor Inn

A real find, a 1650 ale house on Chatteris Fen. The New Bedford river streams past outside. It was cut from the soil by the pub's first residents, Scottish prisoners of war brought in by Cromwell to dig the dykes that drain the fens. These days cosy comfort infuses every corner. Inside, you find low doorways and ceilings, timber-framed walls, raw dark panelling and terracotta-tiled floors. A wood-burner warms the bar, so stop for a pint of cask ale, then feast on delicious fresh local produce served by charming staff, perhaps deep fried whitebait, local venison, pear tarte tatin; breakfast is equally indulgent. Four rooms above the shop fit the mood exactly (not posh, supremely comfy, two small). Expect trim carpets, wicker chairs, crisp white duvets and Indian cotton throws. The suites each have a sofabed and three rooms have fen and river views. Footpaths flank the water; stroll down and you might see mallards or Hooper swans, even a seal (the river is tidal to the Wash). Don't miss Ely (the bishop comes to eat), Cambridge, or the nesting swans at Welney. Brilliant.

Price	£79.50-£99. Suites £115-£155. Singles from £59.50. Extra bed £20.
Rooms	4: 1 double, 1 twin/double, 2 suites.
Meals	Lunch, 2 courses, £13.95. Dinner, 3 courses, £25-£30. Sunday lunch from £11.50.
Closed	Never.
Directions	From Ely A142 west. In Sutton left on B1381 for Earith. Right in southern Sutton, signed Sutton Gault. 1 mile north on left at bridge.

Adam Pickup & Carlene Bunten
Bury Lane, Sutton Gault,
Ely CB6 2BD

Tel	+44 (0)1353 778537
Email	anchorinn@popmail.bta.com
Web	www.anchorsuttongault.co.uk

The Crown Inn

A dreamy inn built of mellow stone that stands on the green in this gorgeous village. Paths lead out into open country, so follow the river up to Fotheringhay, where Mary Queen of Scots lost her head. Back at the pub, warm interiors mix style and tradition to great effect. You can eat wherever you want – in the bar, where a fire roars, in the airy snug with views of the green, or in the orangery, which opens onto a terrace. Wherever you end up, you'll eat well, perhaps langoustines with garlic and dill, saddle of venison with poached pear, Bramley apple and cinnamon crumble. In summer life spills onto the gravelled front, on May Day there's a hog roast for the village fête. Six hand pumps bring in the locals, as do quiz nights, live music and the odd game of rugby on the telly. Bedrooms are excellent. The two courtyard rooms are nice and quiet and come with padded bedheads, pretty art, lovely fabrics and flat-screen TVs; one has a magnificent bathroom. Those in the main house overlook the green. The small room has a four-poster, the big room is perfect for families.

Price	£75. Singles from £55.
Rooms	5 doubles.
Meals	Lunch & dinner £5-£25 (not Sun night or Mon lunch). Restaurant closed first week in January.
Closed	Rarely.
Directions	A1(M), junc. 17, then A605 west for 3 miles. Right on B671 for Elton. In village left, signed Nassington.

Marcus Lamb
8 Duck Street, Elton,
Peterborough PE8 6RQ
Tel   +44 (0)1832 280232
Email inncrown@googlemail.com
Web   www.thecrowninn.org

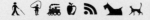

Judges Country House Hotel

This fine old country house is English to its core. It stands in 26 acres of attractive gardens with lawns that sweep down to a small river and paths that weave through private woods. Inside, wonderful interiors sweep you back to grander days. There's an elegant entrance hall that floods with light, a sitting room bar in racing green, and a golden drawing room where doors open to a pretty terrace for lunch in summer. Wander about and find fires primed for combustion, the daily papers laid out in reception, a elegant staircase that rises towards a glass dome. Country-house bedrooms are full of colour. You get bowls of fruit, beautiful beds, gorgeous linen, garden flowers. Bigger rooms have sofas, all have robes in super bathrooms. Back downstairs, there's serious food in the restaurant, perhaps Whitby crab with mango and lemongrass, local venison with chicory and orange, macadamia nut parfait with pears and Earl Grey jelly. If that's not enough, then bring a party and dine in style in the Dom Perignon room surrounded by an irresistible supply of champagne. The Moors are close.

Price	£130-£220. Suites & four-posters £160-£220. Singles from £110. Half-board from £97.50 p.p.
Rooms	21: 14 twins/doubles, 2 singles, 3 four-posters, 2 suites.
Meals	Lunch from £15.95. Dinner, 3 courses, £32.50.
Closed	Never.
Directions	A1(M), then A19 for Middlesbrough. Left onto A67, through Kirklevington, hotel signed left.

Tim Howard
Kirklevington Hall, Kirklevington,
Yarm TS15 9LW

Tel	+44 (0)1642 789000
Email	enquiries@judgeshotel.co.uk
Web	www.judgeshotel.co.uk

Hell Bay

Magical Bryher. In winter, giant rollers crash against high cliffs; in summer, sapphire waters sparkle in the sun. There are sandy beaches, passing sail boats, waders and wild swans, absolute peace. The hotel lazes on the west coast with sublime watery views – there's nothing between you and America – so grab a drink from the bar and wander onto the terrace to watch a vast sky blush at sunset. Inside, you get stripped floors, coastal colours, excellent art and airy interiors that look out to sea. Step outside and find a heated pool in the garden and a courtyard stocked with rosemary and lavender; castaways would refuse rescue. Bedrooms offer beach-house heaven, most with terraces or balconies, most with views of sand and sea. You get tongue-and-groove panelling, walls of windows, crisp fabrics, super bathrooms. In summer dig into crab and lobster straight from the ocean, fresh asparagus from Tresco, succulent strawberries from the island. There's a sauna, a Nintendo Wii for kids, golf for the hopeful. Low-season deals are exceptional. *Surcharge for dogs £12 a night.*

Price	Half-board £135–£320 p.p. Child in parent's room £50 (incl. high tea). Under 2s free.
Rooms	25 suites.
Meals	Lunch £5–£15. Dinner included.
Closed	November to mid-March.
Directions	Ship/helicopter from Penzance, or fly to St Mary's from Bristol, Southampton, Exeter, Newquay or Land's End; boat to Bryher.

Philip Callan
Bryher,
Isles of Scilly TR23 0PR

Tel	+44 (0)1720 422947
Email	contactus@hellbay.co.uk
Web	www.hellbay.co.uk

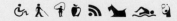

The Beach at Bude

In a fine position above the beach with huge Atlantic views, a fabulous base with beautiful rooms from which to explore this magical stretch of coast. It's just what Bude has been crying out for and it stands in a row of smart Victorian villas that look out over the town, the harbour, the canal, Compass Point and the ocean. You breakfast heartily beneath picture windows in the large, airy dining room/lounge with a New England, uncluttered feel; there's also a library with a good selection of books and board games and a quiet study for workaholics. Bedrooms (three on the ground floor, some right up in the loft) are all a good size: find lime-washed, solid oak furniture, Lloyd Loom chairs and fabulous bathrooms. Some have a private terrace or Juliet balcony, most come with sea views, all have thick Vi-Spring mattresses and lovely white cotton. It's all new, pristine and modern. Sandy surf beaches wait, there's a tidal swimming pool, safe bathing for children, the coastal path and plenty of space to store gear. Explore Bude, there's much more here than you'd think. Brilliant.

Price	£125–£185. Singles £105–£155.
Rooms	15: 12 doubles, 2 twins, 1 twin/double.
Meals	Pubs/restaurants within walking distance.
Closed	Rarely.
Directions	Sent on booking.

Sara Whiteman
Summerleaze Crescent,
Bude EX23 8HN

Tel	+44 (0)1288 389800
Email	enquiries@thebeachatbude.co.uk
Web	www.thebeachatbude.co.uk

The Seafood Restaurant

In 1975 a young chef called Rick Stein opened a restaurant in Padstow. Thirty-five years on and he and wife Jill have three more, a deli and a pâtisserie, a seafood cookery school and 40 beautiful bedrooms. Despite this success his homespun philosophy has never wavered: buy the freshest seafood on the quay from the fisherman, cook it simply and eat it with friends. It is a viewpoint half the country seems to share and The Seafood Restaurant is now a place of pilgrimage, so come to discover this glorious stretch of Cornish coast, walk on the cliffs, paddle in the estuary, then drop into the lively restaurant for a delicious meal, perhaps razor clams with garlic and parsley, chargrilled Dover sole with sea salt and lime, apple and quince tartlet with vanilla ice cream. Book in for the night and a table in the restaurant is yours – though beautiful bedrooms are so seductive you may find them hard to leave. They are scattered about town, some above the restaurant, others over at the bistro or just around the corner. All are immaculate. Expect the best fabrics, gorgeous bathrooms, and the odd terrace with estuary views.

Price	£97–£280.
Rooms	40: 16 doubles, 8 twins/doubles, 16 four-posters.
Meals	Lunch £29.95–£37. Dinner £55.
Closed	Christmas.
Directions	A39, then A389 to Padstow. Follow signs to centre; restaurant on left opposite harbour car park.

Jill & Rick Stein
Riverside,
Padstow PL28 8BY

Tel	+44 (0)1841 532700
Email	reservations@rickstein.com
Web	www.rickstein.com

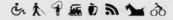

Woodlands Country House

A big house in the country, half a mile west of Padstow, with long views across the fields down to the sea. Pippa and Hugo came west to renovate and have done a fine job. You get an honesty bar in the sitting room, a croquet lawn by the fountain and stripped floors in the airy breakfast room, where a legendary feast is served each morning. Spotless bedrooms are smart and homely, some big, some smaller, all with a price to match, but it's worth splashing out on the bigger ones, which are away from the road and have watery views. Expect lots of colour, pretty beds, floral curtains, Frette linen. One room has a four-poster, another comes with a claw-foot bath, there are robes in adequate bathrooms. All have flat-screen TVs and DVD players, with a library of films downstairs. WiFi runs throughout, there's a computer guests can use, taxis can be ordered – but make sure you book restaurants in advance, especially Rick Stein's or Jamie Oliver's Fifteen. Hire bikes in town and follow the Camel trail, take the ferry over to Rock, head down to the beach, walk on the cliffs. Dogs are very welcome.

Price	£98-£138. Singles from £74.
Rooms	8: 4 doubles, 3 twins/doubles, 1 four-poster.
Meals	Picnics £18. Restaurants in Padstow, 0.5 miles. Breakfast for non-residents £15.
Closed	20 December-1 February.
Directions	On A389, just before Padstow, left for Newquay, then west on B3276. House signed on right in village.

Hugo & Pippa Woolley
Treator,
Padstow PL28 8RU
Tel   +44 (0)1841 532426
Email   info@woodlands-padstow.co.uk
Web   www.woodlands-padstow.co.uk

The Scarlet

A super-cool design hotel which overlooks the sea; a vast wall of glass in reception frames the view perfectly. The Scarlet does nothing by halves – this is a serious contender for Britain's funkiest bolthole – but it also offers a guilt-free destination as it's green to its core. Cutting-edge technology here includes a biomass boiler, solar panels and state-of-the-art insulation. You'll find a couple of swimming pools to insure against the weather, then log-fired hot tubs in a garden from which you can stargaze at night. There's a cool bar, a pool table in the library, then a restaurant that opens onto a decked terrace, where you eat fabulous Cornish food while gazing out to sea. Exceptional bedrooms come with huge views and all have balconies or terraces, private gardens or viewing pods. Expect oak floors from sustainable forests, organic cotton, perhaps a free-standing bath in your room. Some are enormous, one has a dual-aspect balcony, another comes with a rooftop lounge. If that's not enough, there's an ayurvedic-inspired spa, where tented treatment rooms are lit by lanterns. Amazing. *Dogs welcome.*

Price	£190-£295. Suites £265-£450. Half-board from £127.50 p.p. Min. 2 nights at weekends.
Rooms	37: 14 doubles, 11 twins/doubles, 12 suites.
Meals	Lunch, 3 courses, £22.50. Dinner, 3 courses, £42.50.
Closed	4 January-12 February.
Directions	North from Newquay on B3276 to Mawgan Porth. Signed left in village halfway up hill.

Emma Stratton
Tredragon Road,
Mawgan Porth TR8 4DQ

Tel	+44 (0)1637 861800
Email	stay@scarlethotel.co.uk
Web	www.scarlethotel.co.uk

Headland House

A super-cool B&B hotel that stands above Cabris Bay with big views across the water to St Ives. Mark and Fenella refurbished from top to toe, turning their home into a small-scale pleasure dome. Outside, you find sunloungers and a hammock in the lawned garden; inside, there's a snug bar with leather sofas, then a gorgeous breakfast room that floods with light. Here you feast on lavender-scented yoghurt, freshly pressed smoothies, perhaps smoked salmon and scrambled eggs or the full Cornish works; in summer doors open onto a deck for breakfast in the sun. Back inside, seven gorgeous rooms wait. All have the same seaside chic: white walls to soak up the light, pretty fabrics, lovely beds, fabulous bathrooms. Most have sea views, a couple have claw-foot baths, one has its own small garden. There's tea and cake 'on the house' in the afternoon, then a glass of sherry before heading out to St Ives for dinner overlooking the harbour. You can walk down to the beach (glorious), follow the coastal path, or call for a taxi. Leave your car at home and take the sleeper from Paddington. Brilliant.

Price	£85–£139.
Rooms	7 doubles.
Meals	Pubs/restaurants 5-minute walk.
Closed	Rarely.
Directions	Sent on booking.

Mark & Fenella Thomas
Headland Road, Carbis Bay,
St Ives TR26 2NS

Tel	+44 (0)1736 796647
Email	info@headlandhousehotel.co.uk
Web	www.headlandhousehotel.co.uk

Boskerris Hotel

A gorgeous little hotel with glass everywhere framing huge views of ocean and headland. In summer, sofas are strategically placed on the decked terrace so you can gaze out in comfort. Godrevy lighthouse twinkles to the right, St Ives slips into the sea on the left, the wide sands of Carbis Bay and Lelant shimmer between. Back inside, white walls and big mirrors soak up the light. You get bleached boards and smart sofas in the sitting room, fresh flowers and blond wood in the dining room. Airy bedrooms in various sizes are delightfully uncluttered, with silky throws, padded headboards, crisp linen. Eleven rooms have the view, all have fancy bathrooms, some have deep baths and deluge showers. You'll find White Company lotions, Designers Guild fabrics; in one room you can soak in the bath whilst gazing out to sea. Staff are kind, nothing is too much trouble, breakfasts are exceptional. A steep coastal path leads down to St Ives (20 mins), mazy streets snake up to the Tate; and there's a branch line. Sustenance, too: don't miss the Porthminster Beach Café for the fanciest nosh in town.

Price	£115–£240. Singles from £86.25.
Rooms	15: 10 doubles, 3 twins, 1 family room, 1 triple.
Meals	Dinner, 3 courses, about £30.
Closed	Mid-November to mid-February.
Directions	A30 past Hayle, then A3074 for St Ives. After 3 miles pass sign for Carbis Bay, then third right into Boskerris Road. Down hill, on left.

Jonathan & Marianne Bassett
Boskerris Road, Carbis Bay,
St Ives TR26 2NQ

Tel	+44 (0)1736 795295
Email	reservations@boskerrishotel.co.uk
Web	www.boskerrishotel.co.uk

Blue Hayes Private Hotel

The view from the terrace is hard to beat, a clean sweep across the bay to St Ives. You breakfast here in good weather in the shade of a Monterey pine, as if transported back to the French Riviera of the Fifties. As for the rest of the hotel, it's an unadulterated treat, mostly due to Malcolm, whose infectious generosity is stamped over every square inch. Few hoteliers close for four months to redecorate over winter, but that's the way things are done here and the house shines as a result. It comes in ivory white, with the occasional dash of colour from carpet and curtain. The bar has a vaulted ceiling and a wall of glass that runs along the front to weatherproof the view. Big bedrooms are gorgeous, two with balconies, one with a terrace, all with sparkling bathrooms. If you want to eat, light suppers are on hand, though a short stroll into town leads to dozens of restaurants; Alfresco on the harbor is excellent, torches are provided for the journey back. Penzance, Zennor and the New Tate are close as are a host of beaches. There's folk and jazz for the September festival, a great time to visit.

Price	£170–£200. Singles from £110. Suite £230–£240.
Rooms	6: 4 doubles, 1 suite, 1 triple.
Meals	Packed lunch by arrangement. Light suppers from £12. Restaurants within walking distance.
Closed	November–February.
Directions	A30, then A3074 to St Ives. Through Lelant & Carbis Bay, over mini-r'bout (Tesco on left) and down hill. On right immed. after garage on right.

Malcolm Herring
Trelyon Avenue,
St Ives TR26 2AD

Tel	+44 (0)1736 797129
Email	info@bluehayes.co.uk
Web	www.bluehayes.co.uk

Primrose Valley Hotel

Roll out of bed, drop down for breakfast, spin off to the beach, stroll into town. If you want St Ives bang on your doorstep, this is the hotel for you; the sands are a 30-second stroll. Half the rooms have views across the bay, two have balconies for lazy afternoons. Inside, open-plan interiors revel in an earthy contemporary chic, with leather sofas, varnished floors, fresh flowers and glossy magazines. Bedrooms aren't huge, but have lots of style, so come for Hypnos beds, bespoke furniture and good bathrooms; the suite comes with a red leather sofa, hi-tech gadgetry and a fancy bathroom. Andrew and Sue are environmentally aware, committed to sustainable tourism and community projects. Their hugely popular breakfast is mostly sourced within the county, and food provenance is listed on the menu. There's a cool little bar that's stocked with potions from far and wide, then the REN room, small but perfect, for bio-active beauty and skincare therapies. As for St Ives – the Tate and Barbara Hepworth's sculpture garden both wait, as do Alba and Alfresco, a couple of lovely restaurants overlooking the harbour.

Price	£85–£170. Suite £175–£240. Singles from £75. Min. 2 nights at weekends.	
Rooms	9: 6 doubles, 2 twins, 1 suite.	
Meals	Platters £8. Restaurant 200m.	
Closed	Christmas. 3 weeks in January. Open for New Year.	
Directions	From A3074 Trelyon Avenue; before hospital sign slow down, indicate right & turn down Primrose Valley; under bridge, left, then back under bridge; signs for hotel parking.	

	Andrew & Sue Biss
	Primrose Valley,
	St Ives TR26 2ED
Tel	+44 (0)1736 794939
Email	info@primroseonline.co.uk
Web	www.primroseonline.co.uk

The Gurnard's Head

The coastline here is utterly magical and the walk up to St Ives is hard to beat. Secret beaches appear at low tide, cliffs tumble down to the water and wild flowers streak the land pink in summer. As for the hotel, you couldn't hope for a better base. It's earthy, warm, stylish and friendly, with airy interiors, colour-washed walls, stripped wooden floors and fires at both ends of the bar. Logs are piled up in an alcove, maps and art hang on the walls, books fill every shelf; if you pick one up and don't finish it, take it home and post it back. Rooms are warm and cosy, simple and spotless, with Vi-Spring mattresses, crisp white linen, throws over armchairs, Roberts radios. Downstairs, super food, all homemade, can be eaten wherever you want: in the bar, in the restaurant or out in the garden in good weather. Snack on rustic delights – pork pies, crab claws, half a pint of Atlantic prawns – or tuck into more substantial treats, maybe mussels with white wine, pork loin with grain mustard, then lemon posset and rhubarb. Picnics are easily arranged and there's bluegrass folk music in the bar most weeks.

Price	£97.50-£167.50. Singles from £82.50. Half-board from £71.25 p.p.
Rooms	7: 4 doubles, 3 twins/doubles.
Meals	Lunch from £16.50. Dinner, 3 courses, from £26.50. Sunday lunch, 3 courses, £21.
Closed	24 & 25 December & 4 days in mid-January.
Directions	On B3306 between St Ives & St Just, 2 miles west of Zennor, at head of village of Treen.

Charles & Edmund Inkin
Zennor,
St Ives TR26 3DE

Tel	+44 (0)1736 796928
Email	enquiries@gurnardshead.co.uk
Web	www.gurnardshead.co.uk

The Summer House

A glittering find, a small enclave of Mediterranean goodness a hundred yards up from the sea. It's stylish and informal, colourful and welcoming; what's more, it's super value for money. Linda and Ciro, English and Italian respectively, run the place with great affection. Linda, bubbling away out front, is the designer, her breezy interiors warm and elegant with stripped floors, Ciro's art, panelled windows and murals in the dining room (the breakfast chef is a sculptress). Ciro worked in some of London's best restaurants before heading west to go it alone and will whisk up culinary delights for dinner. In good weather you can eat his ambrosial food in a small, lush courtyard garden, perhaps langoustine with mango and chives, rack of lamb with herbes de Provence, warm apple tart with armagnac sorbet. Breakfast – also served in the courtyard when the sun shines – is a feast. Stylish rooms are the final delight: seaside colours, well-dressed beds, freshly cut flowers, flat-screen TVs, super little bathrooms. *Picnic baskets for Minack Theatre by arrangement.*

Price	£120-£150. Singles from £100.
Rooms	5: 4 doubles, 1 twin/double.
Meals	Simple suppers £20 (Mon to Fri). Dinner, 4 courses, £35 (Sat & Sun).
Closed	November-March.
Directions	With sea on left, along harbourside, past open-air pool, then immediate right after Queens Hotel. House 30 yds up on left. Private car park.

Linda & Ciro Zaino
Cornwall Terrace,
Penzance TR18 4HL

Tel   +44 (0)1736 363744
Email   reception@summerhouse-cornwall.com
Web   www.summerhouse-cornwall.com

The Abbey Hotel

This smart little hotel sits above Penzance harbour with views from the front to St Michael's Mount. It dates to 1660 and its blue façade gives way to elegant interiors. It's a great place to escape the world, not least for its lovely garden, where you can sit in blissful silence and dig into afternoon tea or gather for a sundowner before heading next door to the hotel's restaurant for a good meal. Inside, country-house interiors have lots of sparkle. The drawing room is hard to beat. You'll find a roaring fire, walls of books and rugs on stripped floors, then a bust of Lafayette, exquisite art and huge arched windows that rise to the ceiling and open onto the garden. Bedrooms are also lovely – grand, but quirky (in one you pull open a cupboard to find an en suite shower). You sink into big comfy beds wrapped in crisp white linen, there are chandeliers, quilted bedspreads, French armoires and plump-cushioned armchairs. Breakfast is served in a panelled dining room with a fire crackling and assorted busts and statues for company. St Ives, Zennor, Mousehole and the Minack all wait.

Price	£105–£200. Suite £150–£210. Singles from £75. Flat £115–£170.
Rooms	7 + 1: 4 doubles, 1 twin, 1 family room, 1 suite. Self-catering flat for 4.
Meals	Lunch from £6.50. Dinner, 3 courses, about £30.
Closed	Rarely.
Directions	Follow signs to town centre. Up hill (Market Jew St). Left at top, then fork left & 3rd on the left.

Thaddeus Cox
Abbey Street,
Penzance TR18 4AR

Tel	+44 (0)1736 366906
Email	hotel@theabbeyonline.co.uk
Web	www.theabbeyonline.co.uk

Artist Residence Penzance

Distinctly hip, deliciously quirky and overflowing with colour, this groovy little bolthole is hard to resist. The house dates to 1600 and stands on the ley line that connects St Michael's Mount to Stonehenge. You're in the old quarter of town, a stone's throw from the harbour. Inside, Charlie and her staff potter about informally, stopping to chat and point you in the right direction. Downstairs, you find a cute dining room that doubles variously as a sitting room, a clothes shop, an art gallery and a bar – a very sociable spot. Bedrooms are scattered about, each designed by a different artist; many have brightly coloured murals. One has a wall you can write on, another is pretty in pink, yet another shows a cartoon version of the street outside your window; in short, you sleep amid art. Most have compact shower rooms, one has a claw-foot bath. All have smart beds, white linen and toppers for a good night's sleep; family rooms have fridges, too. Back downstairs, lovely breakfasts offer honey-roast ham, local eggs, delicious smoothies. Good pubs and restaurants are very close, too.

Price	£70–£130. Singles from £60.
Rooms	11: 6 doubles, 2 twins/doubles, 3 family rooms.
Meals	Lunch & dinner from £4.50.
Closed	January.
Directions	A30 into Penzance. Follow signs to town centre; up main street; left at top; keep left and on right after 200m.

Charlie Newey
20 Chapel Street,
Penzance TR18 4AW

Tel	+44 (0)1736 365664
Email	penzance@artistresidence.co.uk
Web	www.arthotelcornwall.co.uk

The Cove

You're lost in the lanes west of Penzance with a pirate's cove at the end of the garden. The position here is fabulous, with views from the terrace that shoot out to sea. As for the Cove, well, it's not your average hotel. The trick here is that every apartment comes with a cool little kitchen, so you can look after yourself if you want. Not that you have to – the hotel has a fabulous restaurant and will cater to your every need, from Easter to November. Most people tend to do a bit of both and it works particularly well for young families, so much so there's a kids' club in summer. An airy seaside elegance runs throughout (white walls, coastal art, lots of glass to bring in the light), but the hub of the hotel is the terrace, where loungers circle the pool. Rooms – some huge, others smaller – all have a similar style: sisal matting, aqua blue fabrics, comfy beds, super little bathrooms As for the restaurant, you can nip down for breakfast, lunch or a rather good dinner, perhaps Serrano ham with black figs, poached lobster with a rocket salad, a plate of West Country cheeses.

Price	Studios: £115-£195. Apartments: £115-£375. Min. 7 nights mid-July to Aug.
Rooms	15: 2 studios, 13 apartments.
Meals	Full English brought to you, £9.95. Lunch from £5. Dinner £20-£40. Limited service during the week off season.
Closed	Rarely.
Directions	West from Penzance on B3315 (left in Newlyn). Clearly signed after 3 miles for Lamorna Cove and the hotel.

Lee Magner
Lamorna,
Penzance TR19 6XH

Tel	+44 (0)1736 731411
Email	contact@thecovecornwall.com
Web	www.thecovecornwall.com

The Old Coastguard

The Old Coastguard stands bang on the water in one of Cornwall's loveliest coastal villages. It's a super spot and rather peaceful – little has happened here since 1595, when the Spanish sacked the place. Recently, the hotel fell into the benign hands of Edmund and Charles, past masters at reinvigorating lovely small hotels; warm colours, attractive prices, great food and a happy vibe are their hallmarks. Downstairs, the airy bar and the dining room come together as one, the informality of open plan creating a great space to hang out. There are smart rustic tables, earthy colours, local ales and local art, then a crackling fire in the restaurant. Drop down a few steps to find a bank of sofas and a wall of glass framing sea views; in summer, doors open onto a decked terrace, a lush lawn, then the coastal path weaving down to the small harbour. Bedrooms are lovely: sand-coloured walls, excellent beds, robes in fine bathrooms, books everywhere. Most have the view, eight have balconies. Don't miss dinner: grilled sardines, duck confit, banana tarte tatin. Dogs are welcome. Wonderful.

Price	£110–£195. Half-board from £75 p.p. Ask about seasonal offers.
Rooms	14: 10 doubles, 2 twins/doubles, 1 family room, 1 suite.
Meals	Lunch from £6. Dinner, 3 courses, about £25. Sunday lunch from £12.50.
Closed	One week in early January.
Directions	Take A30 to Penzance then Land's End. Signs to Newlyn & Mousehole. Hotel on left immed. as you enter Mousehole. Limited parking or public car park next door; £2 on departure.

	Charles & Edmund Inkin The Parade, Mousehole, Penzance TR19 6PR
Tel	+44 (0)1736 731222
Email	enquiries@oldcoastguardhotel.co.uk
Web	www.oldcoastguardhotel.co.uk

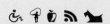

Mount Haven Hotel & Restaurant

A magical hotel with sublime views of St Michael's Mount, an ancient Cornish totem that's been pulling in the crowds for millennia. Most rooms look the right way and have a balcony to boot, but there's a decked terrace in case yours doesn't and the causeway leads over at low tide, so make sure you discover the ancient castle and church. Back at the hotel, sink in to comfy sofas in the bar where huge windows frame the view, making sunsets rather special. Elsewhere, Eastern deities jostle for space, local art hugs the walls, and there's a treatment room for a soothing massage, the profits of which fund an orphanage and medical camp in India. The restaurant comes with big mirrors and doors that open onto a terrace where you eat in good weather; try Newlyn crab cakes, duck breast with a ginger marmalade, then chocolate pave with blood-orange sorbet. Bedrooms are lovely. Most aren't huge, but nearly all have balconies or terraces and those on the top floor have unblemished views. They come with fresh flowers, crisp linen, flat-screen TVs. Bathrooms tend to be small but sweet.

Price	£130-£195. Four-posters & suite £170-£230. Singles from £120.
Rooms	18: 10 doubles, 4 twins/doubles, 1 family room, 2 four-posters, 1 suite.
Meals	Lunch from £5. Dinner, 3 courses, about £30.
Closed	Mid-December to mid-February.
Directions	Leave A30 for Marazion 1 mile east of Penzance at middle roundabout on dual carriageway. Left at T-junction by sea, then through village and signed on right.

Orange & Mike Trevillion
Turnpike Road,
Marazion TR17 0DQ
Tel   +44 (0)1736 710249
Email reception@mounthaven.co.uk
Web   www.mounthaven.co.uk

Bay Hotel

The Bay Hotel sits beneath a vast sky with views to the front of nothing but sea — unless you count the beach at low tide, where buckets and spades are mandatory. Outside, the lawn rolls down to the water, sprinkled with deckchairs and loungers, so grab a book, snooze in the sun or listen to the sounds of the English seaside. Stylish interiors are just the ticket, but you can't escape the view: dining room, conservatory and sitting room look the right way, with big windows to keep your eyes glued to the horizon. Warm colours fit the mood perfectly, there are flowers everywhere, cavernous sofas, a telescope to scan the high seas, a small bar for pre-dinner drinks. Airy bedrooms vary in size. Suites are big — one has it's own balcony — and all have sea views (some from the side). Expect smart whites, leather armchairs, tongue-and-groove bathrooms. As for Ric's delicious food, fish comes straight from the sea, perhaps deep-fried calamari with chilli dip and Cornish sole with anchovy butter, followed by chilled Grand Marnier crème brûlée. The coastal path passes directly outside. Don't miss afternoon tea.

Price	Half-board £73-£120 p.p. Suite £115-£145 p.p.
Rooms	13: 5 doubles, 5 twins/doubles, 3 suites.
Meals	Dinner, 3 courses & coffee, included; non-residents, £34.95.
Closed	December-March (open Christmas & New Year).
Directions	A3083 south from Helston, then left onto B3293 for St Keverne. Right for Coverack after 8 miles. Down hill, right at sea, second on right.

Ric, Gina & Zoe House
North Corner, Coverack,
Helston TR12 6TF

Tel	+44 (0)1326 280464
Email	enquiries@thebayhotel.co.uk
Web	www.thebayhotel.co.uk

The Rosevine

A super-smart family bolthole on the Roseland peninsular with views that tumble across trim lawns and splash into to the sea. Tim and Hazel welcome children with open arms and have created a small oasis where guests of all ages can have great fun. There's a playroom for kids (Xbox, plasma screen, DVDs, toys), an indoor pool, and a beach at the bottom of the hill. High teas are on hand, there are cots and highchairs, babysitters can be arranged. Parents don't fare badly either: an elegant sitting room with sofas in front of the wood-burner; sea views and Lloyd Loom furniture in a light filled restaurant; sun loungers scattered about a semi-tropical garden. Suites and apartments come with small kitchens (fridge, sink, dishwasher, microwave/oven); you can self-cater, eat in the restaurant or mix and match (there's deli menu for posh takeaways). Some rooms are open-plan while others have separate bedrooms. Expect airy, uncluttered interiors, flat-screen TVs, top-notch bed linen and robes in good bathrooms. Eight have a balcony or terrace. St Mawes is close.

Price	Studios £155–£215. Family suites & apartments £175–£385.
Rooms	12: 4 studios, 4 family suites for 2-4, 4 apartments for 2-5. All with kitchenettes.
Meals	Breakfast £3–£12. Lunch from £5. Dinner, 3 courses, about £30.
Closed	January.
Directions	From A390 south for St Mawes on A3078. Signed left after 8 miles. Right at bottom of road; just above beach.

Hazel & Tim Brocklebank
Rosevine, Portscatho,
Truro TR2 5EW

Tel	+44 (0)1872 580206
Email	info@rosevine.co.uk
Web	www.rosevine.co.uk

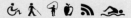

Driftwood Hotel

A faultless position, one of the best, with six acres of garden that drop down to a private beach and coastal paths that lead to cliff-top walks. At the Driftwood, Cape Cod meets Cape Cornwall and airy interiors shine in white and blue. The sitting room is stuffed with beautiful things – fat armchairs, deep sofas, driftwood lamps, a smouldering fire – and there's a telescope in the bar with which to scan the high seas. Best of all are the walls of glass that pull in the spectacular watery views; in summer, doors open onto a decked terrace for breakfast and lunch in the sun. Bedrooms are gorgeous (all but one has a sea view), some big, others smaller, one in a cabin halfway down the cliff with a private terrace. All have the same clipped elegance: big beds, white linen, wicker chairs and white walls to soak up the light. There are Roberts radios on bedside tables, cotton robes in excellent bathrooms. Drop down to the dining room for seriously good food that makes the most of the sea. High teas for children, hampers for beach picnics and rucksacks for walkers, too. *Minimum two nights at weekends.*

Price	£190–£275.
Rooms	15: 11 doubles, 3 twins, 1 cabin.
Meals	Dinner £46 (inc. in room price in low season).
Closed	Early December to early February.
Directions	From St Austell, A390 west. Left on B3287 for St Mawes; left at Tregony on A3078 for approx. 7 miles. Signed left down lane.

Paul & Fiona Robinson
Rosevine, Portscatho,
Truro TR2 5EW

Tel	+44 (0)1872 580644
Email	info@driftwoodhotel.co.uk
Web	www.driftwoodhotel.co.uk

The Nare Hotel

The Nare is matchless, English to its core. It sits above Gerrans Bay with sublime views of sand and sea, and wherever you go, inside or out, something beautiful catches the eye. There are two swimming pools, croquet and tennis, mature gardens that sparkle in summer, a hot tub overlooking an enormous beach. Interiors are equally wonderful – the art in the gallery is worth the trip alone. You'll find crackling fires, a cocktail bar, even a billiard room that doubles as a library. Afternoon tea 'on the house' is served every day by smartly dressed waiters, so sip your Earl Grey out on the terrace and watch the waves roll in. Recently refurbished country-house bedrooms are nothing short of gorgeous. Expect beautiful fabrics, fresh flowers, antique furniture, fabulous bathrooms. Most have watery views (you can lie in bed and gaze out to sea), balconies or terraces. As for the food, the dining room is formal, the Quarterdeck restaurant is less so; expect fabulous fish, lobster every day, game in season or delicious Cornish beef. We haven't even scratched the surface. Out of this world.

Price	£270-£503. Singles £140-£268. Suites £334-£768.
Rooms	37: 21 twins/doubles, 6 singles, 10 suites.
Meals	Lunch from £7. Dinner in brasserie, 3 courses, about £30; in restaurant, 5 courses, £49.50.
Closed	Never.
Directions	A390 west from St Austell, then B3287 to Tregony. Pick up A3078 for St Mawes and hotel signed left after two miles.

Toby Ashworth
Carne Beach, Veryan-in-Roseland,
Truro TR2 5PF

Tel	+44 (0)1872 501111
Email	stay@narehotel.co.uk
Web	www.narehotel.co.uk

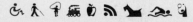

Trevalsa Court Hotel

This Arts and Crafts house has a fine position at the top of the cliffs with sprawling lawns that run down to Cornwall's coastal path; either turn right and amble along to Mevagissey or drop down to the beach with your bucket and spade. Don't dally too long: Trevalsa is a seaside treat – friendly, stylish, seriously spoiling. In summer, you can decamp onto the terrace and lawns and fall asleep in a deckchair, but the view here is weatherproofed by an enormous mullioned window seat in the sitting room, a great place to watch the weather spin by. Elsewhere, you'll find a small bar packed with art, then a panelled dining room where you dig into bistro-style food – homemade fishcakes, coq au vin, chocolate fondant with basil ice cream. Bedrooms are lovely, all recently refurbished. They come in seaside colours with designer fabrics, the odd wall of paper, padded headboards and super new wet rooms. There are TVs and DVD players and most have sea views, while bigger rooms have sofas and spoil you all the way. The Lost Gardens of Heligan are on your doorstep. *Open for Christmas & New Year.*

Price	£105–£185. Singles £75–£95. Suites £195–£235. Half-board £75–£140 p.p. Min. 2 nights at weekends/in high season.
Rooms	14: 9 doubles, 2 twins, 2 singles, 1 suite for 4.
Meals	Dinner £30.
Closed	Rarely.
Directions	B3273 from St Austell signed Mevagissey, through Pentewan to top of the hill, left at the x-roads, over mini r'bout. Hotel on left, signed.

Susan & John Gladwin
School Hill, Mevagissey,
St Austell PL26 6TH

Tel	+44 (0)1726 842468
Email	stay@trevalsa-hotel.co.uk
Web	www.trevalsa-hotel.co.uk

The Cornwall Hotel, Spa & Estate

The Cornwall started life as an Edwardian retreat for the landed gentry, but a recent development of this 43-acre estate has moved the hotel firmly into the 21st century. At its heart is the White House, now a contemporary retreat with fantastic art, seriously good food and warmly stylish design. Here you find a cool little brasserie, an attractive drawing room with sofas in front of the fire, then a super-smart restaurant which overlooks the manicured grounds; doors open onto a terrace in summer. Bedrooms in the main house are seriously fancy, those out back come with balconies overlooking the Pentewan valley. All are lovely, with smart colours, cool bathrooms and technological excess. Elsewhere, a groovy spa, where an indoor infinity pool overlooks a walled garden strewn with sun loungers. You can hire bikes, spin off to the Eden Project or simply take to the coastal path. Whatever you do, come back for some great food, perhaps St Austell Bay mussels, local rib-eye, sticky toffee pudding. There are 22 woodland homes if you want to stay longer and self-cater.

Price	£99–£220. Self-catering £600–£1500 per week.
Rooms	65 + 22: 62 twins/doubles, 2 four-posters, 1 suite. 22 self-catering woodland homes for 4-6. 1 self-catering cottage for 2-4.
Meals	Lunch from £5.95. Dinner £11–£35.
Closed	Never.
Directions	South from St Austell on B3273 for Megavissey. Hotel on right after 1 mile.

Nigel Walker
Pentewan Road, Tregorrick,
St Austell PL26 7AB

Tel	+44 (0)1726 874050
Email	enquiries@thecornwall.com
Web	www.thecornwall.com

The Old Quay House Hotel

You drop down the hill, navigate the narrow lanes, then pull up at this boutique hotel which started life as a seaman's mission. It's a perfect spot, with the estuary lapping directly outside and a sun-trapping terrace for summer dining, as good a place as any from which to watch the boats zip past. Inside, stylish bedrooms spoil you all the way with goose down duvets, beautiful fabrics and seriously spoiling bathrooms (replete with bathrobes, the odd claw-foot tub and maybe a separate shower). Most rooms look the right way, eight have balconies and the view from the penthouse suite is unbeatable. Downstairs great food waits, so trip down to the terrace for a cocktail, then dig into excellent food prepared from a wealth of local ingredients, perhaps Fowey River oysters, Cornish scallops and West Country duck. Fowey is enchanting, bustles with life and fills with sailors for the August regatta. If you want to escape, take the ferry across to Polruan where Daphne du Maurier lived and wrote. You can potter over to spectacular Lantic Bay for a picnic lunch on the beach. *Minimum two nights at weekends in high season.*

Price	£180–£320. Singles from £130.
Rooms	11: 5 doubles, 5 twins/doubles, 1 suite.
Meals	Lunch (April–September) about £15. Dinner £30–£37.50.
Closed	Rarely.
Directions	Entering Fowey, follow one-way system past church. Hotel on right where road at narrowest point, next to Lloyds Bank. Nearest car park 800 yds.

	Anthony Chapman
	28 Fore Street,
	Fowey PL23 1AQ
Tel	+44 (0)1726 833302
Email	info@theoldquayhouse.com
Web	www.theoldquayhouse.com

Bishop's House

Fabulous Fowey. Drop off your luggage, forget the car and be spoilt at this 1802 townhouse, reputedly once the summer home of the Bishop of Truro. It's B&B but not as you know it: find a bursting library, a music room with a grand piano (yes, you can play it), big beds with the crispest white cotton, and charming Elizabeth and Nigel to look after you – impeccably. A cream tea in the terraced garden comes with breathtaking views over the estuary to Polruan, where bobbing boats, whirling gulls and ever-changing light will arrest you for hours; it's the best seat in town for Regatta week. Breakfast here at a time you choose: locally smoked haddock with poached eggs, Cornish bacon, homemade jams and marmalade; on cooler days retreat to the pretty orangery with its wall-to-wall windows. Sleep very peacefully in good-sized bedrooms (most have that view), with fresh flowers, restful colours, thick curtains in elegant fabrics and warm, sparkling bathrooms. And there are ferries, walks, great pubs, sailing, the Eden Centre and Rick Stein's on the doorstep. Delectable.

Price	£150.
Rooms	4: 3 doubles, 1 twin/double.
Meals	Restaurants nearby.
Closed	October-Easter.
Directions	Sent on booking.

Nigel & Elizabeth Wagstaff
Fowey PL23 1HY

Tel	+44 (0)1726 833759
Email	choices@foweyresidences.co.uk
Web	www.foweyresidences.co.uk

The Cormorant Hotel

A sublime position on the side of a wooded hill with the magical Fowey river curling past below. Oyster catchers swoop low across the water, sheep bleat in the fields, sail boats tug on their moorings. The hotel is one room deep, every window looks the right way, and most of the bedrooms have small balconies, where you can doze in the sun and listen to the sound of the river. A terrace sweeps along the front of the house, a finger of lawn runs below, and, inside, the river follows wherever you go. You get fresh flowers in the tiny bar, a wood burner in the gorgeous sitting room, wooden floors in the airy dining room. Super bedrooms come without clutter: light colours, trim carpets, walls of glass, white linen. One has a slipper bath from which you can gaze down on the water. Swim in the pool, tan on its terrace, jump in the hot tub, then dine on fabulous Cornish food, perhaps seared scallops with cauliflower purée, grilled lemon sole with wild garlic, then coconut marshmallow with a pineapple and chilli salsa. There are gardens to explore, but you may well linger.

Price	£110–£250. Singles from £95.
Rooms	14: 11 doubles, 3 twins.
Meals	Lunch from £12. Dinner, à la carte, from £30.
Closed	Rarely.
Directions	A390 west towards St Austell, then B3269 to Fowey. After 4 miles, left to Golant. Into village, along quay, hotel signed right up very steep hill.

	Mary Tozer
	Golant, Fowey PL23 1LL
Tel	+44 (0)1726 833426
Email	relax@cormoranthotel.co.uk
Web	www.cormoranthotel.co.uk

Entry 43   Map 1

Talland Bay Hotel

The position here is magical. First you plunge down rollercoaster lanes, then you arrive at this delicious hotel. Directly in front, the sea sparkles through pine trees, an old church crowns the hill and two acres of lawns end in a ha-ha, where the land drops down to the bay. Vanessa came to renovate and has done so magnificently, breathing new life into this venerable old hotel. There's a sitting room bar in blue and white, a roaring fire in the half-panelled dining room, refurbished bedrooms that take your breath away. Masses of art hangs on the walls, there are vast sofas, polished flagstones, a gravelled terrace for afternoon tea. Follow the coastal path over the hill, then return for an excellent dinner, perhaps chicken liver pâté with pistachio brioche, fillet of sea bream with olives and lemon, hot chocolate fondant with white chocolate sorbet. And so to bed. All rooms have been refurbished and are ready to pamper you rotten. Expect rich colours, vast beds, beautiful linen, the odd panelled wall. One has a balcony, a couple open onto terraces, all have seriously swanky bathrooms.

Price	£115–£205. Suites £185–£225. Singles from £105. Half-board from £87.50 p.p.
Rooms	22: 17 twins/doubles, 3 suites, 2 singles.
Meals	Lunch from £6.95. Dinner £32–£38.
Closed	Never.
Directions	From Looe A387 for Polperro. Ignore 1st sign to Talland. After 2 miles, left at x-roads; follow signs.

Vanessa Rees
Porthallow,
Looe PL13 2JB

Tel	+44 (0)1503 272667
Email	info@tallandbayhotel.co.uk
Web	www.tallandbayhotel.co.uk

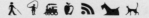

The Tufton Arms

Appleby is an ancient market town, one of the loveliest in the north. It has a fine Norman castle, a Grade II listed high street and a cricket pitch that overlooks the river. This Victorian coaching inn stands in the middle of it all, a hub for the local community. It's a mildly eccentric place, one that mixes traditional décor (almost extinct) with contemporary elegance (a beautiful conquest). Downstairs, you find a smart drawing room, a bar at the front and an attractive dining room for good country fare, while outside a small café in the courtyard/car park comes with a stone terrace. Back inside, bedrooms are the big surprise. All but two rooms have been recently refurbished. Some are hugely grand with half-testers and chandeliers; some are smaller with padded headboards and warm colours; others fall between the two. All have beds dressed in crisp white linen and fluffy white robes in excellent bathrooms. As for Appleby, follow your nose and you won't find a single high street name. Further afield you can play golf, fish the Eden or potter through glorious country.

Price	£135–£210. Singles from £79.50. Half-board from £90 p.p.
Rooms	22: 14 twins/doubles, 3 suites, 5 singles.
Meals	Bar meals from £3.95. Sunday lunch from £16.95. Dinner, 3 courses, £29.50.
Closed	25 & 26 December.
Directions	M6 junc. 38, then north to Appleby on B6260. On high street.

	Nigel Milsom
	Market Square,
	Appleby-in-Westmorland CA16 6XA
Tel	+44 (0)17683 51593
Email	info@tuftonarmshotel.co.uk
Web	www.tuftonarmshotel.co.uk

Augill Castle

A folly castle built in 1841. Outside, five acres of lush gardens are patrolled by a family of free-range hens, whose eggs are served at breakfast each morning. Inside, grand interiors come properly furnished: chesterfield sofas in a vast hall, a grand piano in the music room, an honesty bar in the drawing room, ribbed ceilings, open fires, fine arched windows. The house is run informally: no uniforms, no rules, just Wendy, Simon and their staff to ply you with delicious food, big pillows, massive tubs. A stained-glass window on the staircase shines under a vaulted ceiling, then come wonderful country-house bedrooms. One is enormous, another has a wardrobe in the turret. You'll find beautiful beds, cavernous bathrooms, lattice windows and vintage luggage. All rooms have the view, there are sofas if there's room, interesting art, antique wood, one huge dining table. Perfect for house parties and small weddings. The aptly named Eden Valley waits outside, while the Dales, the Lakes and the High Pennines are all close, making this a great base from which to explore the North.

Price	£160–£180. Family suites £240. Singles from £80.
Rooms	14: 6 doubles, 4 twins/doubles, 4 family suites.
Meals	Dinner, 3 courses, £30 (booking essential). Supper platter £12.50. Afternoon tea £18. Children's high tea £10.
Closed	Never.
Directions	M6 junc. 38; A685 thro' Kirkby Stephen. Before Brough right for South Stainmore; signed on left in 1 mile. Kirkby Stephen station 3 miles.

Simon & Wendy Bennett
South Stainmore,
Kirkby Stephen CA17 4DE

Tel	+44 (0)17683 41937
Email	enquiries@stayinacastle.com
Web	www.stayinacastle.com

The Black Swan

This fabulous small hotel is hard to fault. Bang in the middle of a pretty village surrounded by blistering country it's all things to all men: a smart restaurant, a lively bar, a village shop; they even hold a music festival here in September. A stream runs through an enormous garden, where you can eat in good weather; free-range hens live in one corner. Inside, warm country interiors fit the mood perfectly. You get fresh flowers, tartan carpets, games on the piano, books galore. There's a locals' bar for local ales and a sitting-room bar with an open fire, but the hub of the hotel is the bar in the middle, where village life gathers. You can eat wherever you want, including the airy restaurant at the front where you dig into delicious country food (the meat is from the fields around you), perhaps smoked trout terrine, steak and venison casserole, lemon and ginger syllabub. Excellent bedrooms are fantastic for the money. Expect pretty colours, beautiful linen, smart furniture, super bathrooms. The Lakes and Dales are close, children and dogs are welcome. A very happy place.

Price	£80-£110. Suites £110-£150. Singles £50.
Rooms	14: 11 twins/doubles, 2 suites, 1 single.
Meals	Lunch from £3.95. Dinner, 3 courses, £20-£30.
Closed	Rarely.
Directions	Off A685 between M6 junc. 38 & A66 at Brough.

Alan & Louise Dinnes
Ravenstonedale,
Kirkby Stephen CA17 4NG

Tel	+44 (0)15396 23204
Email	enquiries@blackswanhotel.com
Web	www.blackswanhotel.com

Entry 47   Map 6

The Sun Inn

Extreme pleasure awaits those who book into The Sun. Not only is this ancient inn a delight to behold – thick stone walls, wood-burners, windows onto a cobbled passageway, beer pumps ready for action – but the town itself is dreamy, another jewel of the north. The inn backs onto St Mary's churchyard, where wild flowers prosper and bumble bees ply their trade. Potter across and find 'one of the loveliest views in England, and therefore the world' to quote Ruskin. Herons fish the river, lambs graze the fields, hills soar into a vast sky. Turner painted it in 1825. Back at The Sun, all manner of good things. Warm interiors, recently refurbished, come in elegant country style, keeping the feel of the past while dressing it up in smart clothes. You'll find old stone walls, boarded floors, cosy window seats, newspapers in a rack. Airy, uncluttered bedrooms upstairs are just as good; expect trim carpets, comfy beds, crisp white linen, super bathrooms. Finally, the food – homemade soups, mussels in white wine, loin of local lamb, apple and chocolate pudding. Don't miss it. *Minimum stay two nights if booking Sat night.*

Price	£99–£162. Singles from £76.
Rooms	11: 8 doubles, 1 twin/double, 2 family rooms.
Meals	Lunch from £9.95. Dinner from £14.95. Not Monday lunch.
Closed	Never.
Directions	M6 junc. 36, then A65 for 5 miles following signs for Kirkby Lonsdale. In town centre.

Mark & Lucy Fuller
6 Market Street, Kirkby Lonsdale,
Carnforth LA6 2AU

Tel	+44 (0)15242 71965
Email	email@sun-inn.info
Web	www.sun-inn.info

Number 43

The position here is fabulous: a vast sky, a pretty village, the Kent estuary spilling out to sea. Huge views shoot off to the Lake District, where mountains take to the skies. You're at the end of the road, more likely to be disturbed by commuting birds than a car, so sit on the terrace and watch the train puff across the viaduct or follow a flock of geese as they sweep through the valley. As for Lesley's super-smart B&B, interiors shine after a total renovation. You get glossy books and great views in the sitting room, then an honesty bar in the dining room, where delicious communal breakfasts set you up for the day: freshly squeezed orange juice, baskets of patisserie, porridge with honey and sugar, the full Cumbrian works. Bedrooms vary in size, but all are elegant with warm colours, fabulous linen, excellent beds, sparkling bathrooms. Two have the view, one has a free-standing bath by the window. Platters of meat and cheese can be ordered at night, but there's a legendary fish and chip restaurant (BYO) in the village and a couple of good pubs, too. The Lakes are a 20-minute drive.

Price	£120–£135. Suites £175–£185.
Rooms	6: 1 twin/double, 3 doubles, 2 suites.
Meals	Lunch & dinner platters £14.95. Dinner £22.50, by arrangement, October–March. Pubs in village.
Closed	Never.
Directions	A6 south from Kendal. Right at Milnthorpe, 4 miles to Arnside. Hotel on promenade.

	Lesley Hornsby
	43 The Promenade,
	Arnside LA5 0AA
Tel	+44 (0)15247 62761
Email	lesley@no43.org.uk
Web	www.no43.org.uk

Aynsome Manor Hotel

A small country house with a big heart. It may not be the grandest place in the book but the welcome is genuine, the peace is intoxicating and the value is unmistakable. Stand at the front and a long sweep across open meadows leads south to Cartmel and its priory, a view that has changed little in 800 years. The house, a mere pup by comparison, dates to 1512. Step in to find red armchairs, a grandfather clock and a coal fire in the hall. There's a small bar at the front and a cantilever staircase with cupola dome that sweeps you up to a first-floor drawing room where panelled windows frame the view. Downstairs you eat under an ornate tongue-and-groove ceiling with Georgian colours and old portraits on the walls. You get good country cooking, too, perhaps French onion soup, roast leg of Cumbrian lamb, rich chocolate mousse served with white chocolate sauce. Bedrooms are warm, cosy, simple, spotless, colourful. Some have views over the fields, one may be haunted, another has an avocado bathroom suite. Windermere and Coniston are close. The kippers with lemon at breakfast are a treat. *Minimum two nights at weekends.*

Price	£99–£140. Half-board £73–£90 p.p.
Rooms	12: 5 doubles, 4 twins, 1 four-poster, 2 family rooms.
Meals	Packed lunches by arrangement £8.95. Dinner, 4 courses, £31.
Closed	25 & 26 December; January.
Directions	From M6 junc. 36 take A590 for Barrow. At top of Lindale Hill follow signs left to Cartmel. Hotel on right 3 miles from A590.

Christopher & Andrea Varley
Aynsome Lane, Cartmel,
Grange-over-Sands LA11 6HH

Tel	+44 (0)15395 36653
Email	aynsomemanor@btconnect.com
Web	www.aynsomemanorhotel.co.uk

Masons Arms

A perfect Lakeland inn tucked away two miles inland from Windermere. You're on the side of a hill with huge views across lush fields to Scout Scar in the distance. In summer, all pub life decants onto a spectacular terrace – a sitting room in the sun – where window boxes and flowerbeds tumble with colour. The inn dates from the 16th century and is impossibly pretty. The bar is wonderfully traditional with roaring fires, flagged floors, wavy beams, a cosy snug… and a menu of 40 bottled beers to quench your thirst. Rustic elegance upstairs comes courtesy of stripped floors, country rugs and red walls in the first-floor dining room – so grab a window seat for fabulous views and order delicious food, anything from a sandwich to Cumbrian duck. Apartments (in the pub) and cottages (with bunk beds and sofabeds for children) are a steal; all come with fancy kitchens and breakfast hampers can be arranged. You get cool colours, comfy beds and Bang & Olufsen TVs. Best of all, most have a private terrace; order a meal in the restaurant and they'll bring it to you here. Brilliant. *Minimum two nights at weekends.*

Price	£75–£140. Cottages £110–£165.
Rooms	5 + 2: 5 apartments. 2 self-catering cottages: 1 for 2-4, 1 for 2-6.
Meals	Breakfast hampers £15–£25. Lunch from £6.95. Bar meals from £9.95. Dinner from £14.95.
Closed	Never.
Directions	M6 junc. 36; A590 west, then A592 north. 1st right after Fell Foot Park. Straight ahead for 2.5 miles. On left after sharp right-hand turn.

John & Diane Taylor
Cartmel Fell,
Grange-over-Sands LA11 6NW
Tel   +44 (0)15395 68486
Email   info@masonsarmsstrawberrybank.co.uk
Web   www.strawberrybank.com

The Swan Hotel & Spa

This rather pretty hotel stands on the river Leven, a wide sweep of water that pours out of Windermere on its way south to Morecambe Bay. It's a fabulous spot and the Swan makes the most of it: a stone terrace runs along to an ancient packhorse bridge. The Swan was flooded in the great storm of 2009 and a recent refurbishment has breathed new life into old bones (this is a 17th-century monastic farmhouse). Inside, airy interiors have taken root. There are a couple of sitting rooms, open fires, the daily papers, a lively bar and a good restaurant to keep you going. There's also a spa: hard to miss as the swimming pool shimmers behind a wall of glass in reception. Treatment rooms, a sauna, a steam room and a gym all wait. Pretty bedrooms have the same crisp style: comfy beds, smart white linen, a wall of paper, a sofa if there's room. Those at the front have watery views, the family suites have a dolls house and a PlayStation. Back downstairs, dig into tasty food in the bar or brasserie, perhaps tiger prawn and chickpea broth, Chateaubriand steak with chunky chips, honeycomb cheesecake.

Price	£119–£270. Suites £209–£390.
Rooms	51: 28 doubles, 15 twins/doubles, 8 suites.
Meals	Lunch & dinner £5–£30.
Closed	Never.
Directions	M6 junc. 36, then A590 west. Into Newby Bridge. Over roundabout, then 1st right for hotel.

Sarah Gibbs
Newby Bridge LA12 8NB

Tel	+44 (0)15395 31681
Email	reservations@swanhotel.com
Web	www.swanhotel.com

The Punch Bowl Inn

You're away from Windermere in a pretty village encircled by a tangle of lanes that defeat most tourists. This is a great spot, with views sweeping across a quilt of lush fields and a church that stands next door; bell ringers practise on Friday mornings, the odd bride ambles out in summer. Yet while the Punch Bowl sits in a sleepy village lost to the world, it is actually a seriously funky inn. Rescued from neglect and renovated in great style, it now sparkles with a brilliant mix of old and new. Outside, honeysuckle and roses ramble on stone walls; inside open fires keep you warm in winter. A clipped elegance runs throughout – Farrow & Ball colours, sofas in front of a wood-burner – while Chris Meredith's fabulous food waits in the airy restaurant, perhaps Lancashire cheese soufflé, pan-fried sea bass, bread and butter pudding. Super bedrooms come with beautiful linen, lovely fabrics, Roberts radios, gorgeous bathrooms. Four rooms have big valley views; the vast suite, with double baths, is matchless. There's a sun-trapping terrace, too, but don't miss the lakes and the hills.

Price	£95–£235. Suite £225–£305. Singles from £75.
Rooms	9: 5 doubles, 1 twin/double, 2 four-posters, 1 suite.
Meals	Lunch from £5. Dinner, 3 courses, £30–£35.
Closed	Never.
Directions	M6 junc. 36, then A590 for Newby Bridge. Right onto A5074, then right for Crosthwaite after 3 miles. Pub on southern flank of village, next to church.

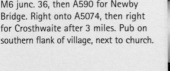

Abigail Lloyd
Crosthwaite, Kendal LA8 8HR

Tel	+44 (0)15395 68237
Email	info@the-punchbowl.co.uk
Web	www.the-punchbowl.co.uk

Gilpin Hotel & Lake House

One of the loveliest places to stay in the country, simple as that. Staff are delightful, the house is a treasure trove, the food is heavenly. Run by two generations of the same family, Gilpin delivers at every turn. Clipped country-house elegance flows throughout: smouldering coals, Zoffany wallpaper, gilded mirrors, flowers everywhere. Afternoon tea, served wherever you want it, comes on silver trays, while the cellar is on display in an exceedingly groovy bar. You're in 20 acres of silence, so throw open doors and sit on the terrace surrounded by pots of colour or stroll through the garden for magnolias, cherry blossom and a fine copper beech as well as the odd pond. Bedrooms are divine with crisp white linen, exquisite fabrics, delicious art; nothing is left to chance. Over half the rooms open onto the garden and a mile away is the new Lake House with six stunning suites by a private lake. As for the food, expect the best, perhaps terrine of rabbit with toasted brioche, Cumbrian veal with a Parmesan crust, passion fruit soufflé with dark chocolate jelly. Unbeatable. *Minimum stay two nights at weekends.*

Price	Half-board £160–£300 p.p. Singles from £210.
Rooms	26: 8 doubles, 12 twins/doubles, 6 suites.
Meals	Lunch £10–£35. Dinner included; non-residents, £58.50.
Closed	Never.
Directions	M6 junc 36, A591 north, then B5284 west for Bowness. On right after 5 miles.

John, Christine, Barnaby & Zoe Cunliffe
Crook Road,
Windermere LA23 3NE

Tel	+44 (0)15394 88818
Email	hotel@gilpinlodge.co.uk
Web	www.gilpinlodge.co.uk

Cedar Manor Hotel

A small country house on the edge of Windermere with good prices, pretty interiors and delicious food. Jonathan and Caroline love their world and can't stop spending money on it. Their most recent extravagance is the coach-house suite, a hedonist's dream; the bathroom is out of this world, the sitting room has a vast sofa, gadgets are sprinkled about (iPod dock, PlayStation, Nespresso coffee machine). The main house, originally a 17th-century cottage, was once home to a retired vicar, hence the ecclesiastic windows. Outside, an ancient cedar of Lebanon shades the lawn. Inside, cool colours and an easy style flourish. There's a beautiful sitting room in brown and cream with clumps of sofas and local art, then a sparkling dining room that overlooks the garden, where you dig into excellent food, perhaps crab cakes, rack of lamb, pear Charlotte with caramel mouse. Bedrooms – some warmly traditional, others nicely contemporary – have Zoffany fabrics, Lloyd Loom wicker and flat-screen TVs; most have fancy bathrooms, some have big views. All things Windermere wait. *Min. two nights at weekends.*

Price	£110–£140. Suites £190-350. Singles from £80.
Rooms	10: 7 doubles, 1 twin, 2 suites.
Meals	Dinner £32.95-£39.95.
Closed	12 December-23 January, but open for New Year.
Directions	From Windermere A591 east out of town for Kendal; hotel on right, next to church, before railway station.

Jonathan & Caroline Kaye
Ambleside Road,
Windermere LA23 1AX

Tel	+44 (0)15394 43192
Email	info@cedarmanor.co.uk
Web	www.cedarmanor.co.uk

Jerichos

You'll be hard-pressed to find better value in Windermere. This is an attractive restaurant with rooms one street away from the middle of town. Chris and Jo had a small restaurant here, wanted something bigger, found this hotel, then spent a king's ransom doing it up. The results are excellent, but it's the way things are done that make it so special: this is a friendly, very personal place. Step inside to find airy interiors with stripped wooden floors, Victorian windows and a splash of colour on the walls. There's a residents' sitting room with a couple of baby chesterfields, then a super restaurant where candles flicker at night. So come for a good meal, perhaps English asparagus, local lamb, milk chocolate panna cotta with rum and raisin ice cream. Spotless bedrooms are very well priced. Those on the first floor have high ceilings, there are leather bedheads, comfy armchairs, fat white duvets and excellent bathrooms, most with fancy showers. Also: iPod docks, cool wallpapers, Lakeland art. The lake is a short stroll: a good way to round off breakfast. *Minimum two nights at weekends.*

Price	£75-£125. Singles from £40.
Rooms	10: 9 doubles, 1 single.
Meals	Dinner, 3 courses, £30-£40. Not Mon & Thurs.
Closed	First 3 weeks in Dec; last 3 weeks in Jan.
Directions	A591 from Kendal to Windermere. Pass train station, don't turn left into town, rather next left 200 yards on. First right and on right after 500m.

Chris & Jo Blaydes
College Road,
Windermere LA23 1BX

Tel	+44 (0)15394 42522
Email	info@jerichos.co.uk
Web	www.jerichos.co.uk

Miller Howe Hotel & Restaurant

The view is breathtaking, one of the best in the Lakes, a clean sweep over Windermere to the majestic Langdale Pikes. As for Miller Howe, it's just as good, an Edwardian country-house hotel made famous by TV chef John Tovey. These days a fine new look is emerging, all the result of a super refurbishment by passionate owners Helen and Martin Ainscough. Inside, new and old combine with ease. Contemporary art and beautiful fabrics blend seamlessly with period features, and the atmosphere is refreshingly relaxed. You can sink into a deep armchair by an open fire and soak up huge views of lake and mountain, then spin into the dining room where walls of glass open onto a dining terrace. Menus bristle with local food, perhaps Lancashire cheese soufflé, Cumbrian lamb, Yorkshire rhubarb crumble. Handsome bedrooms vary in size and style. All are individually designed with handmade fabrics, period furniture and posh TVs, while some have balconies for fabulous views. Cottage suites in the glorious garden offer sublime peace. Perfect whatever the weather. *Minimum two nights at weekends.*

Price	Half-board £105–£155 p.p.
Rooms	15: 7 twins/doubles, 5 doubles, 3 garden suites.
Meals	Lunch from £6.50. Sunday lunch £27.50. Dinner included; non-residents, £45.
Closed	Rarely.
Directions	From Kendal A591 to Windermere. Left at mini-r'bout onto A592 for Bowness; 0.25 miles on right.

	Helen & Martin Ainscough Rayrigg Road, Windermere LA23 1EY
Tel	+44 (0)15394 42536
Email	info@millerhowe.com
Web	www.millerhowe.com

Entry 57　Map 5

Linthwaite House Hotel & Restaurant

The view is magnificent – Windermere sparkling half a mile below, a chain of peaks rising beyond – so it's no great surprise to discover that the terrace acts as a *de facto* sitting room in summer. Linthwaite is a grand Lakeland country house run in informal style. Everything is a treat: wonderful bedrooms, gorgeous interiors, glorious food, attentive staff. The house dates from 1900 and is soundproofed by 15 acres of trim lawns, formal gardens and wild rhododendrons. Totter up through a bluebell wood to find a small lake surrounded by fields where you can fish, swim or retreat to a summer house and fall asleep in the sun. The house is no less alluring with logs piled high by the front door, fires smouldering, sofas waiting and a clipped colonial elegance in the conservatory sitting room. Sublime food is served in elegant dining rooms (one is decorated with nothing but mirrors), while gorgeous country-house bedrooms come in a contemporary uncluttered style. Those at the front have lake views, you can stargaze from the suite. Mountains wait, but you might just decide to stay put. *Minimum two nights at weekends.*

Price	Half-board £126–£204 p.p. Suites £197–£308 p.p. Singles from £155.
Rooms	30: 22 doubles, 5 twins/doubles, 3 suites.
Meals	Lunch from £6.95. Dinner included; non-residents, £52.
Closed	Rarely.
Directions	M6 junc. 36. Take A590 north, then A591 for Windermere. Left at r'bout onto B5284. Past golf course and hotel signed left after 1 mile.

Mike Bevans
Crook Road, Bowness-on-Windermere,
Windermere LA23 3JA

Tel	+44 (0)15394 88600
Email	stay@linthwaite.com
Web	www.linthwaite.com

Holbeck Ghyll Country House Hotel

Holbeck's majestic setting is hard to beat, a sublime position on the side of the hill with huge views tumbling down to Lake Windermere. Acres of gardens abound, there are sweeping lawns, a tennis court and colour in abundance. The house was bought by Lord Lonsdale in 1888. Inside, super-smart country-house interiors reveal grand sitting rooms, golden panelling, roaring fires, rugs on wood floors. Wellington boots stand to attention at the front door, there are mullioned windows, fresh flowers everywhere and a sun terrace for al fresco meals in summer. Best of all is the restaurant – Michelin-starred for 12 years – serving ambrosial food, perhaps roasted scallops with spiced cauliflower, lion of venison with pumpkin purée, nougat glace with a passion fruit sorbet. Bedrooms come with an overdose of elegance. Most in the main house have lake views, while the Potter Suite has a hot tub on its terrace; Madison House and The Sheiling, a couple of cottages, are perfect for families. Wonderful staff know every guest by name. Sunsets are amazing. *Minimum stay two nights at weekends.*

Price	£160–£310. Suites £230–£380. Half-board £290–£510 per room. Cottages £320–£760 (based on 4 sharing).
Rooms	23: 13 twins/doubles, 10 suites, 2 cottages.
Meals	Lunch from £25. Dinner £65. Tasting menu £85.
Closed	Rarely.
Directions	M6 junc. 36, A591 to Windermere. Continue towards Ambleside, past Brockhole Visitor Centre, then right towards Troutbeck (Holbeck Lane). Half a mile on left.

Andrew McPherson
Holbeck Lane,
Windermere LA23 1LU

Tel +44 (0)15394 32375
Email stay@holbeckghyll.com
Web www.holbeckghyll.com

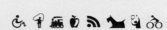

Drunken Duck Inn

The Duck is a Lakeland institution, blissfully hidden away from the crowds. Afternoon tea can be taken in the garden, where lawns roll down to Black Tarn and Greek gods gaze upon jumping fish. You're up on the hill, cradled by woods and highland fell, with huge views from the terrace that shoot across to towering peaks. Roses ramble on the veranda, stone walls double as flowerbeds. As for the Duck, she may be old, but she sure is pretty, so step into a world of airy interiors: stripped floors in the beamed bar, where home-brewed ales are on tap; timber-framed walls in the popular restaurant for super food. Wander at will and find open fires, grandfather clocks, rugs on the floor, exquisite art. Bedrooms come in different shapes and sizes with colours courtesy of Farrow & Ball and peaty water straight off the fell. Rooms in the main house are snug in the eaves; those across the courtyard are seriously indulging. Some have private terraces, one comes with a balcony, several have walls of glass to frame the mighty mountains. Don't miss Duck Tarn for blue heron and brown trout.

Price	£95–£285. Singles from £71.25.
Rooms	17: 15 doubles, 2 twins.
Meals	Lunch from £5. Dinner, 3 courses, £30–£35.
Closed	Christmas Day.
Directions	West from Ambleside on A593, then left at Clappersgate for Hawkshead on B5286. After 2 miles turn right, signed. Up hill to inn.

Stephanie Barton
Barngates,
Ambleside LA22 0NG

Tel	+44 (0)15394 36347
Email	info@drunkenduckinn.co.uk
Web	www.drunkenduckinn.co.uk

Nanny Brow

A beautiful Lakeland Arts & Crafts house which dates to 1903, when architect Francis Whitwell built it for himself. He chose a rather good spot, the view sweeping up the valley with the river Brathay pottering off towards Wrynose Pass. Interiors are no less glorious. Sue and Peter rescued Nanny Brow from neglect and now it shines, a country house reborn. All the lovely old stuff has been painstakingly restored, but the feel is fresh with airy rooms that bask in the light and an easy elegance flowing throughout. The half-panelled sitting room is gorgeous: smart sofas, original windows, ornate ceiling friezes, vases of beautiful flowers. Bedrooms are lovely, too. Some have arch windows that frame the view, all have super-comfy beds, crisp colours, the odd wall of designer paper; gorgeous bathrooms have double-ended baths or walk-in power showers or both. Cumbrian breakfasts set you up for the day, paths through ancient woodlands lead onto the fells. There's a drying room for walkers, secure storage for bikes and excellent restaurants in Ambleside, a mile up the road. *Min. stay two nights at weekends.*

Price	£120–£180. Suites £210–£300. Singles from £110.
Rooms	10: 7 doubles, 3 suites.
Meals	Restaurants 1 mile.
Closed	Never
Directions	West from Ambleside on A593. On right after a mile.

Peter & Susan Robinson
Clappersgate,
Ambleside LA22 9NF
Tel   +44 (0)15394 33232
Email   unwind@nannybrow.co.uk
Web   www.nannybrow.co.uk

Borrowdale Gates

This super hotel sits peacefully in Borrowdale, 'the loveliest square mile in Lakeland' to quote Alfred Wainwright. High peaks encircle you, sheep grace the fields, the river Derwent potters past close by. The view from the top of High Seat is one of the best in the Lakes with Derwent Water sparkling under a vast sky, but the lowland walking is equally impressive: long or short, high or low, Borrowdale always delivers. At the end of the day, roll back down to this deeply comfy hotel and recover in style. Downstairs, big windows follow you around and there are sofas and armchairs scattered about to make the most of the view. You get binoculars, the daily papers, afternoon tea in front of roaring fires. Bedrooms are immaculately traditional. Expect warm colours, super beds, smart bathrooms, armchairs or sofas if there's room. Some open onto terraces, several have small balconies, most have the view. As for the restaurant, a wall of glass looks out over the village and beyond, a perfect spot for a tasty meal, perhaps sweet potato soup, fell-bred lamb, sticky toffee pudding. *Minimum two nights at weekends.*

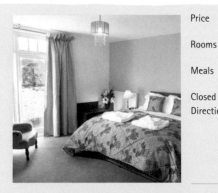

Price	Half-board £97–£132 p.p. Suites £150 p.p. Singles from £97.
Rooms	25: 12 doubles, 3 twins, 3 twins/doubles, 4 singles, 3 suites.
Meals	Light lunches from £8. Dinner included; non-residents, £30–£39.
Closed	January.
Directions	M6 to Penrith, A66 to Keswick, then B5289 south for 4 miles. Right at humpback bridge, through Grange, hotel on right.

Colin Harrison
Grange-in-Borrowdale,
Keswick CA12 5UQ

Tel	+44 (0)17687 77204
Email	hotel@borrowdale-gates.co.uk
Web	www.borrowdale-gates.com

The Cottage in the Wood

Small is beautiful at the Cottage in the Wood, where delicious food, attractive prices and a winning position on the side of Whinlatter Pass have won a devoted band of happy guests. This 17th-century white-washed building sits on the side of a forested hill, with three-mile views from dining-room windows across the valley to Skiddaw; a terrace for summer meals looks the right way. Inside, chic simplicity is the virtue: an airy sitting room, a fire that burns on both sides, books and games to keep you amused, windows galore in the restaurant. Excellent food, with roots and herbs foraged from the forest, hits the spot. Try beetroot and red wine spelt with goats curd, wood pigeon with wild mushroom tortellini and British artisan cheeses. Airy bedrooms vary in size; some are big, some are small, all are spotless with honest prices. Expect crisp linen, flat-screen TVs and big white towels in super bathrooms (and a wet room in the garden room). Also, a drying room for walkers, secure storage for bicycles, a burn that tumbles down the hill and starry skies on clear nights. *Minimum two nights at weekends.*

Price	£110–£150. Suite £180. Singles from £88.
Rooms	9: 6 doubles, 2 twins/doubles, 1 suite.
Meals	Lunch from £14.95. Sunday lunch £25. Dinner £36–£55. Not Sunday night or Monday.
Closed	January.
Directions	M6 junc. 40, A66 west to Braithwaite, then B5292 for Lorton. On right after 2.5 miles (before visitor centre).

Kath & Liam Berney
Braithwaite,
Keswick CA12 5TW

Tel	+44 (0)17687 78409
Email	relax@thecottageinthewood.co.uk
Web	www.thecottageinthewood.co.uk

Swinside Lodge Hotel

Swinside is a dream — a small, intimate country house that sits in silence at the foot of Cat Bells. Fells rise, spirits soar, and Derwent Water, Queen of the Lakes, is a short stroll through the woods. Kath and Mike came back from France to take up the reigns of this ever-popular hotel and they haven't stopped; sash windows have been replaced, bedrooms have been given a makeover, fancy bathrooms are now de rigueur. Downstairs, you'll find fresh flowers and comfy sofas in the yellow drawing room, shelves of books and a jukebox in the sitting room, red walls and gilt-framed mirrors in the airy dining room, where windows frame views of Skiddaw. Super food waits in the restaurant, exactly what you want after a day on the fells — tasty fishcakes, local lamb, chocolate mousse. Upstairs, a new regime is taking shape in the bedrooms with warm colours, golden throws and padded window seats spreading a cool country elegance wherever they go. Outside, a host of characters visit the garden: a woodpecker, red squirrels, roe deer. Wonderful. *Children over 12 welcome.*

Price	Half-board £94–£152 p.p.
Rooms	7: 5 doubles, 2 twins/doubles.
Meals	Dinner, 4 courses, included; non-residents, £45. Packed lunches £9.
Closed	Christmas & New Year.
Directions	M6 junc. 40. A66 west past Keswick, over r'bout, then 2nd left for Portinscale & Grange. Follow signs to Grange for 2 miles (not right hand turns). House signed on right.

Mike & Kathy Bilton
Newlands,
Keswick CA12 5UE

Tel	+44 (0)17687 72948
Email	info@swinsidelodge-hotel.co.uk
Web	www.swinsidelodge-hotel.co.uk

The Pheasant

A 15th-century coaching inn with Sale Fell and Wythop Woods rising behind. A glorious English garden looks the right way, so grab a deckchair and settle in for an early evening drink; heaven on a good day. Interiors are no less beautiful. This is an extremely comfortable country-house inn with open fires in elegant sitting rooms and a fabulous bar, a treasured relic of times past; a couple of Thompson sketches hang on the wall (he exchanged them for drink). Cosseting bedrooms, warm in yellow, come with pretty pine beds, crisp linen, Roberts radios and robes in spotless bathrooms. Most are in the main house; two in a nearby garden lodge are dog-friendly. There's lots to do: Skiddaw to be scaled, and Bassenthwaite, the only lake in the Lake District, close. So explore by day, then return for an excellent dinner. You eat either in the elegant bistro at the front (period colours, oak flooring) or the airy dining room at the back (fresh flowers, big art). Wherever you go, the food is delicious, perhaps peat-smoked salmon, saddle of Lakeland lamb, Irish whiskey crème brûlée. A treat. *Min. stay two nights at weekends.*

Price	£150–£210. Singles from £90.
Rooms	15: 8 twins/doubles, 6 doubles, 1 single.
Meals	Bistro lunch & dinner £5–£30. Restaurant: dinner, 3 courses, £35. À la carte £40–£50.
Closed	Christmas Day.
Directions	From Keswick A66 north-west for 6 miles. Hotel on left, signed.

	Matthew Wylie Bassenthwaite Lake, Cockermouth CA13 9YE
Tel	+44 (0)17687 76234
Email	info@the-pheasant.co.uk
Web	www.the-pheasant.co.uk

Entry 65   Map 5

The Peacock at Rowsley

The Peacock dates to 1652. It was once the dower house to Haddon Hall and stands by the bridge in the middle of the village. It opened as a coaching inn 200 years ago and its lawns run down to the river Derwent. Fishermen come to try their hand, but those who want to walk can follow the river up to Chatsworth. Later, sweep back over gentle hills and return for a night at this rather swish hotel. Old and new mix harmoniously inside. Imagine mullioned windows, hessian rugs, aristocratic art, then striking colours that give a contemporary feel. French windows in the restaurant open onto a pot-festooned terrace in summer, while the fire in the bar smoulders all year. Rooms come in different shapes and sizes, all with a surfeit of style: crisp linen, good beds, Farrow & Ball colours, the odd antique. Serious food waits in the restaurant, perhaps squab pigeon with chocolate jelly, Derbyshire rib-eye with Madeira sauce, ginger crème brûlée with pear sorbet. Three circular walks start from the front door, so you can walk off any excess in the hills that surround you. *Minimum stay two nights at weekends.*

Price	£155–£257.50. Singles from £85. Half-board from £107.50 p.p.
Rooms	16: 6 doubles, 7 twins, 1 four-poster, 2 singles.
Meals	Lunch from £4.50. Dinner £55. Sunday lunch £20.50–£27.50.
Closed	Rarely.
Directions	A6 north through Matlock, then to Rowsley. On right in village.

Jenni MacKenzie
Bakewell Road, Rowsley,
Matlock DE4 2EB

Tel	+44 (0)1629 733518
Email	reception@thepeacockatrowsley.com
Web	www.thepeacockatrowsley.com

Cavendish Hotel

Chatsworth House stands a mile or two across the fields from this smart estate hotel. You can rise leisurely, scoff your bacon and eggs, then follow footpaths over, a great way to arrive at one of Britain's loveliest houses; those who do find fabulous gardens and a jaw-dropping collection of art. As for the Cavendish, it comes in warm country-house style. Sofas wait in front of a roaring fire in the golden sitting room, art from the 'big house' hangs on the walls, there's afternoon tea on the lawn in summer. Lovely bedrooms come in different shapes and sizes, some with pretty florals, others in period colours. None are small, all but one have country views and some are seriously swanky. You'll find robes in decent bathrooms, lots of colour, a sofa if there's room. Back downstairs you can eat in the Garden room (more informal, big views) or in the elegant restaurant, perhaps mushroom risotto with truffle foam, Chatsworth beef with blue cheese bon bons, tart tatin with star anise ice cream. Outside, the Peak District waits, so bring your walking boots. Fishing can be arranged, too.

Price	£169-£219. Suite £286. Singles from £133.
Rooms	24: 20 doubles, 2 twins, 1 family room, 1 suite.
Meals	Continental breakfast £9.50, full English £18.90. Lunch from £5.95. Dinner £30-£45.
Closed	Never.
Directions	M1 junc. 29, A617 to Chesterfield, A619 to Baslow. On left in village.

Philip Joseph
Church Lane, Baslow,
Bakewell DE45 1SP

Tel	+44 (0)1246 582311
Email	info@cavendish-hotel.net
Web	www.cavendish-hotel.net

The George

Charlotte Brontë set part of *Jane Eyre* here. She called the village Morton, referred to this hotel as The Feathers and stole the name of an old landlord for her heroine. These days a copy of her famous novel sits on the shelves of 'the smallest library in the world', which occupies a turret in the sitting room. The bigger turret, equally well employed, is now the bar. The George, a 500-year-old ale house, has grown in stature over time and a smart refurbishment recently propelled it into the 21st century. As a result, wood floors, stone walls and heavy beams mix with purple sofas, fancy wallpaper and Lloyd Loom furniture. It's an unexpected marriage that works rather well, making this small hotel quite a find in the northern Peak District. Airy bedrooms are good value for money. They are full of colour, have spotless bathrooms, excellent beds are dressed in crisp linen; those at the back are quietest. As for the food, a good meal waits in the dining room, so scale Arbor Low, then return to smoked salmon, chestnut and venison pudding, chocolate pave with hazelnut macaroons.

Price	£95–£198. Singles from £70.
Rooms	24: 17 doubles, 4 twins/doubles, 3 singles.
Meals	Lunch from £4.75. Dinner, 3 courses, £36.50.
Closed	Never.
Directions	In village at junction of A6187 and B6001, 10 miles west of M1 at Sheffield.

Philip Joseph
Main Road, Hathersage,
Hope Valley S32 1BB

Tel	+44 (0)1433 650436
Email	info@george-hotel.net
Web	www.george-hotel.net

The Culbone

This lovely little restaurant with rooms has fantastic views that stretch for miles across these mighty moors. You can walk straight out – the path to Robber's Bridge cuts through the garden. Mark and Jack have come to be a part of their community: to source their food from nearby farms; to give locals land for an allotment; to offer jobs to those who live here; to run the place with the needs of the community in mind. This is pretty big stuff and it's carried off with nonchalant aplomb, as if everyone else is doing it; they're not. Predictably, the locals love it, not least for Jack's wonderful food, anything from a spectacular Toulouse sausage sandwich to grilled sea bass with harissa and fennel. If eating the food isn't enough, Jack runs a cookery school and will teach you how prepare his dishes; he'll even take you down to the farm, into the forest to forage or down to the river to fish: total immersion! Back at the inn you find whitewashed walls and contemporary furniture, then pretty bedrooms (not huge) with lots of comfort; one opens onto its own terrace. Dogs are welcome.

Price	£85–£125. Half-board from £65 p.p.
Rooms	5: 4 doubles, 1 twin/double.
Meals	Lunch from £6.50. Dinner, 3 courses, £25–£35.
Closed	Never.
Directions	West from Porlock on A39 and on right after 5 miles.

Mark Sanders & Jack Scarterfield
Porlock,
Minehead TA24 8JW

Tel	+44 (0)1643 862259
Email	mark@pipspubs.com
Web	www.theculbone.com

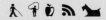

The Old Rectory Hotel Exmoor

The coastal road from Lynton is a great way in, a rollercoaster lane that sweeps though woods clinging to the hill with the sea below. Wash up at the Old Rectory and find a warmly stylish hotel that must qualify as one of the quietest in England. Three acres of matured gardens wrap around you, only birdsong disturbs you, though Exmoor deer occasionally come to drink from the pond. Inside, Huw and Sam, corporate escapees who have taken to the hills, have put their elegant mark on the place: uncluttered interiors, Farrow & Ball colours and a revamp of the marvellous conservatory, where a 200-year old vine provides grapes for the cheese board. There are books, an open fire in the snug sitting room and wonderful bedrooms scattered about with big beds, crisp linen, cool colours and flat-screen TVs; one has a balcony, most have super-cool bathrooms. Spin into the restaurant for an excellent meal, perhaps local asparagus, Exmoor pork, bread and butter pudding. Afternoon tea is on the house and served in the garden in good weather. *Minimum two nights at weekends in high season.*

Price	£160–£170. Suites £185. Half-board £100–£125 p.p.
Rooms	10: 3 doubles, 4 twins/doubles, 3 suites.
Meals	Dinner, 4 courses, £36.
Closed	November–March.
Directions	M5 junc. 27, A361 to South Molton, then A399 north. Right at Blackmore Gate onto A39 for Lynton. Left after 3 miles, signed Martinhoe. In village, next to church.

Huw Rees & Sam Prosser
Martinhoe, Parracombe,
Barnstaple EX31 4QT

Tel	+44 (0)1598 763368
Email	info@oldrectoryhotel.co.uk
Web	www.oldrectoryhotel.co.uk

Heasley House

The sort of place you chance upon, only to return again and again. Everything here is lovely. It's a beautiful house in a sleepy village lost in a wild Exmoor valley, with stylish interiors, delicious food and attractive prices. Inside, Paul and Jan have overseen a total refurbishment, recovering the grandness of a Georgian mine captain's house, then dressing it up in contemporary clothes. You find stripped boards, stone walls, timber frames, a frieze on the fireplace. Harmonious colours run throughout, fires burn in the sitting rooms, there is original art, a fancy bar and fresh flowers everywhere. Airy bedrooms are more than comfy with big beds, good linen and lovely bathrooms. Those at the front have country views, those in the eaves have beams. All have flat-screen TVs, DVD players, bathrobes and armchairs. Spin down to the restaurant for a feast of local Devon produce, perhaps fennel soup with smoked salmon, Exmoor lamb with puy lentils, rhubarb and orange crumble with clotted cream. Paths lead out, so follow the river into the woods or head north for cliffs at the coast. Brilliant – and so hospitable.

Price	£150. Suite £170. Singles from £110.
Rooms	7: 6 twins/doubles, 1 suite.
Meals	Dinner £26-£32.
Closed	Christmas Day, Boxing Day & February.
Directions	M5 junc. 27, A361 for Barnstaple. After South Molton right for North Molton, then left for Heasley Mill.

Paul & Jan Gambrill
Heasley Mill,
South Molton EX36 3LE

Tel	+44 (0)1598 740213
Email	enquiries@heasley-house.co.uk
Web	www.heasley-house.co.uk

Northcote Manor

A divine retreat at the top of a hill built on the site of a 15th-century monastery. Those who want peace in glorious country will be in heaven. You wind up a one-mile drive, through a wood that bursts with colour in spring, then emerge onto a plateau of lush rolling hills. The house is as lovely as the land that surrounds it, built of local stone, wisteria wanders along the walls. There are sweeping lawns, a walled garden and a tennis court with country views. Inside, fires roar: in the airy hall, which doubles as the bar; in the country-house drawing room that floods with light; in the sitting room where you gather for pre-dinner drinks. Super food waits in a lovely dining room, steps lead down to a pretty conservatory, and doors open onto a gravelled terrace for summer breakfasts and exquisite views. Bedrooms are no less appealing, all recently refurbished in contemporary country-house style. Expect padded bedheads, mahogany dressers, flat-screen TVs, silky throws. Lovely walks start from the front door; Exmoor and North Devon's coasts are fabulously close. *The Sanctuary, a licensed venue, available for weddings.*

Price	£160–£215. Suites £260. Singles from £110. Half-board (min. 2 nights) from £115 p.p. per night.
Rooms	16: 5 doubles, 3 twins/doubles, 1 four-poster, 7 suites.
Meals	Lunch from £12.50. Dinner, 3 courses, £45. Sunday lunch from £18.50.
Closed	Rarely.
Directions	M5 junc. 27, A361 to S. Molton. Fork left onto B3227; left on A377 for Exeter. Entrance 4.1 miles on right, signed.

Richie Herkes
Burrington,
Umberleigh EX37 9LZ

Tel	+44 (0)1769 560501
Email	rest@northcotemanor.co.uk
Web	www.northcotemanor.co.uk

Percy's Country Hotel

Percy's — a restaurant with rooms on an organic farm — teems with life: pigs roam freely through 60 acres of woodland, sheep graze open pasture, ducks and chickens supply the tastiest eggs. As for this Devon longhouse, it's a cool little hideaway that sits in deep peace. It blends old world wonders with contemporary flair and those clever enough to come find wood-burners to keep them toasty, a zinc bar for a glass of good wine, then a terrace with fabulous views, where you can eat in good weather. And food at Percy's matters. Tina grows her own vegetables, rears her own meat, then conjures up delicious meals, perhaps Cornish scallops with home-cured bacon, home-reared lamb with a rosemary jus, lemon tart and lavender ice cream; there are days in summer when everything you eat comes from the land around you. As for the bedrooms, they're equally lovely — warm and stylish with super beds, leather sofas, spotless bathrooms and flat-screen TVs. Pull yourself away to explore: six ponds attract masses of wildlife, you can even help on the farm. A great place for families and small groups. Dogs are welcome.

Price	£140-£180. Suite £210. Half-board from £105 p.p.
Rooms	7: 6 twins/doubles, 1 suite.
Meals	Dinner, 3 courses, £40.
Closed	Never.
Directions	From Okehampton A3079 for Metherell Cross. After 8.3 miles, left. Hotel on left after 6.5 miles.

Tina & Tony Bricknell-Webb
Coombeshead Estate, Virginstow,
Beaworthy EX21 5EA

Tel	+44 (0)1409 211236
Email	info@percys.co.uk
Web	www.percys.co.uk

Lewtrenchard Manor

A magnificent Jacobean mansion, a wormhole back to the 16th century. Sue and James have returned to this fine country house, which they established 20 years ago as one of the loveliest hotels in the land. Inside, the full aristocratic monty: a spectacular hall with a cavernous fireplace, a dazzling ballroom with staggering plasterwork. There are priest holes, oak panelling, oils by the score. Best of all is the 1602 gallery with its majestic ceiling and grand piano; 'Onward Christian Soldiers' could have been written in the library. Bedrooms are large. Most tend to be warmly traditional (the four-poster belonged to Queen Henrietta Maria, wife of Charles I), but some are contemporary with chic fabrics and fancy bathrooms. All have jugs of iced water, garden flowers and bathrobes. Delicious food waits — perhaps lemon sole, loin of venison, peanut parfait with banana sorbet — and there's a chef's table where you can watch the kitchen at work on a bank of TVs. Outside, a Gertrude Jekyll garden and an avenue of beech trees that make you feel you're in a Hardy novel. *Min. stay two nights at weekends.*

Price	£155–£270. Suites £295–£310. Singles from £120. Half-board from £122.50 p.p.
Rooms	14: 4 doubles, 6 twins/doubles, 4 suites.
Meals	Lunch: bar meals from £5.25; restaurant from £19.50. Dinner, 4 courses, £47.50. Children over seven welcome in restaurant.
Closed	Rarely.
Directions	From Exeter, exit A30 for A386. At T-junc., right, then 1st left for Lewdown. After 6 miles, left for Lewtrenchard. Keep left and house on left after 0.5 miles.

Sue, James, Duncan & Joan Murray
Lewdown,
Okehampton EX20 4PN

Tel	+44 (0)1566 783222
Email	info@lewtrenchard.co.uk
Web	www.lewtrenchard.co.uk

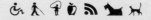

Tor Cottage

At the end of the track, a blissful valley lost to the world. This is a fabulous hideaway wrapped up in 28 acres of majestic country; those who like to be pampered in peace will love it here. Hills rise, cows sleep, streams run, birds sing. Bridle paths lead onto the hill and wild flowers carpet a hay meadow, but be warned – big rooms in converted outbuildings are the lap of rustic luxury and you may dawdle. Each comes with a wood-burner and private terrace: one is straight out of *House and Garden*, another has ceilings open to the rafters. Best of all is the cabin in its own valley – a wonderland in the woods – with a hammock in the trees, a stream passing below, the odd deer pottering past. Breakfast is served in the conservatory or on the terrace in good weather: homemade muesli, local sausages, farm-fresh eggs. You can have smoked salmon sandwiches by the pool for lunch or spark up the barbeque and cook your own dinner; all rooms have fridges and microwaves, so you don't have to go out. Maureen spoils you rotten, her staff couldn't be nicer. A wonderful place.

Price	£150. Singles £98. Cabin £155. Min. stay 2 nights.	
Rooms	5: 2 doubles, 1 twin/double, 1 suite, 1 woodland cabin for 2.	
Meals	Picnic platters £16. Pubs/restaurants 3 miles.	
Closed	Mid-December to end of January.	
Directions	In Chillaton keep pub & PO on left, up hill towards Tavistock. After 300 yards right down bridleway (ignore No Access signs).	

Maureen Rowlatt
Chillaton,
Lifton PL16 0JE

Tel	+44 (0)1822 860248
Email	info@torcottage.co.uk
Web	www.torcottage.co.uk

The Horn of Plenty

This country-house hotel has been thrilling guests for 40 years and it doesn't take long to work out why; the view, the food, the staff and the rooms: all deliver in spades. The house goes back to 1860 and was built for the captain of the mines, who could peer down the valley and check his men were at work; these days it's the Tamar snaking through the hills below that catches the eye. Inside you find the essence of graceful simplicity: stripped floors, gilt mirrors, exquisite art and flowers everywhere. Bedrooms are just as good. Some have terraces that look down to the river, others come in country-house style with vast beds, old armoires, shimmering throws and rugs on stripped floors; bathrooms are predictably divine. As for the food, well, it's the big draw, so expect to eat well, perhaps Falmouth Bay scallops with a carrot purée, Devonshire lamb with a Madeira sauce, then milk chocolate and hazelnut mousse with a passion fruit and banana parfait. Best of all are the staff, who couldn't be more helpful. Tavistock, Dartmoor and The Eden Project are all within striking distance.

Price	£95–£295. Singles from £85. Half-board from £82.50 p.p.
Rooms	10 twins/doubles.
Meals	Lunch £19-50–£24.50. Dinner £49.50.
Closed	Never.
Directions	West from Tavistock on A390 following signs to Callington. Right after 3 miles at Gulworthy Cross. Signed left after 0.75 miles.

Julie Leivers & Damien Pease
Gulworthy,
Tavistock PL19 8JD

Tel	+44 (0)1822 832528
Email	enquiries@thehornofplenty.co.uk
Web	www.thehornofplenty.co.uk

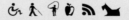

The Henley Hotel

A small house above the sea with fabulous views, super bedrooms and some of the loveliest food in Devon. Despite such credentials it's Martyn and Petra who shine most brightly, and their kind, generous approach makes this a memorable place to stay. Warm Edwardian interiors come with stripped wood floors, seagrass matting, Lloyd Loom wicker chairs, the odd potted palm. Below, the Avon estuary slips gracefully out to sea: at high tide surfers ride the waves; at low tide you can walk on the sands. There's a pretty garden with a path tumbling down to the beach, binoculars in each room, a wood-burner in the snug and good books everywhere. Bedrooms are a steal (one is huge). Expect warm yellows, crisp linen, tongue-and-groove panelling and robes in super little bathrooms. As for Martyn's table d'hôte dinners, expect something special. Fish comes daily from Kingsbridge market, you might have warm crab and parmesan tart, roast monkfish with a lobster sauce, then hot chocolate soufflé with fresh raspberries. Gorgeous Devon is all around. Don't miss it. *Minimum two nights at weekends.*

Price	£120–£144. Singles from £80. Half-board option (min. 3 nights).
Rooms	5: 2 doubles, 3 twins/doubles.
Meals	Dinner £36.
Closed	November–March.
Directions	From A38, A3121 to Modbury, then B3392 to Bigbury-on-Sea. Hotel on left as road slopes down to sea.

Martyn Scarterfield & Petra Lampe
Folly Hill, Bigbury-on-Sea,
Kingsbridge TQ7 4AR

Tel	+44 (0)1548 810240
Email	thehenleyhotel@btconnect.com
Web	www.thehenleyhotel.co.uk

Burgh Island Hotel

Burgh is unique – grand English Art Deco trapped in aspic. Noel Coward loved it, Agatha Christie wrote here. It's much more than a hotel – you come to join a cast of players – so bring your pearls and come for cocktails under a stained-glass dome. By day you lie on steamers in the garden, watch gulls wheeling above, dip your toes into Mermaid's pool or try your hand at a game of croquet. At night you dress for dinner, sip vermouth in a palm-fringed bar, then shuffle off to the ballroom and dine on delicious organic food while the sounds of swing and jazz fill the air. Follow your nose and find flowers in vases four-feet high, bronze ladies thrusting globes into the sky, walls clad in vitrolite, a 14th-century smugglers inn. Art Deco bedrooms are the real thing: Bakelite telephones, ancient radios, bowls of fruit, panelled walls. Some have claw-foot baths, others have balconies, the Beach House suite juts out over rocks. There's snooker, tennis, massage, a sauna. You're on an island; either sweep across the sands at low tide or hitch a ride on the sea tractor. *Minimum two nights at weekends.*

Price	Half-board £400–£430 per room; suites £485–£640.
Rooms	25: 10 doubles, 3 twins/doubles, 12 suites.
Meals	Lunch £48. Dinner included; non-residents, £60. 24-hour residents' menu from £10.50.
Closed	Rarely.
Directions	Drive to Bigbury-on-Sea. At high tide you are transported by sea tractor, at low tide by Landrover. Walking over the beach takes 3 minutes. Eco-taxis can be arranged.

	Deborah Clark & Tony Orchard Burgh Island, Bigbury-on-Sea, Kingsbridge TQ7 4BG
Tel	+44 (0)1548 810514
Email	reception@burghisland.com
Web	www.burghisland.com

Seabreeze

A 16th-century teahouse with rooms on Slapton Sands: only in England. The sea laps ten paces from the front door, the rolling hills of Devon soar behind, three miles of beach shoot off before your eyes. Seabreeze is a treat: cute, relaxed, a comforting dash of homespun magic. Step inside and the first thing you notice is a mountain of irresistible cakes. Carol and Bonni bake the old-fashioned way. It's all homemade and utterly delicious: hot scones, Victoria sponge, banana and chocolate chip brownies. The tearoom itself – white walls, pretty art, tables topped with maps – is warmed by a wood-burner in winter, but in summer you decamp onto the terrace, where sea and sky fuse before you. Both rooms have the view and come in seaside colours with jars of driftwood, padded bedheads and window seats. Outside, there's loads to do: buckets and spades on the beach, cliff walks to great pubs, kayaks for intrepid adventures. Epic breakfasts set you up for the day, while the Start Bay Inn for tasty seafood suppers is yards away. There's surf school at Bigbury or sailing at Salcombe. *Minimum two nights at weekends in high season.*

Price	£100–£140.
Rooms	2: 1 double, 1 twin/double.
Meals	Lunch from £4. Dinner by arrangement. Restaurants in village.
Closed	Never.
Directions	A379 south from Dartmouth to Torcross. House on seafront in village.

Carol Simmons & Bonni Lincoln
Torcross,
Kingsbridge TQ7 2TQ
Tel   +44 (0)1548 580697
Email   info@seabreezebreaks.com
Web   www.seabreezebreaks.com

Plantation House

Plantation House is a small hotel where great food and cool interiors go hand in hand. To some this makes it a restaurant with rooms, but whatever it is, all who stay agree on one thing – it's a great little place to seek solace from the outside world. A lovely vibe follows you around wherever you go. Downstairs, a fire smoulders in the sitting-room bar; upstairs, Georgian windows frame views of hill and forest. Bedrooms pamper you rotten. Two are huge, the rest are merely big. They come with stunning bathrooms, lovely beds, crisp linen and warm colours. You get padded bedheads, sound systems, bowls of fruit. As for Richard's food, it bursts with flavour, perhaps turbot with crab and Chardonnay bisque, crispy Devon duckling, cider and bramley apple jus, then chocolate espresso tart, cappuccino praline sauce and hazelnut ice cream. Soft fruits, vegetables and potatoes all come from the garden in summer, as do home-laid eggs at breakfast. The river Erme passes across the road, so follow it down to the sea and discover Wonwell Beach. Further afield you'll find Dartmoor and Dartmouth, Salcombe and Slapton Sands. Wonderful.

Price	£125–£180. Suite £240. Singles from £69.
Rooms	8: 5 doubles, 1 twin, 1 single, 1 suite.
Meals	Dinner, 5 courses, £36.
Closed	Never.
Directions	A38, then A3121 for Ermington. In village on western fringe.

Richard Hendey
Totnes Road, Ermington,
Ivybridge PL21 9NS
Tel   +44 (0)1548 831100
Email   info@plantationhousehotel.co.uk
Web   www.plantationhousehotel.co.uk

Fingals

People love the individualism of Fingals and the easy-going among us are the happiest there. Richard runs things in a rare laissez-faire style; Sheila is impossibly kind. Guests wander around as if at home, children and dogs potter about. Dinner (local and mostly organic) is served in one of two panelled dining rooms and you can choose to eat with fellow guests if you fancy. You may find yourself next to an earl, a comedian or a fascinating 'nobody', all drawn in by the charm of this place. Breakfast is served until 11am – a nice touch if you've stayed up late making friends in the honesty bar. The setting is a handsome Queen Anne farmhouse next to a stream with a small indoor pool, a sauna, a grass tennis court and books and art all over the place. Rooms are full of personality and have been spruced up in a mix of styles; the eco suite with its sunken bath overlooking the stream is impeccable. It is generous, engaging, occasionally chaotic and, although it may not appeal to everyone, there are legions of devoted fans. Don't miss Greenway by the Dart – Agatha Christie's atmospheric home. *Min. two nights at weekends.*

Price	£75–£210. Self-catering: £400–£1,400 per week.
Rooms	6 + 3: 6 doubles. 1 self-catering barn for 6, 1 self-catering mill for 5, 1 self-catering suite for 4.
Meals	Dinner £30.
Closed	Mid-January to mid-March.
Directions	From Totnes A381 south; left for Cornworthy; right at x-roads for Cornworthy; right at ruined priory towards Dittisham. Down steep hill, over bridge. Sign on right.

Richard & Sheila Johnston
Dittisham,
Dartmouth TQ6 0JA

Tel   +44 (0)1803 722398
Email info@fingals.co.uk
Web   www.fingals.co.uk

Browns Hotel

Browns is all things to all men, a trendy little eatery bang in the middle of town. You can pop in for coffee, stay for lunch, drop by for a beer or book in for a slap-up dinner. The building goes back to 1812 but the interiors are unmistakably contemporary, with sofas by the fire in the bar and Philippe Starck chairs in the airy restaurant. An open-plan feel runs throughout and fine Georgian windows look onto the high street, so sink into a comfy armchair and watch the world go by. Colours come courtesy of Farrow & Ball, big seaside oils hang on the walls, flames leap from a pebbled fire, stripped floors mix with sandstone tiles. Bedrooms upstairs may not be huge but they're clean, comfortable and pretty. Expect padded bedheads, flat-screen TVs, tub leather armchairs and warm colours. Rooms at the back are quieter, but all have radios, good bathrooms and a book that spills local secrets (the best walks and beaches, which ferries to use). Bistro-style food waits in the restaurant: super paella, local sea bass, fish tagine. And the river is close. *Minimum two nights at weekends.*

Price	£95-£165. Four-poster £185. Singles from £75 (Sunday-Thursday).
Rooms	10: 8 doubles, 1 twin, 1 four-poster.
Meals	Lunch from £6.95. Dinner, 3 courses, about £25.
Closed	First 2 weeks in January.
Directions	Into Dartmouth on A3122. Left at 1st r'bout, straight over 2nd r'bout, then 3rd right (Townstal Road). Down into town. On right.

James & Clare Brown
27-29 Victoria Road,
Dartmouth TQ6 9RT

Tel	+44 (0)1803 832572
Email	enquiries@brownshoteldartmouth.co.uk
Web	www.brownshoteldartmouth.co.uk

The Cary Arms at Babbacombe Bay

The Cary Arms hovers above Babbacombe Bay with huge views of water and sky that shoot off to Dorset's Jurassic coast. It's a cool little place – half seaside pub, half dreamy hotel – and it makes the most of its spectacular position: five beautiful terraces drop downhill towards a small jetty, where locals fish. The hotel has six moorings in the bay, you can charter a boat and explore the coast. Back on dry land the bar comes with stone walls, wooden floors and a fire that burns every day. In good weather you eat on the terraces, perhaps a pint of prawns, Dover sole, wet chocolate cake; groups of friends can enjoy their own barbecues, too. Dazzling bedrooms come in New England style. All but one opens onto a private terrace or balcony, you get decanters of sloe gin, flat-screen TVs, fabulous beds, super bathrooms (one has a claw-foot bath that looks out to sea). Back outside, you can snorkel on mackerel reefs or hug the coastline in a kayak. If that sounds too energetic, either head to the treatment room (do book) or sink into a deck chair on the residents' sun terrace. *Minimum two nights at weekends.*

Price	£170–£270. Suite £320–£370. Cottages £900–£2,995 per week.
Rooms	8 + 4: 6 doubles, 1 twin/double, 1 family suite. 4 self-catering cottages for 2–8.
Meals	Lunch from £7.95. Dinner £25–£35.
Closed	Never.
Directions	From Teignmouth south on A379; 5 miles to St Mary Church, thro' lights, left into Babbacombe Downs Rd. Follow road right; left downhill.

Jen Podmore
Beach Road, Babbacombe,
Torquay TQ1 3LX

Tel	+44 (0)1803 327110
Email	enquiries@caryarms.co.uk
Web	www.caryarms.co.uk

Kingston House

It's hard to know where to begin with this stupendous house – the history in one bathroom alone would fill a small book. "It's like visiting a National Trust home where you can get into bed," says Elizabeth, your gentle, erudite host. Set in a flawless Devon valley, completed in 1730 for a wealthy wool merchant, Kingston is one of the finest surviving examples of early 18th-century English architecture and stands in 16 acres of blissful peace. Many original features remain, including numerous open fires, murals peeling off the walls, a sitting room in the old chapel (look for the drunken cherubs). The craftsman who carved the marble hallway later worked on the White House, the marquetry staircase is the best in Europe, and the magnificent bed in the Green Room has stood there since 1830. The cooking is old school as befits the house, perhaps smoked salmon soufflé, rack of lamb, tarte au citron; vegetables come from the garden, free-range hens provide for breakfast. Come in May for 6,000 tulips in the gardens. And there's a small pool with a jet stream so you can swim 20 miles.

Price	£180-£200. Singles from £110.
Rooms	3: 2 four-posters, both en suite. 1 twin/double with separate bath.
Meals	Dinner, 3 courses, £40.
Closed	Christmas & New Year.
Directions	From A38, A384 to Staverton. At Sea Trout Inn left fork for Kingston; halfway up hill right fork; at top, ahead at x-roads. Left thro' pillars at formal garden.

Michael & Elizabeth Corfield
Staverton,
Totnes TQ9 6AR

Tel	+44 (0)1803 762235
Email	info@kingston-estate.co.uk
Web	www.kingston-estate.co.uk

Prince Hall Hotel

A small country house lost to the world on beautiful Dartmoor. You spin down an avenue of beech trees, note the majestic view, then decant into this warm and friendly bolthole. It's one of those places that brilliantly blends informality with good service: lovely staff look after you during your stay. Potter about and find a sitting-room bar where you can sink into sofas in front of a wood-burner; binoculars in the drawing room, where long views are framed by shuttered windows; then a smart white restaurant where you gather for delicious local food, perhaps pea soup with poached asparagus, rack of Dartmoor lamb, vanilla panna cotta with rhubarb soup. Bedrooms are all different, but it's worth splashing out on the big ones at the back which have the view. They're altogether grander and come with smart beds, warm colours, excellent bathrooms, perhaps a sofa, too. Those at the side are simpler, but earthy walkers will find much rest here. Outside, lawns run down to fields, the river passes beyond, then moor and sky. Dogs are very welcome.

Price	£135–£190. Singles from £95. Half-board from £85 p.p. Min. 2 nights at weekends.
Rooms	8: 4 doubles, 4 twins/doubles.
Meals	Lunch from £5.95. Dinner £33.95–£39.95.
Closed	Never.
Directions	A38 to Ashburton, then follow signs through Poundsgate & Dartmeet. Hotel signed on left 1 mile before Two Bridges.

Fi & Chris Daly
Two Bridges, Princetown,
Yelverton PL20 6SA

Tel	+44 (0)1822 890403
Email	info@princehall.co.uk
Web	www.princehall.co.uk

Lydgate House Hotel

You're in 36 acres of heaven, so come for the wonder of Dartmoor: deer and badger, fox and pheasant, kingfisher and woodpecker, all live here. A 30-minute circular walk takes you over the East Dart river, up to a wild hay meadow where rare orchids flourish, then back down to a 12th-century clapper bridge: utterly sensational. Herons dive in the river by day; you may get a glimpse from the conservatory as you dig into your locally cured bacon and eggs. The house is a dream, a nourishing stream of homely comforts: a drying room for walkers, deep white sofas, walls of books, a wood-burner in the sitting room, the sound of the river when the river is full. Karen cooks the sort of food you'd hope for after a day on the moors, perhaps leek and potato soup, whole lemon sole, a raspberry and cinnamon torte or a plate of Tavistock cheeses. Bedrooms – two are huge – are warm and cosseting with crisp florals, comfy beds and Radox in the bathrooms. Finally, moonwort grows in the hay meadow. Legend says if gathered by moonlight it unleashes magical properties; clearly someone has.

Price	£85–£120. Singles £45–£55.
Rooms	7: 4 doubles, 1 twin/double, 2 singles.
Meals	Dinner, 3 courses, £27.50.
Closed	January.
Directions	From Exeter A30 west to Whiddon Down, A382 south to Moretonhampstead, B3212 west to Postbridge. In village, left at pub. House signed straight ahead.

Stephen & Karen Horn
Postbridge,
Yelverton PL20 6TJ

Tel	+44 (0)1822 880209
Email	info@lydgatehouse.co.uk
Web	www.lydgatehouse.co.uk

Mill End

Another Dartmoor gem. Mill End is flanked by the Two Moors Way, one of the loveliest walks in England. It leads along the river Teign, then up to Castle Drogo – not a bad way to follow your bacon and eggs. As for the hotel, inside is an elegant country retreat. There are timber frames, nooks and crannies, bowls of fruit, pretty art. Warm, uncluttered interiors are just the ticket, with vases of flowers on plinths in the sofa'd sitting room and smartly upholstered dining chairs in the airy restaurant. Bedrooms come in country-house style: white linen, big beds, moor views, the odd antique. You might find a chandelier, a large balcony or padded window seats. All come with flat-screen TVs, some have big baths stocked with lotions. Back down in the restaurant, where the mill wheel turns in the window, you find delicious food, perhaps mushroom and tarragon soup, Dartmoor lamb with fondant potato and rosemary jus, chocolate tart. Little ones have their own high tea at 6pm. In the morning there's porridge with cream and brown sugar, as well as the usual extravagance. Dogs are very welcome.

Price	£90–£110. Suites £130–£210. Singles from £75. Half-board from £85 p.p.
Rooms	15: 9 doubles, 2 twins,1 family, 3 suites.
Meals	Lunch from £8, Mon-Sat. Sunday lunch from £15.95. Dinner £38–£42.
Closed	2 weeks in Jan.
Directions	M5, then A30 to Whiddon Down. South on A382, through Sandy Park, over small bridge and on right.

Peter & Sue Davies
Chagford,
Newton Abbot TQ13 8JN

Tel	+44 (0)1647 432282
Email	info@millendhotel.com
Web	www.millendhotel.com

The Lamb Inn

This 16th-century inn is nothing short of perfect, a proper local in the old tradition with gorgeous rooms and the odd touch of quirkiness to add authenticity to earthy bones. It stands on a cobbled walkway in a village lost down Devon's tiny lanes, and those lucky enough to chance upon it will leave reluctantly. Outside, all manner of greenery covers its stone walls; inside there are beams, but they are not sandblasted, red carpets with a little swirl, sofas in front of an open fire and rough-hewn oak panels painted black. Boarded menus trumpet wonderful award-winning food – carrot and orange soup, whole baked trout with almond butter, an irresistible tarte tatin. There's a cobbled terrace, a walled garden, an occasional cinema, an open mic night... and a back bar, where four ales are hand-pumped. Upstairs, six marvellous bedrooms elate. One is large with a bath and a wood-burner in the room, but all are lovely with super-smart power showers, sash windows that give village views, hi-fis, flat-screen TVs, good linen and comfy beds. Dartmoor waits but you may well linger. There's Tiny, the guard dog, too.

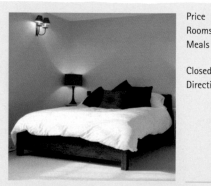

Price	£65–£105.
Rooms	6: 5 doubles, 1 twin/double.
Meals	Lunch from £8. Dinner, 3 courses, £20–£30. Sunday lunch from £8.90.
Closed	Rarely.
Directions	A377 north from Exeter. 1st right in Crediton, left, signed Sandford. 1 mile up & in village.

	Mark Hildyard & Katharine Lightfoot Sandford, Crediton EX17 4LW
Tel	+44 (0)1363 773676
Email	thelambinn@gmail.com
Web	www.lambinnsandford.co.uk

The Lazy Toad Inn

This lovely little inn is humble and gracious and not like those fancy places that always want to blow their own trumpets. It's a way of life. Clive rears sheep and grows masses of food on their land behind, then Mo helps to cook it up to keep the locals smiling. You're in a tiny Devon village, close to the church, where you'll find a river you can walk along. Back at the pub there's a cobbled courtyard, then a small lawn behind; in good weather both make a lovely spot for lunch. Inside, a warm cottage style runs throughout: painted settles, a wood-burner, the odd sofa, good art. Bedrooms above have irresistible prices; one is small, one is big, the other in the middle (two more are coming soon). You get pretty furniture, colourful throws, painted beams and Farrow & Ball colours; one has a funky bathroom. Back in the bar, find local ales, Devon wines, even home-made cordials. As for the food, some of which is foraged, well, we've left the best for last, perhaps goats cheese soufflé, shoulder of Devon lamb, home-grown rhubarb mousse. Exeter is five miles away, but it feels like a hundred. Fabulous.

Price	£75–£95. Singles £55–£75.
Rooms	3 doubles.
Meals	Lunch from £5.35. Bar meals from £10.95. Dinner from £14.00. Sunday lunch, 3 courses, £25.
Closed	Last 3 weeks in January.
Directions	North from Exeter on A377 for Crediton. Over roundabout at Cowley, then 1st right for Brampford Speke. Right again after 1 mile and in village.

Mo & Clive Walker
Brampford Speke,
Exeter EX5 5DP

Tel	+44 (0)1392 841591
Email	thelazytoadinn@btinternet.com
Web	www.thelazytoadinn.co.uk

Southernhay House

A gorgeous small hotel on the loveliest square in town, a short stroll from the cathedral. The house dates to 1805 and was built for a major returning from the Raj. These days interiors sparkle, all the result of a wonderful refurbishment. It's proved hugely popular with locals – the restaurant was brimming the day we visited – and those clever enough to check in for the night find some deeply spoiling bedrooms. Downstairs, French windows at the back of the house draw you out to a small terrace. You can eat here when the sun shines, though the house is weatherproofed with a smart restaurant and a cool little bar should the rain dare to fall. Potter about and find electric blue sofas, 50s starlets framed on the wall, old style radiators and beautiful art. Delicious bedrooms wait upstairs – some are bigger, all are lovely. Expect grand colours, sumptuous fabrics, Indian art and hi-tech gadgetry. Fancy bathrooms come as standard, though bigger rooms have free-standing baths. Don't miss the food – Brown Windsor soup, Dover sole, damson gin jelly and cream. Exeter, Dartmoor and the south coast wait.

Price	£150–£240.
Rooms	10 doubles.
Meals	Lunch, 2 courses, £16.90. À la carte dinner £20–£35.
Closed	Never.
Directions	Sent on booking.

Deborah Clark & Tony Orchard
36 Southernhay East,
Exeter EX1 1NX

Tel	+44 (0)1392 439000
Email	home@southernhayhouse.com
Web	www.southernhayhouse.com

Magdalen Chapter

Where on earth do we start? It might be simpler to confine ourselves to a bald statement of facts to describe this contemporary wonderland. An open fire, terrazzo floors, big warm colours and the odd sofa greet you in the entrance hall. Contemporary art hangs on every wall. There's a curated library, where you can sit and flick through glossy pages; a sitting-room bar with a funky fireplace and a Hugo Dalton mural; an interior courtyard with walls of glass that looks onto a gorgeous garden. The brasserie is magnificent, open to the rafters with white pods of light hanging on high and an open kitchen on display; in summer, glass doors fly open and you eat on the terrace, perhaps seafood spaghetti or a good steak. There are deckchairs on the lawn, a small kitchen garden, treatment rooms for stressed-out guests; there's even a small swimming pool that comes with a wood-burner. Bedrooms have an uncluttered, contemporary feel: iPads, flat-screen TVs, black-and-white photography, handmade furniture. Bathrooms are excellent; expect power showers, big vats of REN lotions and white bathrobes.

Price	£150-£300. Singles from £105.
Rooms	59: 52 doubles, 2 twins/doubles, 5 singles.
Meals	Lunch from £8. Dinner from £12.95; à la carte about £30.
Closed	Never.
Directions	Sent on booking.

Fiona Moores
Magdalen Street,
Exeter EX2 4HY

Tel	+44 (0)1392 281000
Email	magdalen-ge@chapterhotels.com
Web	www.themagdalenchapter.com

Combe House Devon

Combe is matchless, an ancient house on a huge estate, the full aristocratic monty. You spin up a long drive, pass the odd Arabian horse dawdling in the fields, then skip through the front door and enter a place of architectural wonder. A fire smoulders in the vast panelled hall, the muralled dining room gives huge country views, the sitting-room bar in racing green opens onto the croquet lawn. Best of all is the way things are done: the feel is more home than hotel with a battalion of lovely staff on hand to attend to your every whim. Wander around and find medieval flagstones, William Morris wallpaper, Victorian kitchen gardens that provide much for the table; expect home-buzzed honey and fresh eggs from a roving band of exotic chickens. Rooms are stately with wonderful beds, stunning bathrooms and outstanding views, while the vast suite, once the laundry press, is the stuff of fashion shoots. There are 3,500 acres to explore, then ambrosial food waiting on your return, but it's Ruth and Ken who win the prize; they just know how to do it. Dogs are very welcome. *Minimum two nights at weekends.*

Price	£215–£375. Suites £425–£450. Half-board from £159.50 p.p. Cottage £425–£450 (B&B per night).
Rooms	15 + 1: 10 twins/doubles, 1 four-poster, 4 suites. Thatched cottage for 2 with walled garden.
Meals	Lunch from £9. Cream tea from £9. Dinner £52. Sunday lunch £37.
Closed	Rarely.
Directions	M5 junc. 29, then A30 to Honiton. Follow signs to Heathpark, then Gittisham. Hotel signed in village.

Ruth & Ken Hunt
Gittisham,
Honiton EX14 3AD

Tel	+44 (0)1404 540400
Email	stay@combehousedevon.com
Web	www.combehousedevon.com

Masons Arms

Lose yourself in tiny lanes, follow them down towards the sea, pass the Norman church, roll up at the Masons Arms. It stands in a village half a mile back from the pebble beach surrounded by glorious country, with a stone terrace at the front from which to gaze upon lush hills. It dates back to 1350 – a cider house turned country pub – and the men who cut the stone for Exeter Cathedral drank here, hence the name. Inside, simple, authentic interiors are just the thing: timber frames, low beamed ceilings, pine cladding, whitewashed walls and a roaring fire over which the spit roast is cooked on Sundays. Some bedrooms are above the inn, others are behind on the hill. Those in the pub are small but cosy (warm yellows, check fabrics, leather bedheads, super bathrooms); those behind are bigger, quieter and more traditional; they overlook a garden and share a private terrace with valley views that tumble down to the sea. Footpaths lead out – over hills, along the coast – so follow your nose, then return for super food: seared scallops, lamb cutlets, saffron and honey crème brûlée.

Price	£85–£145. Suites £165–£185.
Rooms	21: 8 doubles, 6 twins/doubles, 6 four-posters, 1 family room.
Meals	Lunch from £7.50. Bar meals from £9.95. Dinner, 3 courses, £20–£25. Sunday lunch from £9.95.
Closed	Never.
Directions	Branscombe is signed off A3052 between Seaton & Sidmouth. In village.

John McKitterick
Branscombe,
Seaton EX12 3DJ

Tel	+44 (0)1297 680300
Email	masonsarms@staustellbrewery.co.uk
Web	www.masonsarms.co.uk

Alexandra Hotel & Restaurant

Everything here is lovely, but the view is hard to beat, a clean sweep up the Jurassic coast towards Portland Bill. The hotel overlooks Lyme Bay; the only thing between you and it is the lawn. Below, the Cobb curls into the sea, the very spot where Meryl Streep withstood the crashing waves in *The French Lieutenant's Woman*; in summer, steamers pepper the garden and guests fall asleep, book in hand, under an English sun. As for the hotel, it's just as good. Kathryn, ex-Firmdale, bought it from her mother and has refurbished brilliantly. You get stripped wood floors, windows everywhere, an airy bar for pre-dinner drinks, an attractive sitting room with plenty of books. The dining room could double as a ballroom, the conservatory brasserie opens onto a terrace; both provide excellent sustenance; try crab and lime fishcakes, saddle of venison, pear tart tatin with vanilla ice cream. Beautiful rooms are the final treat, most have the view. Expect super beds, padded headboards, robes in wonderful bathrooms. Lyme, the beach and the fossil-ridden coast all wait.

Price	£177–£225. Singles from £85. Half-board £120–£147.50 p.p.
Rooms	25: 19 twins/doubles, 2 singles, 3 family rooms, 1 family apartment.
Meals	Lunch from £9.90. Dinner in brasserie from £9.90; in restaurant, 3 courses, £41.50.
Closed	Rarely.
Directions	In Lyme Regis up hill on high street; keep left at bend; on left after 200m.

Kathryn Haskins
Pound Street,
Lyme Regis DT7 3HZ

Tel   +44 (0)1297 442010
Email   enquiries@hotelalexandra.co.uk
Web   www.hotelalexandra.co.uk

The Abbot's House

Charmouth – epicentre of Dorset's Jurassic coast – was a model village built by the monks of Forde Abbey in medieval times. This was its principal house and Charles II slept here after his defeat at the Battle of Worcester in 1651; some B&B. Inside, imperious panelling survives (along with 15th-century graffiti), as do ancient flagstones and a piece of plaster moulding now framed on a wall. Nick and Sheila have renovated in great style, their warm interiors a delightful mix of old and new. You find cross beams and regal reds in the cosy sitting room, then an airy breakfast room, where tables come with en suite sofas so you can sit with the papers after your bacon and eggs. Three lavish bedrooms are laden with luxury: period colours, beautiful fabrics, pressed linen, gorgeous bathrooms, technological excess, and freshly baked biscuits every day. Excellent local restaurant wait: Mark Hix in Lyme for fish and oysters, the River Cottage Canteen at Axminster, then Wild Garlic in Beaminster (Mat Frolas won Masterchef in 2009). Back in Charmouth, the beach, rich with fossils, is close.

Price	£120–£140. Min. 2 nights at weekends/in high season.
Rooms	3 doubles.
Meals	Pub/restaurant within 200 yds.
Closed	Christmas & New Year.
Directions	Charmouth is 2 miles east of Lyme Regis, off A35. House on southern side of main street.

Nick & Sheila Gilbey
The Street,
Charmouth DT6 6QF

Tel	+44 (0)1297 560339
Email	info@abbotshouse.co.uk
Web	www.abbotshouse.co.uk

The Bull Hotel

With Dorset's star firmly on the rise, it was only a matter of time before a funky hotel appeared on the radar. Step forward The Bull, a sparkling bolthole that comes in cool hues and which stands on the high street in the middle of town. It's smart enough for a masked ball on New Year's Eve, and informal enough for ladies who lunch to pop in unannounced. It's a big hit with the locals and lively most days; at weekends the bar rocks. All of which makes it a lot of fun for guests passing through. Gorgeous rooms wait upstairs; French and English country elegance entwine with a touch of contemporary flair. Expect beautiful beds, pashmina throws, old radiators, perhaps an armoire. Most come in airy whites, some have striking wallpaper, maybe a claw-foot bath at the end of the bed. There are digital radios, flat-screen TVs, super little bathrooms.. Back downstairs – stripped floorboards, Farrow & Ball walls, sofas in the bar, candles everywhere – dig into brasserie-style food; moules frites is on the menu every Wednesday night. Lyme Regis and Chesil Beach are close. *Minimum two nights at weekends.*

Price	£85–£195. Four-poster £155–£195. Family room £170–£210. Singles £75–£115. Suite £205–£265.
Rooms	19: 10 doubles, 1 twin, 3 four-posters, 3 family rooms, 1 single, 1 suite.
Meals	Lunch, 2 courses, from £12. Dinner, 3 courses, around £30. Sunday lunch £19.
Closed	Never.
Directions	On main street in town. Car park at rear.

Nikki & Richard Cooper
34 East Street,
Bridport DT6 3LF

Tel	+44 (0)1308 422878
Email	info@thebullhotel.co.uk
Web	www.thebullhotel.co.uk

The Greyhound Inn

It's hard to fault this fabulous inn. It sits in one of Dorset's loveliest villages, lost in a lush valley with big views that shoot uphill. Outside, roses, clematis and lavender add the colour; inside rustic interiors have a warm traditional feel. You find stone walls, old flagstones, gilt mirrors and a wood-burner to keep things cosy. There's a lively locals' bar where you can grab a pint of Butcombe, then sink into a Chesterfield, then a lovely little restaurant with old beams and curios, where you dig into delicious food. The feel here is delightfully relaxed and you can eat wherever you want, so spin onto the terrace in good weather and feast on local food, perhaps clam chowder, venison Wellington, almond tart with vanilla ice cream. Six lovely rooms wait in an old skittle alley. They're not huge, but nor is their price, and what they lack in space, they make up for in comfort and style with fluffy duvets, crisp white linen, iPod docks and painted beams. Not that you'll linger, you'll be too busy having fun in the pub. The Cerne Abbas giant is close, the walking exceptional.

Price	£90–£100. Singles from £80.
Rooms	6 doubles.
Meals	Lunch from £6. Dinner, 3 courses, about £30 (not Sunday evening).
Closed	Never.
Directions	South from Sherborne on A352. In Cerne Abbas right for Sydling. Left at ford for village.

Alice Draper
26 High Street, Sydling St Nicholas,
Dorchester DT2 9PD

Tel	+44 (0)1300 341303
Email	info@dorsetgreyhound.co.uk
Web	www.dorsetgreyhound.co.uk

The New Inn Cerne Abbas

The New Inn is most certainly new; it may date to the 16th century, but Jeremy has recently spent the best part of a year refurbishing the place and now it shines. Gone are the swirly green carpets; in their place local slate has been laid in the bar. Lots of lovely old stuff remains — timber frames, mullioned windows, the odd settle — but the feel is fresh with warm colours, engineered oak floors and a smart new bar, where you can order a pint of Dorset Gold or a glass of good wine. An open-plan feel runs throughout and you dig into local food wherever you want, perhaps fish from Brixham, local game, sticky toffee pudding. Bedrooms — some in the main house, others in the old stables — are good value for money. You'll find Hypnos mattresses, blond wood furniture and super little bathrooms. Those in the converted stables feel more contemporary: ground-floor rooms open onto the terrace, where you eat in good weather; those above are built into the eaves. A couple of suites come with double-ended baths in the room. Don't miss the Cerne Abbas Giant. *Minimum stay two nights at weekends.*

Price	£90–£120. Singles from £75.
Rooms	12: 7 doubles, 3 twins/doubles, 2 suites.
Meals	Lunch & dinner £5–£35.
Closed	Christmas Day.
Directions	Village just off A352 between Dorchester and Sherborne.

	Jeremy & Vanessa Lee
	14 Long Street,
	Cerne Abbas DT2 7JF
Tel	+44 (0)1300 341274
Email	info@thenewinncerneabbas.co.uk
Web	www.thenewinncerneabbas.co.uk

BridgeHouse Hotel

Beaminster — Emminster in Thomas Hardy's *Tess* — sits in a lush Dorset valley. From the hills above, rural England goes on show: quilted fields lead to a country town, the church tower soars towards heaven. At BridgeHouse stone flags, mullioned windows, old beams and huge inglenooks sweep you back to a graceful past. This is a comfortable hotel in a country town — intimate, friendly, quietly smart. There are rugs on parquet floors, a beamed bar in a turreted alcove, a sparkling dining room with Georgian panelling. Breakfast is served in the brasserie, where huge windows look onto the lawns, so watch the gardener potter about as you scoff your bacon and eggs. Delicious food — local and organic — is a big draw, perhaps seared scallops, Gressingham duck, champagne sorbet. And so to bed. Rooms in the main house are bigger and smarter, those in the coach house are simpler and less expensive; all are pretty with chic fabrics, crisp linen, flat-screen TVs and stylish bathrooms. There are river walks, antique shops and Dorset's Jurassic coast. *Minimum stay two nights at weekends.*

Price	£126–£200. Singles from £76.
Rooms	13: 6 twins/doubles, 2 four-posters, 1 single. Coach House: 3 doubles, 1 family room.
Meals	Lunch from £12.50. Dinner à la carte £15–£40.
Closed	Never.
Directions	From Yeovil A30 west; A3066 for Bridport to Beaminster. Hotel at far end of town as road bends to right.

Mark & Jo Donovan
3 Prout Bridge,
Beaminster DT8 3AY

Tel	+44 (0)1308 862200
Email	enquiries@bridge-house.co.uk
Web	www.bridge-house.co.uk

Plumber Manor

A grand old country house that sits in a couple of acres of green and pleasant land with the river Develish running through. It dates from 1650 and comes with mullioned windows, huge stone flags and a fine terrace for afternoon tea. An avenue of horse chestnuts leads up to the front door. Inside, a pair of labradors rule the roost. Interiors pay no heed to designer trends – Plumber is old-school, defiantly so, viz. the first-floor landing with its enormous sofa, its gallery of family oils and the grand piano thrown in for good measure. Bedrooms are split between the main house and converted barns. The latter tend to be bigger and are good for people with dogs. Décor is dated – 1980s florals – as are most bathrooms, though a couple now sparkle in travertine splendour. The family triumvirate of Brian (in the kitchen), Richard (behind the bar) and Alison (simply everywhere) excel in the art of old-fashioned hospitality. Delicious country food waits in the restaurant, perhaps seared scallops with pea purée, rack of lamb with rosemary and garlic, lemon meringue pie. Bulbarrow Hill is close. *Pets by arrangement.*

Price	£150-£220. Singles from £115.
Rooms	16: 2 doubles, 13 twins/doubles, all en suite. 1 twin/double with separate bath.
Meals	Sunday lunch £27.50. Dinner £28-£35.
Closed	February.
Directions	West from Sturminster Newton on A357. Across traffic lights, up hill & left for Hazelbury Bryan. Follow brown tourism signs. Hotel signed left after 2 miles.

Richard, Alison & Brian Prideaux-Brune
Plumber,
Sturminster Newton DT10 2AF

Tel	+44 (0)1258 472507
Email	book@plumbermanor.com
Web	www.plumbermanor.com

Stapleton Arms

A perfect village inn: loads of style, lovely staff, super food, excellent prices. The Stapleton started life as a Georgian home, becoming an inn after the war. These days its warm, hip interiors carry a streak of country glamour. Downstairs, amid the happy vibe, find sofas in front of the fire, a piano for live music, a restaurant with shuttered windows and candles in the fireplace. You can eat whatever you want wherever you want; delicious pork pies wait at the bar, but it's hard to resist a three-course feast, perhaps Welsh rarebit with sautéed field mushrooms, Beef Wellington with horseradish mash, Mississippi mud pie. There's a beer menu to beat all others (ale matters here) and on Sundays groups can order their own joint of meat; there's always a menu for kids, too. Super rooms are soundproofed to ensure a good night's sleep. All have beautiful linen, fresh flowers, happy colours, fantastic showers. Also: maps and wellies if you want to walk, a DVD library for all ages, and a playground for kids in the garden. Wincanton is close for the races. Dogs are very welcome. One of the best.

Price	£80–£120. Singles £72–£96.
Rooms	4: 3 doubles, 1 twin/double.
Meals	Lunch & bar meals from £7. Dinner from £10.50.
Closed	Rarely.
Directions	A303 to Wincanton. Into town right after fire station, signed Buckhorn Weston. Left at T-junction after 3 miles. In village, pub on right.

Rupert & Victoria Reeves
Church Hill, Buckhorn Weston,
Gillingham SP8 5HS

Tel	+44 (0)1963 370396
Email	relax@thestapletonarms.com
Web	www.thestapletonarms.com

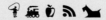

Castleman Hotel & Restaurant

It's a little like stepping into the pages of a Hardy novel: an untouched corner of idyllic Dorset, a 400-year-old bailiff's house, sheep grazing in lush fields and a rich cast of characters. The Castleman — a country-house restaurant with rooms — is a true one-off: quirky, intimate, defiantly English. It pays no heed to prevailing fashions, not least because the locals would revolt if it did. Barbara runs the place with relaxed informality, though touches of grandeur are hard to miss: a panelled hall, art from Chettle House, a magnificent Jacobean ceiling in one of the sitting rooms. Potter about and find a cosy bar, fresh flowers everywhere, books galore. The restaurant has garden views though your eyes will attend only to Barbara's deliciously old-fashioned English food, perhaps potted shrimp terrine, haunch of local venison, meringues with chocolate mousse and toasted almonds. Smart homely bedrooms fit the bill perfectly: eminently comfortable, delightfully priced; a couple have claw-foot baths. Magical Dorset will fill your days with splendour.

Price	£90–£105.
Rooms	8: 4 doubles, 1 four-poster, 1 twin, 1 twin/double, 1 family.
Meals	Sunday lunch £23. Dinner, 3 courses, about £27.
Closed	February.
Directions	A354 north from Blandford Forum. 3rd left (about 4 miles up) and on left in village.

Barbara Garnsworthy
Chettle,
Blandford Forum DT11 8DB

Tel	+44 (0)1258 830096
Email	enquiry@castlemanhotel.co.uk
Web	www.castlemanhotel.co.uk

The King John Inn

You're on the Dorset/Wiltshire border, lost in blissful country, with paths that lead up into glorious hills. Tumble back down to this super inn. Alex and Gretchen have refurbished every square inch and the place shines. Expect airy interiors, a smart country feel, a sun-trapping terrace and a fire that crackles in winter. Originally a foundry, it opened as a brewery in 1859, and, when beer proved more popular than horseshoes, the inn was born. You'll find three local ales on tap but great wines, too – Alex loves the stuff and has opened his own shop across the courtyard – take home a bottle if you like what you drink. As for the food, it's as local as can be with game straight off the Rushmore estate and meat from over the hill; the sausages are a thing of rare beauty. Country-house bedrooms are the final treat. Some are bigger than others, three are in the Coach House, all come with wonderful fabrics, padded headboards, crisp white linen and super bathrooms (one has a slipper bath). In summer, a terraced lawn gives views over a couple of rooftops onto the woods. A perfect spot.

Price	£120–£170.
Rooms	8: 6 doubles, 2 twins/doubles.
Meals	Lunch from £12.95. Bar meals from £8.95. Dinner from £13.95.
Closed	Rarely.
Directions	South from Salisbury on A354, then right onto B3081 at roundabout after 8 miles. In village on right.

Alex & Gretchen Boon
Tollard Royal,
Salisbury SP5 5PS

Tel	+44 (0)1725 516207
Email	info@kingjohninn.co.uk
Web	www.kingjohninn.co.uk

La Fosse at Cranborne

Cranborne was home to Robert Cecil, Earl of Salisbury, the Tudor spymaster who moved King James onto the throne when Elizabeth died in 1603. Under his patronage the village grew into a market town with a garrison to protect a plentiful supply of royal visitors; these days the village has returned to its sleepy roots and is all the better for it. Mark and Emmanuelle arrived three years ago, he to cook, she to polish and shine. It's a small affair, a restaurant with rooms that has resisted the urge for all-out contemporary design. Instead, you find something more homespun: a bar that doubles as reception; sofas in front of a wood-burner; travel books to sweep you away; maps galore for glorious walking. Bedrooms upstairs, recently refurbished, have a super style: warm yellows, pretty fabrics, comfy beds and crisp white linen, smart little bathrooms with underfloor heating. Best of all is the restaurant for Mark's rustic cooking... game terrine, roast shoulder of veal, Capricorn goat's cheese with plum compote. Spin west a few miles to Hambledon Hill (a prehistoric hill fort) for huge country views.

Price	£85. Singles from £49.
Rooms	6: 3 doubles, 2 twins/doubles, 1 suite.
Meals	Dinner (Mon-Sat) & Sunday lunch £19.95-£25.95.
Closed	Never.
Directions	A338 to Fordingbridge, then B3078 into Cranborne. Right at village shop and on right.

Emmanuelle & Mark Hartstone
The Square, Cranborne,
Wimborne BH21 5PR

Tel	+44 (0)1725 517604
Email	lafossemail@gmail.com
Web	www.la-fosse.com

The Priory Hotel

The lawns of this 16th-century priory run down to the river Frome. Behind, a church rises, beyond, a neat Georgian square, and a stone-flagged courtyard leads up to the hotel. Step in to warm country-house interiors: a grand piano in the drawing room, a first-floor sitting room with garden views, and a stone-vaulted dining room in the old cellar. Best of all is the terrace, where you can sit in the sun and watch yachts drift past – a perfect spot for lunch in summer. Bedrooms in the main house come in different sizes, some cosy under beams, others grandly adorned in reds and golds. Also: mahogany dressers, padded window seats, bowls of fruit, the odd sofa. Bathrooms – some dazzlingly opulent – come with white robes. Eight have river views, others look onto the garden or church. Rooms in the boathouse, a 16th-century clay barn, are lavish, with oak panelling, stone walls, the odd chest and sublime views. Four acres of idyllic gardens have climbing roses, a duck pond and banks of daffs. Corfe Castle and Studland Bay are close. A wonderful slice of old England. *Minimum two nights at weekends.*

Price	£205-£300. Suites £335-£365. Half-board (obligatory at weekends) from £130 p.p.
Rooms	18: 13 twins/doubles, 5 suites.
Meals	Lunch from £29. Dinner £44.50.
Closed	Never.
Directions	West from Poole on A35, then A351 for Wareham and B3075 into town. Through lights, 1st left, right out of square, then keep left. Entrance on left beyond church.

Jeremy Merchant
Church Green,
Wareham BH20 4ND

Tel	+44 (0)1929 551666
Email	reservations@theprioryhotel.co.uk
Web	www.theprioryhotel.co.uk

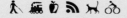

Urban Beach Hotel

Urban beach operates to different rules. The spirit here is infectious: very friendly with buckets of style – surfer chic in Bournemouth with seven miles of sandy beach waiting at the end of the road. Inside, gaze upon a total renovation. Walls have been removed downstairs to create one large airy room and the bar/restaurant now comes with a ceiling rose and plaster moulding to complement chrome stools and the odd decorative surf board. There are big circular leather booths, driftwood lamps, a house guitar and surf movies projected onto a wall in the bar. In summer, doors open onto a decked terrace for cocktails, fresh fruit smoothies and barbecues in the sun. Lovely bedrooms, some big, some smaller, are all fitted to the same spec: flat-screen TVs, crushed velvet curtains, wonderful bathrooms. Drop down for a good breakfast: freshly squeezed orange juice, hot croissants, the full cooked works. A brasserie-style menu runs all day. It's a 20-minute seaside walk into Bournemouth town centre. *Minimum two nights at weekends (three nights bank holidays).*

Price	£97–£180. Singles from £72.
Rooms	12: 9 doubles, 1 twin/double, 2 singles.
Meals	Lunch & dinner £5–£25.
Closed	Never.
Directions	South from Ringwood on A338; left for Boscombe (east of centre). Over railway, right onto Centenary Way. Keep with the flow (left, then right) to join Christchurch Rd; 2nd left (St John's Rd); 2nd left.

Mark & Fiona Cribb
23 Argyll Road,
Bournemouth BH5 1EB

Tel	+44 (0)1202 301509
Email	reception@urbanbeach.co.uk
Web	www.urbanbeach.co.uk

Captain's Club Hotel

A sparkling hotel on the banks on the Stour, where a tiny ferry potters along the river dodging swans and ducks. The hotel has its own launch and those who want to skim across to the Isle of White can do so in style. Back on dry land, locals flock in day and night and the big bar hums with merry chatter as they sink into sofas, sip cocktails or dig into a crab sandwich. There's live music every night, newspapers at reception and doors that open onto a pretty terrace, perfect in good weather. Bedrooms all have river views and come in an uncluttered contemporary style, with low-slung beds, crisp white linen, neutral colours and excellent bathrooms. None are small, some are huge with separate sitting rooms, apartments have more than one bedroom, thus perfect for families and friends. Residents have free access to the spa (hydrotherapy pool, sauna, four treatment rooms). Dinner comes in an ultra-airy restaurant, where you dig into tasty brasserie-style food, perhaps goats cheese soufflé, Gressingham duck, pear mousse with Kir royale sorbet. Pretty Christchurch is a short walk upstream. *Minimum two nights at weekends.*

Price	£199-£259. Apartments £289-£649.
Rooms	29: 17 doubles, 12 apartments for 2-6.
Meals	Bar meals all day from £6. Restaurant lunch from £15; dinner £30-£35.
Closed	Never.
Directions	M27/A31 west, then A338/B3073 south into Christchurch. At A35 (lights at big r'about) follow one-way system left. Double back after 100m. Cross r'bout heading west and 1st left into Sopers Lane. Signed left.

	Timothy Lloyd & Robert Wilson
	Wick Ferry, Wick Lane,
	Christchurch BH23 1HU
Tel	+44 (0)1202 475111
Email	reservations@captainsclubhotel.com
Web	www.captainsclubhotel.com

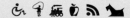

Rose & Crown

An idyllic village of mellow stone where little has changed in 200 years. The Rose and Crown dates from 1733 and stands on the green, next to the village's Saxon church. Roses ramble above the door in summer, so pick up a pint and search out the sun on the gravelled forecourt. Inside is just as good. You can sit at settles in the tiny locals' bar and roast away in front of the fire while reading the *Teesdale Mercury*, or seek out sofas in the peaceful sitting room and tuck into afternoon tea. Bedrooms are lovely. Those in the converted barn are less posh but have padded headboards and tumble with colour; those in the main house come with stylish furnishings and vibrant colours; all have Bose sound systems, quietly fancy bathrooms and lots of other extras. Delicious food can be eaten informally in the brasserie (smoked salmon soufflé, confit of duck, sticky toffee pudding) or grandly in the panelled dining room (farmhouse ham with fresh figs, grilled sea bass, honey and whisky ice cream). High Force waterfall and Hadrian's Wall are close and there's a drying room for walkers.

Price	£150-£190. Suites £210-£225. Singles from £95. Half-board from £110 p.p.
Rooms	12: 6 doubles, 4 twins, 2 suites.
Meals	Lunch & bar meals from £12. Dinner, 3 courses, from £35. Sunday lunch £18.95.
Closed	22-26 December.
Directions	From Barnard Castle B6277 north for 6 miles. Right in village towards green. Inn on left.

Christopher & Alison Davy
Romaldkirk,
Barnard Castle DL12 9EB
Tel   +44 (0)1833 650213
Email   hotel@rose-and-crown.co.uk
Web   www.rose-and-crown.co.uk

The Pier at Harwich

You're bang on the water, overlooking the historic Ha'penny Pier, with vast skies and watery views that shoot across to Felixstowe. The hotel was built in 1862 in the style of a Venetian palazzo and has remained in continuous service ever since. Inside are boarded floors, big arched windows, a granite bar and travel posters framed on the walls. Eat informally in the bistro downstairs (fish pie, grilled bream, beef stew and dumplings) or grab a window seat in the first-floor dining room and tuck into lobster bisque while huge ferries glide past outside. The owners took over the adjoining pub several years ago and have carved out a pretty lounge with port-hole windows, leather sofas, coir matting, timber frames, even a piano. Bedrooms are scattered about, some above the sitting room, others in the main house. All are pretty, with padded bedheads, seaside colours, crisp white linen, super bathrooms; if you want the best view in town, splash out on the Mayflower suite. Don't miss the blue flag beach at Dovercourt for exhilarating walks, or the Electric Palace, the second oldest cinema in Britain.

Price	£117-£215. Suite £190. Singles from £92.
Rooms	14: 13 doubles, 1 suite.
Meals	Lunch from £9.95. Sunday lunch £29. Dinner à la carte £25-£40.
Closed	Never.
Directions	M25 junc. 28, A12 to Colchester bypass, then A120 to Harwich. Head for quay. Hotel opposite pier.

Chris & Vreni Oakley & Nick Chambers
The Quay,
Harwich CO12 3HH

Tel	+44 (0)1255 241212
Email	pier@milsomhotels.com
Web	www.milsomhotels.com

The Mistley Thorn

This Georgian pub stands on the high street and dates back to 1746, but inside you find a fresh contemporary feel that will tickle your pleasure receptors. The mood is laid-back with a great little bar, an excellent restaurant and bedrooms that pack an understated punch. Downstairs, an open-plan feel sweeps you through high-ceilinged rooms that flood with light. Expect tongue-and-groove panelling, Farrow & Ball colours, blond wood furniture and smart wicker chairs. Climb up to excellent rooms for smartly dressed beds, flat-screen TVs, DVD players and iPod docks. You get power showers above double-ended baths, those at the front have fine views of the Stour estuary, all are exceptional value for money. Back down in the restaurant dig into delicious food; Sherri runs a cookery school next door and has a pizzeria in town. Try smoked haddock chowder, Debden duck with clementine sauce, chocolate mocha tart (if you stay on a Sunday or Monday, dinner is free). Constable country is all around. There's history, too; the Witch-Finder General once lived on this spot.

Price	£90–£120. Singles from £75.
Rooms	7: 4 doubles, 3 twins/doubles.
Meals	Lunch from £6.25. Set lunch £11.95 & £14.95. Dinner, 3 courses, about £25.
Closed	Rarely.
Directions	From A12 Hadleigh/East Bergholt exit north of Colchester. Thro' East Bergholt to A137; signed Manningtree; continue to Mistley High St. 50 yards from station.

David McKay & Sherri Singleton
High Street, Mistley,
Manningtree CO11 1HE

Tel	+44 (0)1206 392821
Email	info@mistleythorn.co.uk
Web	www.mistleythorn.co.uk

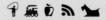

The Sun Inn

An idyllic village made rich by mills in the 16th century. These days you can hire boats on the river, so order a picnic at the inn, float down the glorious Stour, then tie up on the bank for lunch al fresco. You're in the epicentre of Constable country; the artist attended school in the village and often returned to paint St Mary's with its soaring tower; it stands directly opposite. As for The Sun, you couldn't hope to wash up in a better place. Step in to find open fires, boarded floors, timber frames and an easy elegance. A panelled lounge comes with sofas and armchairs, the bar is made from a slab of local elm and the dining room is beamed and airy, so come for fabulous food inspired by Italy: Calabrian salami, pheasant ravioli, spaghetti with chilli and lemon, venison stew with red wine and shallots. Rooms are gorgeous: creaking floorboards, timber-framed walls, a panelled four-poster. Those at the back (a recent addition) are bigger and come in grand style, but all are lovely with crisp linen and power showers in excellent bathrooms. There's afternoon tea on arrival if you book in advance.

Price	£75–£150. Singles from £70.
Rooms	7: 5 doubles, 1 twin/double, 1 four-poster.
Meals	Lunch & dinner from £12. Bar meals from £6.85. Sunday lunch £24.
Closed	25 & 26 December.
Directions	A12 north past Colchester. 2nd exit, signed Dedham. In village opposite church.

Piers Baker
High Street, Dedham,
Colchester CO7 6DF

Tel	+44 (0)1206 323351
Email	office@thesuninndedham.com
Web	www.thesuninndedham.com

Maison Talbooth

Exceptional service, beautiful interiors, a sublime position overlooking Dedham Vale. This small country house packs a polished punch. Once a rectory, it is now a pleasure dome, so step into a golden hall where plump sofas come dressed in fine fabrics and big windows frame the view. The suites are equally majestic. Some on the ground floor have doors onto terraces where hot tubs wait, others at the front have huge views over Constable country. All come primed to pamper you rotten: exceptional bathrooms, fabulous beds, vintage wallpaper, gilt-framed mirrors. But don't linger. The pool house is magnificent, its pool heated to 85°F every day of the year; have a swim, and then dry off by the fire, on the terrace, with a cider. Back inside: an honesty bar, a steam room and sauna. In the evening you're chauffeured to the family's restaurants (both within half a mile): Milsoms for bistro food served informally; Le Talbooth for something more serious overlooking the river. There are treatment rooms back at the hotel, a tennis court with a view, and scrumptious breakfast served in bed.

Price	£210–£420. Singles from £170.
Rooms	12 suites.
Meals	Dinner at Milsoms £25; at Le Talbooth £35–£50.
Closed	Never.
Directions	North on A12 past Colchester. Left to Dedham, right after S bend. Maison Talbooth is on right; follow brown signs.

Paul & Geraldine Milsom
Stratford Road, Dedham,
Colchester CO7 6HN

Tel	+44 (0)1206 322367
Email	maison@milsomhotels.com
Web	www.milsomhotels.com

Tudor Farmhouse Hotel

The Forest of Dean is one of England's best-kept secrets, a magical world of woodland walks, medieval castles, meandering rivers and bleating sheep. This pretty hotel stands in a pocket of silence, a great base from which to explore. You're in the middle of a tiny village, but views from a gorgeous garden – stone walls, postage-stamp lawn, a couple of cottages forming a courtyard – are of field and woods. Inside, airy interiors, exposed stone and whitewashed walls are the order of the day, though timber frames and low beams in the house bear testament to its Tudor roots. Bedrooms are scattered about. An ancient staircase leads up to a half-tester and a four-poster; those in a converted barn are simpler altogether; super garden suites come in beautiful cottages. All mix stone walls, the odd beam, trim carpets and good bathrooms. Back downstairs, you'll find delicious food in the restaurant, perhaps smoked salmon, fillet of beef, a fabulous plate of local cheese. Don't miss Puzzle Wood or Clearwell Caves. You can also kayak on the Wye or join a guide and forage in the forest.

Price	£90–£150. Suites £160–£190. Singles from £80.
Rooms	23: 13 doubles, 3 twins, 2 four-posters, 3 suites.
Meals	Lunch from £4. Sunday lunch from £14.50. Dinner, 3 courses, £30–£35.
Closed	2-9 January.
Directions	West from Gloucester on A40, south for Monmouth on A4136. Left onto B4028. Leave Coleford for Chepstow on B4228 and Clearwell signed right after a mile.

Colin & Hari Fell
High Street,
Clearwell GL16 8JS

Tel   +44 (0)1594 833046
Email   info@tudorfarmhousehotel.co.uk
Web   www.tudorfarmhousehotel.co.uk

Three Choirs Vineyards

England's answer to the Napa Valley. After 15 years of tilling the soil (very sandy, good drainage), Thomas's 75 acres of Gloucestershire hillside now produce 300,000 bottles a year. There are regular tastings, a shop in which to buy a bottle or two, and paths that weave through the vines – a perfect stroll after a good meal. What's more, three fabulous lodges wait down by the lake, all with decks and walls of glass. You'll find claw-foot baths and comfy beds, so camp out in grand savannah style and listen to the woodpeckers. Rooms up at the restaurant are smart and spacious with terraces that overlook the vineyard. They come with padded bedheads, walls of colour, leather armchairs, flat-screen TVs and good little bathrooms. Finally, the restaurant: claret walls, an open fire, lovely views. Excellent food waits, perhaps goat's cheese soufflé with beetroot crisps, spiced monkfish with mango purée, sticky toffee pudding with cinnamon ice cream. World wines are on the list, but you'll plump for something from the vines that surround you; there's a microbrewery, too. Wonderful.

Price	£135–£195. Singles from £105. Half-board from £105 p.p. (min. 2 nights). Min. 2 nights at weekends.
Rooms	11: 6 doubles, 2 twins, 3 vineyard lodges.
Meals	Lunch from £7.50. Dinner à la carte about £35.
Closed	Christmas & New Year.
Directions	From Newent north on B4215 for about 1.5 miles. Follow brown signs to vineyard.

Thomas Shaw
Castle Tump,
Newent GL18 1LS

Tel	+44 (0)1531 890223
Email	info@threechoirs.com
Web	www.three-choirs-vineyards.co.uk

Corse Lawn House Hotel

Baba is old-school, so is Corse Lawn. The service is excellent, the food is delicious and generous prices make it a must for those in search of an alternative to contemporary minimalism. This fine Queen Anne manor house was built on the ruins of a Tudor inn where Cromwell is thought to have slept before the battle of Worcester (1651). It is now the hub of a small community. The Rotary Club dine once a week, shooting parties gather in winter, locals come to celebrate. At the front, a willow dips its branches into the country's last surviving coach-wash; in summer you can sit out under parasols and dig into a cream tea while ducks glide by. Inside, slightly eccentric furnishings prevail. There are palms in the swimming pool, a sofa'd bistro for light meals, an open fire in the sitting room, a paddock at the back for visiting horses. Big bedrooms are eminently comfortable and come in warm colours with crisp linen, bowls of fruit, fresh milk and leaf tea; the four-poster looks onto the pond. As for the food, it's utterly delicious: game terrine, grilled lobster, sticky toffee pudding.

Price	£120–£150. Suites £185. Singles £75–£95. Half-board from £80 p.p.
Rooms	18: 13 twins/doubles, 2 four-posters, 3 suites.
Meals	Lunch & dinner £10–£35.
Closed	Christmas Day & Boxing Day.
Directions	West from Tewkesbury on A438 for Ledbury. After 3 miles left onto B4211. Hotel on right after 2 miles.

Baba Hine
Corse Lawn,
Gloucester GL19 4LZ

Tel	+44 (0)1452 780771
Email	enquiries@corselawn.com
Web	www.corselawn.com

Beaumont House

Beaumont House delivers exactly what you'd want of a small B&B hotel: stylish bedrooms, excellent breakfasts, good value for money, owners who care. Fan and Alan have lived all over the world and came back to England to set up the sort of hotel they like to stay in themselves. After a fine refurbishment, the house shines. Outside, a trim garden gives plenty of scope for summer sundowners before heading into town for an excellent meal. Inside, there's a beautiful sitting room with huge windows and a rather tempting honesty bar. Spotless bedrooms come over three floors. Some are simpler with attractive prices, others are nothing short of extravagant, but all have good bathrooms, so every budget will be happy here. Compact, airy doubles on the lower ground floor are perfect for short stays, while rooms above come with striking design, vast padded headboards, blond-wood furniture and flat-screen TVs. Breakfast is served in an elegant dining room (high ceilings, garden views), while Cheltenham is a 15-minute stroll; there's room service off a short menu in the week in case you want to stay put.

Price	£89–£249. Singles from £69.
Rooms	16: 10 doubles, 3 twins/doubles, 1 family room, 2 singles.
Meals	Restaurants within walking distance. Room service Mon–Thurs eve.
Closed	Rarely.
Directions	Leave one-way system in centre of town for Stroud (south) on A46. Straight ahead, through lights and right at 1st mini-roundabout. On left after 500m.

Alan & Fan Bishop
56 Shurdington Road,
Cheltenham GL53 0JE

Tel	+44 (0)1242 223311
Email	reservations@bhhotel.co.uk
Web	www.bhhotel.co.uk

The Bradley

An early Victorian villa, three windows wide. It was bought in 1918 by Chris's great aunt Madge, who ran it as a home for poor widows returning from the colonies. In the mid-50s an uncle turned it into studios. Now Chris and Sue are continuing the family tradition, restoring it to former glories as a delightful guest house emerges. Downstairs, a couple of vast reception rooms act as the hub of the house. Expect high ceilings, sparkling chandeliers, a roaring fire, cabinets stuffed with interesting things. You get period colours, the daily papers, an Arabian landscape painted by General Rodney Brown. Bedrooms upstairs are a treat. The smallest comes with its own decked balcony, the biggest has a vast four-poster. All have fancy bathrooms; four more rooms are planned for the second floor. Breakfast is served in style with local eggs and bacon. As for dining out, Chris and Sue (who couldn't be nicer) have tried every restaurant in town in order to report back. Try Almanac, Flynn's Bistro or The Emerald for great Thai food. There's a welcoming glass of prosecco on arrival, too.

Price	£85-£115. Four-poster £150. Singles from £80.
Rooms	5: 2 twins/doubles, 2 doubles, 1 four-poster.
Meals	Restaurants within 400m.
Closed	Rarely.
Directions	Leave one-way system to the west, joining St George's Road, signed M5 north. Second left and on left after school.

Chris & Sue Light
19 Royal Parade, Bayshill Road,
Cheltenham GL50 3AY

Tel	+44 (0)1242 519077
Email	thebradleyguesthouse@googlemail.com
Web	www.thebradleyhotel.co.uk

The Montpellier Chapter

The Montpellier Chapter stands at the vanguard of a new movement in cool hotels: loads of style, attractive prices, excellent service from staff who care. It mixes old-fashioned hospitality (you are met in reception and shown to your room) with new technology (you browse the wine list on an iPad). More than anything else, it's a great place to be as it fills with happy locals who bring an infectious buzz. Follow your nose and find a library bar, a Victorian conservatory and a funky interior courtyard for breakfast in good weather. The style is contemporary, the building is a grand Victorian townhouse that's been meticulously restored. Bedrooms – some big, others smaller – spoil you all the way with super-comfy beds, an excess of technology and bathrooms that take your breath away. You get iPods full of local info, Nespresso coffee machines, even a complimentary mini-bar. Excellent comfort food waits in the restaurant, perhaps scallops cooked with garlic and herbs, Shepherd's pie with swede mash, tarte tatin with crème chantilly. And there's an electric car to whisk you around town.

Price	£140–£245. Suite £400.
Rooms	61: 55 doubles, 5 twins/doubles, 1 suite.
Meals	Bar lunch from £7. Restaurant lunch &dinner £12.50–£15. À la carte from £25.
Closed	Never.
Directions	Leave one-way system to the west, joining St George's Road, signed M5 north. Second left and hotel on right at top.

James Partridge
Bayshill Road, Montpellier,
Cheltenham GL50 3AS

Tel	+44 (0)1242 527788
Email	montpelier@chapterhotels.com
Web	www.chapterhotels.com

Wesley House Restaurant

A 15th-century timber-framed house on Winchcombe's ancient high street; John Wesley stayed in 1755, hence the name. Not satisfied with one excellent restaurant, Matthew has opened another bang next door. The elder statesman comes in traditional style with sofas in front of a roaring fire, candles flickering on smartly dressed tables and a fine conservatory for delicious breakfasts with beautiful views of town and country. Next door, the young upstart is unashamedly contemporary with a smoked-glass bar, faux-zebra-skinned stools and alcoves to hide away in. Both buildings shine with original architecture: timber frames, beamed ceilings, stone flags and stripped boards. Quirky bedrooms up in the eaves tend to be cosy, one has a balcony with views over rooftops to field and hill. All come in a warm country style with good beds, pretty fabrics, small showers, smart carpets and wonky floors. Back downstairs, dig into food as simple or rich as you want, anything from fish cakes or a good burger to a three-course feast. The Cotswolds Way skirts the town, so bring your walking boots.

Price	£90–£100. Singles from £65. Half-board (for 1-night stays on Sat) £92.50–£102.50 p.p.
Rooms	5: 1 twin, 1 twin/double, 3 doubles.
Meals	Bar & grill: lunch & dinner from £9.50 (not Sun or Mon). Restaurant: lunch from £13, dinner £20–£25 or £39.50 on Sat. Not Sun nights (except B&B).
Closed	Never.
Directions	From Cheltenham B4632 to Winchcombe. Restaurant on right. Drop off luggage, parking nearby.

Matthew Brown
High Street, Winchcombe,
Cheltenham GL54 5LJ

Tel	+44 (0)1242 602366
Email	enquiries@wesleyhouse.co.uk
Web	www.wesleyhouse.co.uk

Lords of the Manor

This 1650 mansion is fit for a king, but was originally built for a rector. The setting is dreamy, eight acres of lush lawns and formal gardens, then the river Eye and a 19th-century skating pond. Inside, interiors come in grand style, so step in to find parquet flooring, mullioned windows, roaring fires and porters' chairs in a sitting-room bar. Views from the drawing room spin down to the river, old oils adorn the walls, beautiful fabrics come courtesy of Osborne & Little. There's a complimentary wine tasting for guests on Saturday evenings, not a bad way to choose your tipple before sitting down to a Michelin-starred dinner... perhaps breast of mallard with fig purée, line-caught sea bass with roasted scallops, prune and armagnac soufflé with Earl Grey tea mousse. Super-smart bedrooms come in contemporary country-house style with fine linen, excellent art, padded bedheads, bowls of fruit. Some are huge, others smaller. Expect flat-screen TVs and iPod docks, and fancy bathrooms with robes and power showers. Church bells chime on Sunday, the walking is divine. *Minimum two nights at weekends.*

Price	£199–£390. Suites £495. Half-board from £160 p.p.
Rooms	26: 22 twins/doubles, 4 suites.
Meals	Dinner, 3 courses, £65. Tasting menu £85.
Closed	Never.
Directions	North from Cirencester on A429 for 17 miles, then left for The Slaughters. In Lower Slaughter left over bridge. Into Upper Slaughter and hotel on right in village.

Paul Thompson
Upper Slaughter,
Cheltenham GL54 2JD

Tel	+44 (0)1451 820243
Email	reservations@lordsofthemanor.com
Web	www.lordsofthemanor.com

The Wheatsheaf Inn

The Wheatsheaf stands at the vanguard of a cool new movement: the village local reborn in country-house style. It's a winning formula with locals and travellers flocking in for a heady mix of laid-back informality and chic English style. The inn stands between pretty hills in this ancient wool village on the Fosse Way. Inside, happy young staff flit about, throwing logs on the fire, ferrying food to diners, or simply stopping for a chat. Downstairs, you find armchairs in front of smouldering fires, noble portraits on panelled walls, cool tunes playing in the background. Outside, a smart courtyard garden draws a crowd in summer, so much so it has its own bar; English ales, jugs of Pimm's and lovely wines all wait. Back inside, beautiful bedrooms come as standard, some bigger than others, all fully loaded with comfort and style. Expect period colours, Hypnos beds, Bang & Olufsen TVs, then spectacular bathrooms with beautiful baths and/or power showers. As for the food, you feast on lovely local fare, perhaps devilled kidneys, coq au vin, pear and almond tart. Don't miss it.

Price	£130–£200. Singles from £100.
Rooms	14 doubles.
Meals	Continental breakfast included; cooked extras £5–£9. Lunch from £9. Dinner, 3 courses, about £30. Bar meals from £5.
Closed	Never.
Directions	In village centre, off A429 between Stow & Burford.

Sam & Georgina Pearman
West End, Northleach,
Cheltenham GL54 3EZ

Tel	+44 (0)1451 860244
Email	reservations@cotswoldswheatsheaf.com
Web	www.cotswoldswheatsheaf.com

The Dial House Hotel

Bourton – Venice of the Cotswolds – is bisected by the river Windrush; willow branches bathe in its waters, ducks preen for tourists. Dial House is equally alluring, a sublime retreat set back from the high street. It dates from 1698, but skip past the trim lawns and hanging baskets and find the old world made new. Mullioned windows and stone fireplaces shine warmly, the fire crackles, armchairs are dressed in Zoffany fabrics, Cole & Son wallpaper sparkles on some walls. You're in the middle of the village with a peaceful garden at the back in which to escape the summer hordes. You can eat here in good weather or just pull up a deckchair and read in the sun. Stripped floors in the restaurant, cool colours in the bar and bedrooms in different shapes and sizes: grand four-posters in the main house; airy pastels and silky quilts in the coach house; small but sweet garden rooms with fancy little bathrooms. There's fabulous food, too, perhaps langoustine cannelloni, Scottish beef, then a magnificent caramel soufflé. *Minimum two nights at weekends.*

Price	£155–£250.
Rooms	14: 11 doubles, 2 four-posters, 1 suite.
Meals	Lunch from £7. Dinner, 3 courses, about £45.
Closed	Rarely.
Directions	From Oxford A40 to Northleach, then right onto A429 for Bourton. Right into village and hotel set back from High St opp. main bridge.

Martyn & Elaine Booth
High Street, Bourton-on-the-Water,
Cheltenham GL54 2AN

Tel	+44 (0)1451 822244
Email	info@dialhousehotel.com
Web	www.dialhousehotel.com

The New Inn at Coln

The New Inn is old – 1632 to be exact – but well-named nonetheless; a top-to-toe renovation has recently swept away past indiscretions. These days, it's all rather smart. The pub stands in a handsome Cotswold village with ivy roaming on original stone walls and a sun-trapping terrace where roses bloom in summer. Inside, airy interiors come with low ceilings, painted beams, flagged floors and fires that roar. There are padded window seats, eastern busts, gilt mirrors and armchairs in the bar. Bedrooms are a treat, all warmly elegant with perfect white linen, flat-screen TVs and good little bathrooms (a couple have claw-foot baths). There are wonky floors and the odd beam in the main house, while those in the old dovecote come in bold colours and have views across water meadows to the river; walks start from the front door. Bibury, Burford and Stow are all close, so spread your wings, then return for a wonderful meal, perhaps grilled goat's cheese with poached pear, roasted lemon sole with pink grapefruit, vanilla panna cotta with plum crumble. Just the ticket for a relaxing weekend.

Price	£140-£160. Singles from £130. Half-board from £90 p.p.
Rooms	14 doubles.
Meals	Lunch from £5.95. Dinner, 3 courses, about £30. Sunday lunch from £13.95.
Closed	Never.
Directions	From Oxford A40 past Burford, then B4425 for Bibury. Left after Aldsworth to Coln St Aldwyns.

Stuart Hodges
Main Street, Coln St Aldwyns,
Cirencester GL7 5AN

Tel	+44 (0)1285 750651
Email	info@new-inn.co.uk
Web	www.new-inn.co.uk

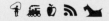

Horse & Groom

The Horse and Groom delivers in spades: a warm welcome, stylish interiors, the sort of food you want to eat, and wines and beers for all. The inn stands at the top of the hill with views to the side that pour over the Cotswolds. Inside, cool colours, stripped floors, open fires and the odd stone wall for a modern rustic feel. Outside you can sit under the shade of damson trees and watch chefs gather eggs from the coop or carrots from the kitchen garden. Uncluttered bedrooms are wonderfully plush and come in contemporary country-house style with beautiful linen, pretty art, a padded window seat or two. One room is huge, the garden room opens onto the terrace, and those at the front are soundproofed to minimise noise from the road. This is a hive of youthful endeavour, with two brothers at the helm. Will cooks, Tom pours the ales, and a cheery conviviality flows. Delicious food hits the spot and is much prized by canny locals, so come for pea and home cured ham soup, Indonesian spiced tamworth pork shoulder, sautéed greens and sesame noodles, Granny G's toffee meringue. *Minimum two nights at weekends.*

Price	£120–£170. Singles £80. Half-board from £70 p.p.
Rooms	5 doubles.
Meals	Lunch & dinner from £11.50. Not Sunday eve.
Closed	Christmas Day & New Year's Eve.
Directions	West from Moreton-in-Marsh on A44. Climb hill in Bourton-on-the-Hill; pub at top on left. Moreton-in-Marsh railway station 2 miles away.

Tom & Will Greenstock
Bourton-on-the-Hill,
Moreton-in-Marsh GL56 9AQ

Tel	+44 (0)1386 700413
Email	greenstocks@horseandgroom.info
Web	www.horseandgroom.info

Lower Brook House

The village is a Cotswold jewel, saved from tourist hordes by roads too narrow for coaches. Lower Brook is no less alluring, a fine example of a small 21st-century country-house hotel. It was built in 1624 to house workers from one of the 12 silk mills that made Blockley rich. Step in and find the past on display: flagged floors, mullioned windows, timber-framed walls and heaps of vintage luggage. Logs smoulder in a huge inglenook in winter, while excellent bedrooms (one is small) come in crisp country-house style with beautiful fabrics, pristine linen and bowls of fresh fruit. All but one overlook the garden, views fly up the hill. Back outside, roses climb on golden walls, colour bursts from beds in summer and a small lawn runs down to a shaded terrace for afternoon tea in good weather. Walks start from the front door, so scale the ridge and dive into the country. Come home to Anna's delicious cooking, perhaps squid with a chilli jam, chicken with a Muscat jus, chocolate fondant with clotted cream; breakfast treats include smoothies, croissants and freshly squeezed juice. *Minimum two nights at weekends.*

Price	£80-£190.
Rooms	6: 3 doubles, 2 twins, 1 four-poster.
Meals	Dinner £15-£30.
Closed	Christmas.
Directions	A44 west from Moreton-in-Marsh. At top of hill in Bourton-on-the-Hill, right, signed Blockley. Down hill to village; on right.

Julian & Anna Ebbutt
Lower Street, Blockley,
Moreton-in-Marsh GL56 9DS

Tel	+44 (0)1386 700286
Email	info@lowerbrookhouse.com
Web	www.lowerbrookhouse.com

Seagrave Arms

A cute little Cotswold inn. The ingredients are simple: lovely Georgian interiors, delicious local food and super rooms with honest prices. Inside, ancient flagstones lead through to the bar; you'll find a roaring fire, local ales, window seats and half-panelled walls. Next door is the charming little restaurant, where you dig into the freshest food. The Seagrave is a founding member of the Sustainable Restaurant Association, and 90% of its meat and vegetables come from local farms. Bedrooms are scattered about, some in the main house, others in the converted stables (dog friendly). They may differ in size, but all have the same cool style with Farrow & Ball colours, crisp white linen and excellent bathrooms with REN lotions. You'll find a sofa if there's room, perhaps a double-ended bath. Spin back down for some lovely food – in summer you decant onto a gravelled terrace and small lawned garden – perhaps Windrush Valley goats cheese tart, Madgetts Farm duck with star anise, rhubarb crumble and clotted-cream ice cream. The Cotswold Way is close, a good way to atone.

Price	£95–£115.
Rooms	8 doubles.
Meals	Lunch from £5.95. Dinner, 3 courses, about £30. Not Monday.
Closed	Never.
Directions	Leave A44 at Broadway for B4632 towards Stratford-upon-Avon. In village.

Kevin & Sue Davies
Friday Street, Weston Subedge,
Chipping Campden GL55 6QH

Tel	+44 (0)1386 840192
Email	info@seagravearms.co.uk
Web	www.seagravearms.co.uk

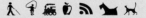

The Malt House

A wonderfully pretty Cotswold village of sculpted golden stone. The Malt House sits in the middle of it all, delightful inside and out. An impeccable country garden runs down to a stream, beyond which fruit trees blossom in spring. There's a summer house, a croquet lawn and Lloyd Loom furniture: pull up a seat and snooze in the sun. Equally impressive is Judi's kitchen garden which provides freshly cut flowers for beautiful bedrooms and summer fruits for the breakfast table. Inside, clipped country-house interiors are just the thing: parquet flooring, sparkling wallpaper, mullioned windows and a mantelpiece that almost touches the ceiling. There are original beams, books and papers, an honesty bar and sofas by the fire. Spotless bedrooms are warmly elegant and hugely comfortable: big mirrors, Jane Churchill silks, Italian fabrics, crisp white linen. You'll find maps for walkers, a list of local restaurants, hot water bottles and umbrellas to keep you dry. Breakfast is a feast: fresh fruit salad, homemade granola, hot bread straight from the oven, the full cooked works. *Minimum two nights at weekends May-August.*

Price	£120-£150. Suite from £160.
Rooms	7: 1 double, 4 twins/doubles, 1 four-poster, 1 suite.
Meals	Pub 200 yards. Dinner by arrangement (min. 12 guests).
Closed	One week over Christmas.
Directions	From Oxford A44 through Moreton-in-Marsh; right on B4081 for Chipping Campden. Entering village 1st right for Broad Campden. Hotel 1 mile on left.

	Judi Wilkes
	Broad Campden,
	Chipping Campden GL55 6UU
Tel	+44 (0)1386 840295
Email	info@malt-house.co.uk
Web	www.malt-house.co.uk

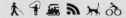

The Cotswold House Hotel & Spa

A deeply cool hotel – fabulous gardens, wonderful art, bedrooms that pack a beautiful punch. It stands on the high street in one of the Cotswolds prettiest villages, an ornament in golden stone with a wool-packers hall that dates to 1340. As for the hotel, it stretches back through stunning gardens to a smart spa with treatment rooms, a hammam, even a hydrotherapy pool. There's a croquet lawn, a beautiful terrace, deep borders packed with colour, deck-chairs and sun loungers scattered about. Inside, a clipped elegance runs throughout: a pillared entrance hall, a restaurant filled with contemporary art, an airy brasserie that's open all day. Bedrooms spoil you rotten. Huge beds have shimmering throws, you get Bang & Olufsen TVs, armchairs or sofas, then seriously fancy bathrooms. A couple have Italian stone baths, another a shower for two. As for the suites, some have open fires or hot tubs on private terraces. Lovely food waits downstairs, perhaps salmon fish cakes, a good steak, a plate of local cheeses. Don't miss Broadway Tower for extraordinary views. *Min. stay two nights at weekends.*

Price	£200-£240. Suites & cottage rooms £270-£320. Singles from £190.
Rooms	30: 11 doubles, 10 twins/doubles, 6 suites, 3 cottage rooms.
Meals	Lunch from £6. Dinner: brasserie from £12.50; dining room, 3 courses, £35.
Closed	Never.
Directions	From Oxford, A44 north for Evesham. 5 miles after Moreton-in-Marsh, right on B4081 to Chipping Campden. Hotel in square by town hall.

Thomas Greenall
The Square,
Chipping Campden GL55 6AN

Tel	+44 (0)1386 840330
Email	reservations@cotswoldhouse.com
Web	www.cotswoldhouse.com

Chewton Glen

Chewton Glen is one of England's loveliest country-house hotels. It opened in 1964 with eight bedrooms; now it has 58. Despite this growth it still remains wonderfully intimate, and with two staff for every guest there's sublime service too. As for the hotel, it has everything you'd ever want: a pillared swimming pool, a hydrotherapy spa, a golf course, a tennis centre, vast parkland gardens. There's beauty at every turn: stately sitting rooms, roaring fires, busts and oils, flowers everywhere. Bedrooms are exemplary, as their price demands. Some come in country-house style, most bask in contemporary splendour. Expect marble bathrooms, private balconies, designer fabrics, faultless housekeeping. Fires burn, Wellington boots wait at the front door, four gardeners tend the estate. The food in Vetiver, the new restaurant, is predictably exquisite – perhaps twice-baked Emmental soufflé, Thai-spiced Christchurch lobster, Charantais melon soup. You can atone in style: a walk on the beach, mountain biking in the New Forest. Afternoon tea is served on the croquet terrace in summer. Hard to beat. *Minimum two nights at weekends.*

Price	£280–£470. Suites £470–£1,482.
Rooms	58: 5 doubles, 30 twins/doubles, 23 suites.
Meals	Full English breakfast: £26. Lunch, 2 courses, £20. Dinner, 3 courses, £45–£65. Tasting menu 79.50. Light meals available throughout the day.
Closed	Never.
Directions	A337 west from Lymington. Through New Milton for Christchurch. Right at r'bout, signed Walkford. Right again; hotel on right.

Andrew Stembridge
Christchurch Road,
New Milton BH25 6QS

Tel	+44 (0)1425 275341
Email	reservations@chewtonglen.com
Web	www.chewtonglen.com

The Mill at Gordleton

A 400-year-old mill that sits in two acres of English country garden with Avon Water tumbling over the weir; ducks, lampreys, Indian runners and leaping trout all call it home. It's an idyllic spot, the terrace perfect for summer suppers, with the stream brushing past below. Inside, find low ceilings, wonky walls, busts and mirrors, jars of shells. Colour tumbles from pretty fabrics, a fire roars in reception, a panelled bar serves pre-dinner drinks. Bedrooms are full of character. One is above the wheel house and comes with mind-your-head beams. You get pretty throws, sheets and blankets, bowls of fruit. Three rooms have watery views (you can fall asleep to the sound of the river), two have small sitting rooms, most have fancy new bathrooms, and while a lane passes outside, you are more likely to be woken by birdsong. Downstairs, the size of the restaurant bears testament to its popularity. The seven chefs use the best local produce: look forward to tiger prawns with lemon grass, Hampshire pork braised in cider, an irresistible passion fruit soufflé. The coast is close. *Minimum two nights at weekends April-October.*

Price	£150–£195. Suites £150–£245. Singles from £115.
Rooms	8: 3 doubles, 3 twins/doubles, 2 suites.
Meals	Lunch from £6.95. Sunday lunch from £21.50. Dinner £22.50–£27.50; à la carte about £40.
Closed	Christmas Day.
Directions	South from Brockenhurst on A337 for 4 miles. After 2nd roundabout 1st right, signed Hordle. On right after 2 miles.

Liz Cottingham
Silver Street, Sway,
Lymington SO41 6DJ

Tel	+44 (0)1590 682219
Email	info@themillatgordleton.co.uk
Web	www.themillatgordleton.co.uk

The Montagu Arms Hotel

Beaulieu, an ancient royal hunting ground, was gifted to Cistercian monks by King John in 1204. Their abbey took 40 years to build and you can walk over to see its ruins in the nearby grounds of Palace House, seat of the Montagu family since 1538. As for the village, its tiny high street is a hotchpotch of 17th-century timber-framed houses that totter by the tidal estuary drinking in views of river and sky. The hotel itself dates back to 1742, but was re-modelled in 1925. Interiors reveal a grand country house with roaring fires, painted beams, a library bar and a courtyard garden, where you can eat in summer. Bedrooms, some overlooking the water, come in smart traditional style. Expect thick fabrics, crisp linen, marble bathrooms, the very best beds. Back downstairs, sip pre-dinner drinks in front of the fire in the drawing room, then spin across to the panelled dining room with its Michelin star to feast on hand-dived scallops, roast venison from the Beaulieu estate, milk chocolate mousse with lavender ice cream. Wonderful walking from the front door may help you atone. *Minimum two nights at weekends.*

Price	£158-£258. Four-posters £198-£338. Suites £288-£448. Singles from £145. Half-board from £124 p.p.
Rooms	22: 9 doubles, 3 twins/doubles, 4 four-posters, 6 suites.
Meals	Lunch £6.50-£25. Sunday lunch £29.50. Dinner, 3 courses, £65.
Closed	Never.
Directions	South from M27, junc. 1 to Lyndhurst on A337, then B3056 for Beaulieu. Left into village and hotel on right.

Sunil Kanjanghat
Palace Lane, Beaulieu,
Brockenhurst SO42 7ZL

Tel	+44 (0)1590 612324
Email	reservations@montaguarms.co.uk
Web	www.montaguarmshotel.co.uk

The Woolpack Inn

It's hard to fault this cool little inn. It's one of those rare places that ticks every box: friendly locals, pretty interiors, super food, lovely rooms. It stands blissfully lost in deepest Hampshire in the smallest hamlet in Britain. Its brick and flint exterior dates to 1880 and views from the front shoot across fields to a distant church; there are terraces at the front and the side, perfect for a pint in summer. Inside, you find a clean, contemporary take on a traditional English inn. A fire roars, there are warm colours, rugs on stone floors and the wine cellar is on display behind a wall of glass. Up in the restaurant, rustic charm is the order of the day with lots of wood, smart booths and candles everywhere, and the food is excellent; tuck into crispy fried squid, shoulder of lamb, honey and lemon tart. Bedrooms in the old skittle alley are great value. Expect exposed walls, the odd beam, Farrow & Ball colours and excellent bathrooms. There's a wood-fired oven on the terrace for pizza in summer, while Sunday lunch is madly popular – don't forget to book. Winchester is close.

Price	£85-£105. Family suite £145.
Rooms	7 doubles.
Meals	Lunch & dinner £5.95-£30. Sunday lunch from £13.95.
Closed	Never.
Directions	On B3046 between Alresford and Basingstoke, 4 miles north of Alresford.

Andrew Cooper
Totford, Northington,
Alresford SO24 9TJ

Tel	+44 (0)845 293 8066
Email	info@thewoolpackinn.co.uk
Web	www.thewoolpackinn.co.uk

Entry 132   Map 3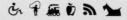

Orles Barn

Everything here is new – apart from the ancient walls, the wooden beams and the odd 17th-century window. Richard and Kelly bought a wreck, ploughed in love and money, and now have a cute little restaurant with rooms. Expect warm colours, a chic style and excellent food mostly sourced from local producers. The house – ancient red brick draped in wisteria – stands 200 metres back from the A40, but once inside you can't hear a thing. Pretty bedrooms overlook the back garden, too, assuring a good night's sleep. They each come with one patterned wall, armchairs or sofas, smart fabrics and soft colours. One is smaller, two have double-ended baths in the room, a couple of suites are dog friendly. Back downstairs, an open fire burns in the lovely bar, where you stop for drinks before slipping into the airy restaurant for Dan Wall's delicious food, perhaps white onion soup with parmesan oil, pot roast chicken with tomato and sage sauce, dark chocolate and banana tart with chocolate ice cream. Hereford, the Forest of Dean and the Black Mountains are close. There's jazz on Sundays in summer, too.

Price	£130–£180. Half-board from £90 p.p. Min. stay 2 nights at weekends April-Sept.
Rooms	6: 3 doubles, 3 suites.
Meals	Lunch from £5.50. Sunday lunch £19–£22. Dinner, 3 courses, about £35. 7-course tasting menu £55.
Closed	Never
Directions	On A40/A49 junction, ignore Ross turn off, and take road between BP petrol station and A40. Orles Barn is 100 yards on left.

Kelly & Richard Bailey
Wilton,
Ross-on-Wye HR9 6AE
Tel   +44 (0)1989 562155
Email   reservations@orles-barn.co.uk
Web   www.orles-barn.co.uk

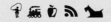

Glewstone Court Country House Hotel & Restaurant

Those in search of the small and friendly will love it here. Bill and Christine run Glewstone with great style, instinctively disregarding the bland new world in favour of a more colourful landscape. Their realm is this attractive country house, once owned by Guy's Hospital. Inside, an eclectic collection of art and antiques fills the rooms. Eastern rugs cover stripped wood floors, resident dogs snooze in front of the fire, and guests gather in the drawing-room bar to eat, drink and make merry. Outside, there's croquet on the lawn in the shade of an ancient Cedar of Lebanon, while back inside a fine Regency staircase spirals up to a galleried landing. Warmly comfortable bedrooms await. A couple are huge, those at the front have long views across the beautiful Wye Valley to the Forest of Dean, those at back overlook cherry orchards; one room on the ground floor opens onto a private garden. Fabulous food, mostly local – Hereford Beef, Marches Lamb – is served at lunch and dinner every day with traditional Sunday lunch popular with locals. The Brecon Beacons and the Cotswolds are not far away.

Price	£125–£150. Singles £70–£85.
Rooms	9: 6 doubles, 1 four-poster, 1 single, 1 suite.
Meals	Lunch from £12.50. Dinner, 3 courses, about £30. Sunday lunch £20.
Closed	25-27 December.
Directions	From Ross-on-Wye A40 towards Monmouth. Right 1 mile south of Wilton r'bout for Glewstone. Hotel on left after 0.5 miles.

Christine & Bill Reeve-Tucker
Glewstone,
Ross-on-Wye HR9 6AW

Tel	+44 (0)1989 770367
Email	glewstone@aol.com
Web	www.glewstonecourt.com

Wilton Court Restaurant with Rooms

A Grade-II listed stone house with a Grade-I listed mulberry tree; in season, its berries are turned in sorbets and pies. The house dates all the way back to 1510 and looks across the river to Wye; herons dive, otters swim, kingfishers nest. Roses ramble on the outside, happy guests potter within. This may not be the fanciest place in the book, but Roger and Helen go the extra mile, and, with good prices, a pretty position on the river and a restaurant for great food; Wilton Court has won itself a devoted following. Bedrooms upstairs come in different shapes and sizes. Splash out on the more expensive ones for watery views, William Morris wallpaper, lots of space, perhaps a four-poster. A couple of rooms are small, but so are their prices and you can lose yourself in the rest of the hotel. Drop down for a drink in the smart panelled bar, then nip across to the airy conservatory/dining room for super food, perhaps langoustine tagliatelli, Raglan lamb, fragipane tart. A small garden across the lane drops down to the river for summer sundowners. Ross is a five-minute stroll. *Minimum two nights at weekends.*

Price	£125-£165. Suite £145-£185. Singles from £90. Half-board from £82.50 p.p. (min. 2 nights).
Rooms	10: 3 doubles, 5 twins/doubles, 1 four-poster, 1 family suite.
Meals	Lunch from £12.75. Sunday lunch £16.50-£18.50. Dinner, 3 courses, about £35. 7-course tasting menu £52.50.
Closed	First 2 weeks of January.
Directions	South into Ross at A40/A49 Wilton roundabout. 1st right into Wilton Lane. Hotel on right.

Roger & Helen Wynn
Wilton Lane, Wilton,
Ross-on-Wye HR9 6AQ

Tel	+44 (0)1989 562569
Email	info@wiltoncourthotel.com
Web	www.wiltoncourthotel.com

Castle House

Hereford's loveliest hotel stands 200 paces from the city's magnificent 11th-century cathedral, home to the Mappa Mundi. It's English to its core with a beautiful garden that overlooks what remains of the old castle's moat; in summer you can eat out here watching ducks glide by. Inside, the lap of luxury waits: a fine staircase, painted paneling, a delicious restaurant for the best food in town. Big bedrooms are lavish. Those in the main house are more traditional (the top-floor suite runs all the way along the front of the house); those in the townhouse (a 30-second stroll) are distinctly 21st century. All have a smart country-house feel with beautiful fabrics, super-comfy beds, crisp white linen, excellent bathrooms. Seriously good food, much from the owner's nearby farm, waits in the restaurant, perhaps goats cheese ravioli, pan-fried sea bass, rhubarb mousse with ginger ice cream. You can atone with a stroll along the river Wye, which runs through the park behind. Pop-up opera, guided walks and Evensong in the cathedral all wait. Don't miss the Three Choirs Festival in July.

Price	£150–£230. Singles from £130.
Rooms	Main house: 1 double, 4 singles, 11 suites. Townhouse: 3 doubles, 5 suites.
Meals	Lunch from £5. Dinner, 3 courses, about £35. Sunday lunch from £18.50.
Closed	Never.
Directions	Follow signs to Hereford city centre, then City Centre east. Right off Bath St into Union St, through St Peters Sq to Owen's St, then right into St Ethelbert St. Hotel on left as road veers right.

Michelle Marriott-Lodge
Castle Street,
Hereford HR1 2NW

Tel	+44 (0)1432 356321
Email	info@castlehse.co.uk
Web	www.castlehse.co.uk

The Wellington

A magical little brasserie with rooms in a pretty village just north of London. Everything here is a treat: an ancient inn, beautiful design, super bedrooms, staff who care. The village dates to Roman times and was mentioned in the Domesday Book. As for the Wellington, Chris, Fiona and Liz have renovated with huge flair. They stripped it back to its bare bones, kept all the lovely old bits, then added 21st-century colour and style. Vast panes of glass connect 700-year-old timber frames, light floods in, so do the locals, who come for good food and wine; both are served informally. Follow their lead and find a zinc-topped bar, raw oak panelling and a fire that burns on both sides. There are beamed ceilings, stripped floors, candles galore, a stone terrace for summer. Bedrooms above are gorgeous: exposed brick walls and timber frames mix with iPod docks and espresso machines. Some have baths in the room, you get big beds, cushioned window seats, local art. Back downstairs, great food waits amid the happy hum, perhaps tiger prawns, rib-eye steak, lemon and thyme crème brûlée. Hatfield House is close.

Price	£100–£120. Singles from £90.
Rooms	6: 1 four-poster, 5 doubles.
Meals	Lunch from £5. Dinner, 3 courses, about £25.
Closed	Never.
Directions	A1(M) junc. 6, then north for 1 mile. At 3rd roundabout left for Welwyn. 1st left (signed Welwyn shops). In village by church.

Fiona & Chris Gerard & Liz Gouldie
1 High Street,
Welwyn AL6 9LZ

Tel	+44 (0)1438 714036
Email	info@wellingtonatwelwyn.co.uk
Web	www.wellingtonatwelwyn.co.uk

The George Hotel

The George is a kingly retreat; Charles II stayed in 1671 and you can sleep in his room with its panelling and high ceilings. The house, a grand mansion in the middle of tiny Yarmouth, has stupendous views of the Solent; Admiral Sir Robert Holmes took full advantage of them when in residence, nipping off to sack passing ships. These days traditional interiors mix with contemporary flourishes. Ancient panelling and stone flags come as standard in the old house, but push on past the crackling fire in the bar to find an airy brasserie with walls of glass that open onto the terrace. You can eat here in summer, next to the castle walls, with sailboats zipping past – a perfect spot for black truffles and scrambled eggs, New Forest venison with peppercorn butter, fig tart with honey and almond ice cream. Bedrooms come in country-house style, some with crowns above the bed, others with fabulous views. Two rooms have balconies that overlook the water, but smaller rooms at the back have the same homely style. Head off to Osborne House, Cowes for the regatta or The Needles for magical walks. *Minimum two nights at weekends.*

Price	£190-£287. Singles from £99.
Rooms	17 twins/doubles, 2 singles.
Meals	Lunch & dinner from £20.
Closed	Rarely.
Directions	Lymington ferry to Yarmouth, then follow signs to town centre.

Jeremy Wilcock
Quay Street,
Yarmouth PO41 0PE

Tel	+44 (0)1983 760331
Email	res@thegeorge.co.uk
Web	www.thegeorge.co.uk

Seaview Hotel

Everything here is a dream. You're 50 yards from the water in a small seaside village that sweeps you back to a nostalgic past. Locals pop in for a pint, famished yachtsmen float in for a meal, those in the know drop by for a luxurious night in indulging rooms. The bar has nautical curios nailed to its walls, the terrace buzzes with island life in summer, the restaurants hum with the contented sighs of happy diners. There's a battalion of kind staff, who book taxis, carry bags and send you off in the right direction for excursions. Interior designer Graham Green oversaw the fabulous refurbishment; some rooms come in smart country-house style (upholstered four-posters, padded headboards), others are contemporary (cool colours, fancy bathrooms). New apartments have blossomed from a converted bank next door, with the Vault suite maintaining many of the original features. Don't miss the food. The hotel has its own farm – home-reared meat, home-grown vegetable's, home-laid eggs, while the crab ramekin is an island institution. There's a treatment room, too, for expert pampering. *Minimum two nights at weekends.*

Price	£125-£255. Suites £295.
Rooms	29: 14 twins/doubles, 3 four-posters. New wing: 4 doubles, 3 twins/doubles, 5 family suites.
Meals	Lunch & dinner £5-£35.
Closed	Christmas Day & Boxing Day.
Directions	From Ryde B3330 south for 1.5 miles. Hotel signed left.

	Dean Bailey
	High Street,
	Seaview PO34 5EX
Tel	+44 (0)1983 612711
Email	reception@seaviewhotel.co.uk
Web	www.seaviewhotel.co.uk

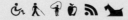

Entry 139   Map 3

Priory Bay Hotel

An imperious position one field up from the sea with paths that lead down to a long private sandy beach, perfect for summer sunbathing. Medieval monks made this land their home, Tudor farmers and Georgian gentry followed. The house dates from the 14th century and stands in 70 acres that flank the coast. The drawing room is gorgeous with high ceilings, a baby grand and huge windows that frame sea views. You can eat in a Regency dining room or in the brasserie-style restaurant (there's a terrace for good weather); try Isle of Wight asparagus; local lobster; praline chocolate finger. You'll find leather armchairs in the bar, a children's playroom and golf clubs for the six-hole course. In summer, sun loungers flank the pool and croquet hoops stand on the lawn. Bedrooms have an uncluttered feel: seaside colours, tongue-and-groove bathrooms, a sofa if there's room. Some are enormous with timber frames, while in-room treatments can be arranged. Alternatively, sleep under canvas in the grounds; think luxurious yurts with en suite bathrooms and private terraces that look out to sea. *Ask about falconry courses.*

Price	£160–£300. Singles from £90. Min 2 nights at weekends.
Rooms	18: 16 twins/doubles, 2 family rooms, 2 barns for 6.
Meals	Lunch £30. Dinner, 3 courses, £35.
Closed	Never.
Directions	South from Ryde on B3330. Through Nettlestone and hotel signed left and left again.

Andrew Palmer
Priory Road,
Seaview PO34 5BU

Tel	+44 (0)1983 613146
Email	enquiries@priorybay.co.uk
Web	www.priorybay.co.uk

The Bull Hotel

Peacefully wedged between the M20 and M26, pretty Wrotham and its rambling old coaching inn sit on Kent's glorious North Downs, smack-bang on the Pilgrim's Way. Refurbishment of the Bull, also the village hub, has been a labour of love, with Martin and Lygia sprucing up their tardis-like interiors whenever the coffers allowed. The final flurry has seen some lovely bedrooms come to life; oak floors, period fireplaces and ceiling timbers were all revealed. Creature comforts are plentiful: crisp linen, smart beds, deep leather sofas and old-fashioned radiators, while good bathrooms have underfloor heating, power showers and Duck Island lotions. Downstairs, in a bar once frequented by Battle of Britain pilots (note the stamps on the ceiling), you find Dark Star ales, interesting wines and good seasonal food, perhaps venison sausages or a 30-day-aged fillet steak, then an orange and almond cake. It's a great country bolthole for the modern-day pilgrim and for Eurotunnel/port-bound travellers. Walks start from the front door and National Trust gems – Knole Park and Churchill's Chartwell – are close.

Price	£79–£129. Singles from £69.
Rooms	11: 8 doubles, 2 twins, 1 four-poster.
Meals	Lunch from £6.50. Bar meals from £9. Dinner, 3 courses, £25–£35. Sunday lunch from £12.
Closed	Rarely.
Directions	Sent on booking.

Martin Deadman
Bull Lane, Wrotham,
Sevenoaks TN15 7RF

Tel +44 (0)1732 789800
Email info@thebullhotel.com
Web www.thebullhotel.com

Hever Castle Luxury Bed & Breakfast

Hever is out of this world, a magical slice of English DNA. This 14th-century moated castle was home to Anne Boleyn, second wife to Henry VIII, mother of Elizabeth I. It is one of those places that thrills at every turn. It has all the regal trimmings: 625 acres of green and pleasant land, fabulous formal gardens, a 38-acre lake you can walk around. You stay in the Astor Wing, built in Tudor style in 1903; gorgeous bedrooms, recently refurbished, are fit for a king. Expect period colours, panelled walls, perhaps a golden chaise longue or a glimpse of the castle through leaded windows. Lots have pretty wallpaper, one has a vaulted ceiling, several have four-poster beds, while bigger rooms have sofas. Bathrooms are predictably divine, some with claw-foot baths, others with walk-in power showers; a few have both. But don't linger; entrance to the castle and gardens is included in your very attractive price. You can boat on the lake, have picnic dinners, they even host the odd spot of jousting. There's golf, too, and a good pub in the village for dinner. Unbeatable.

Price	£140–£180. Singles from £95.
Rooms	21: 16 twins/doubles, 3 four-posters, 2 singles.
Meals	Picnic lunches by arrangement. Restaurants within 0.25 miles.
Closed	Rarely.
Directions	Castle signed west out of Edenbridge.

Roland Smith
Hever,
Edenbridge TN8 7NG
Tel   +44 (0)1732 861800
Email   stay@hevercastle.co.uk
Web   www.hevercastle.co.uk

Cloth Hall Oast

Sweep up the rhododendron-lined drive to this immaculate Kentish oast house and barn. For 40 years Mrs Morgan lived in the 15th-century manor next door where she tended both guests and garden; now she has turned her perfectionist's eye upon these five acres. There are well-groomed lawns, a carp-filled pond, pergola, summer house, heated pool and flower beds full of colour. In fine weather enjoy breakfast on the deck overlooking the pond. Light shimmers through swathes of glass in the dining room; there are off-white walls and pale beams that soar from floor to rafter. Mrs Morgan is a charming and courteous hostess and is always nearby to lend a helping hand. There are three bedrooms for guests: a four-poster on the ground floor, a triple and a queen-size double on the first. Colours are soft, fabrics are frilled but nothing is busy or overdone; you are spoiled with good bathrooms and fine mattresses, crisp linen, flowered chintz... and a Michelin starred restaurant in the village. Return to the sitting room for guests, made snug by a log fire on winter nights. *No credit cards.*

Price	£90-£125.
Rooms	3: 1 four-poster, 1 triple, 1 double.
Meals	Dinner from £25, by arrangement. Pub & restaurant 1 mile.
Closed	Christmas.
Directions	Leave village with windmill on left, taking Golford Road east for Tenterden. After a mile right, before cemetery. Signed right.

Katherine Morgan
Course Horn Lane,
Cranbrook TN17 3NR
Tel   +44 (0)1580 712220
Email   clothhalloast@aol.com
Web   www.clothhalloast.co.uk

Elvey Farm

This ancient farmhouse stands in six acres of blissful peace, half a mile up a private drive. It's a deeply rural position, a nostalgic sweep back to old England. White roses run riot on red walls, a thick vine shades the veranda, trim lawns run up to colourful borders. Inside you find timber frames at every turn, but the feel is airy and contemporary with smart furniture sitting amid stripped boards and old beams. Bedrooms come in similar vein. The two in the main house are big and family-friendly, while those in the stable block have chunky beds, small sitting rooms and excellent wet rooms; two have slipper baths. Best of all are two seriously cool new rooms in the granary. Expect timber-framed walls in state-of-the-art bathrooms and massive beds under original rafters; one room comes with a hot tub in a secret garden. As for the restaurant, locally sourced Kentish fare offers delicious rustic treats: hunter's pâté, slow-roasted pork, tarte tatin with honeycomb ice cream. The Greensand Way runs through the grounds, Leeds Castle is close, the *Darling Buds of May* was filmed in the village.

Price	£105–£245. Singles from £85. Half-board from £74.50 p.p.
Rooms	11: 1 double, 1 four-poster. Stables: 2 suites for 4, 3 suites for 2. Oast: 2 doubles. Granary: 2 suites.
Meals	Dinner, 3 courses, about £30. Sunday lunch from £12.95.
Closed	Never.
Directions	M20 junc. 8; A20 to Lenham. At Charing r'bout 3rd exit for A20 Ashford. Right at lights to Pluckley. Bypass village, down hill, right at pub, right and right again.

Jeff Moody & Simon Peek
Pluckley,
Ashford TN27 0SU

Tel	+44 (0)1233 840442
Email	bookings@elveyfarm.co.uk
Web	www.elveyfarm.co.uk

Entry 144   Map 4

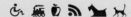

Wife of Bath

With Canterbury on your doorstep, you'd guess this restaurant took its name from Chaucer's famous tale, but the wife in question belonged to the original owner, whom he met in Bath. Named in her honour, it opened in 1963 to great acclaim, one of the first restaurants with rooms to appear in the country. Over the years it has reinvented itself several times, always keeping its reputation for fabulous food; current chef, Robert Hymers, has been at the helm for 16 years. A recent refurbishment has brought Georgian interiors back to life. Expect airy whites, timber frames, the odd roll of fancy wallpaper. There's a bar for cocktails, after which you are whisked through to feast on super food, perhaps watercress and nettle soup with grated horseradish, pressed shoulder of lamb with pistachio pesto, warm pear tart with rosemary ice cream. Bedrooms give every reason to make the most of the wine list, so knock back a good claret, then retire to pretty rooms (crisp linen, Farrow & Ball colours, the odd beam and bathrobes). Great walks start from the village; Ashford is close for Eurostar.

Price	£95–£115. Singles from £75.
Rooms	5: 3 doubles, 1 twin, 1 four-poster.
Meals	Lunch £17–£20. Dinner, 3 courses, £35–£40.
Closed	Sunday & Monday nights.
Directions	M20 junc. 10, then A2070 & immediately right for Wye. Follow signs for 3 miles into Wye. Left in village; on left.

Mark Rankin
4 Upper Bridge Street, Wye,
Ashford TN25 5AF

Tel	+44 (0)1233 812232
Email	relax@thewifeofbath.com
Web	www.thewifeofbath.com

The Relish

It's not just the super-comfy interiors that make The Relish such a tempting port of call. There's a sense of generosity here: a drink on the house each night in the sitting room; tea and cakes on tap all day; free internet throughout. This is a grand 1850s merchant's house on the posh side of town with warmly contemporary interiors; wind up the cast-iron staircase to find bedrooms that make you smile. Hypnos beds with padded headboards wear crisp white linen and pretty throws. You get a sense of space, a sofa if there's room, big mirrors and fabulous bathrooms. All are great value for money. Downstairs there are candles on the mantelpieces above an open fire, stripped wooden floors and padded benches in the dining room; in summer, you can decamp onto the terrace for breakfast, a four-acre communal garden stretching out beyond. You're one street back from Folkestone's cliff-top front for huge sea views; steps lead down to smart gardens and the promenade. There are takeaway breakfasts for early Eurostar departures and a local restaurant guide in every room. *Minimum two nights at weekends in summer.*

Price	£95–£125. Four-poster £145. Singles from £69.
Rooms	10: 2 twins/doubles, 6 doubles, 1 four-poster, 1 single.
Meals	Restaurants nearby.
Closed	22 December–2 January.
Directions	In centre of town, from Langholm Gardens, head west on Sandgate Road. 1st right into Augusta Gardens/Trinity Gardens. Hotel on right.

Chris & Sarah van Dyke
4 Augusta Gardens,
Folkestone CT20 2RR

Tel	+44 (0)1303 850952
Email	reservations@hotelrelish.co.uk
Web	www.hotelrelish.co.uk

Wallett's Court Country House Hotel & Spa

A fabulous position at the end of England, with sweeping fields heading south towards white cliffs; you can follow paths across to a lighthouse for rather good views. The hotel stands opposite a Norman church on land gifted by William the Conqueror to his brother Odo. The current building dates from 1627, but recent additions include an indoor swimming pool which opens onto the garden, and cabins for treatments hidden in the trees. Eight acres of grounds include lush lawns, a tennis court, a boules pitch and a climbing frame for kids. Timber-framed interiors come with contemporary art on ancient brick walls, a fire roars in a sitting-room bar and sublime food waits in the whitewashed restaurant – perhaps Shetland scallops, honey-glazed duck, a delicious banana tarte tatin. Bedrooms are scattered about, some grandly traditional with four-posters in the main house, others simpler and quieter in the outbuildings; the suites above the pool come in contemporary style. Canterbury cathedral, Sandwich golf course and Dover Castle are close. *Minimum two nights at weekends half-board.*

Price	£95–£170. Singles £95–£140.
Rooms	16: 12 twins/doubles, 4 suites.
Meals	Afternoon tea from £8.95. Sunday lunch from £16.95. Dinner, 3 courses, £39.95.
Closed	Rarely.
Directions	From Dover A2 & A20, then A258 towards Deal. Right, signed St Margaret's at Cliffe. House 1 mile on right, signed.

	Chris, Lea & Gavin Oakley
	Dover Road, Westcliffe,
	Dover CT15 6EW
Tel	+44 (0)1304 852424
Email	mail@wallettscourt.com
Web	www.wallettscourt.com

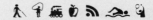

The White Cliffs Hotel & Trading Co.

You're lost in the last folds of England with the beach at the bottom of the hill and the White Cliffs of Dover soaring above, so climb up for views that stretch across to France. This pretty weatherboard hotel stands a mile back from the water with a fine Norman church across the road that's shielded by a curtain of lush trees. Inside, airy interiors come with stripped floors, sandblasted beams, contemporary art and an open fire in the sitting room/bar. Best of all is the walled garden with climbing roses, colourful borders and a trim lawn that plays host to Sunday lunch in summer. Bedrooms are all over the place. Those in the main house are bigger and more sophisticated, and come in bold colours with silky curtains, gilt mirrors and the odd four-poster. Garden rooms are altogether more simple, but good value for money. Expect summer colours, wooden beds, trim carpets and crisp linen. In the restaurant there's meat from Kent, fish from local waters and a children's menu, too. Dover Castle and Sandwich are close and you can use the pool and spa at Wallett's Court, the other half of Gavin's empire.

Price	£99-£109. Family suites £129. Singles from £54.
Rooms	15: 4 doubles, 1 triple, 1 four-poster. Mews cottages: 4 doubles, 1 twin, 2 singles, 2 family suites.
Meals	Lunch from £4.50. Dinner, 3 courses, £25-£30.
Closed	Rarely.
Directions	M20/A20 into Dover, then A2 north. At roundabout, right for Deal, then right again for St Margaret's. Right in village; hotel on left.

Chris, Lea & Gavin Oakley
High Street, St Margaret's-at-Cliffe,
Dover CT15 6AT

Tel	+44 (0)1304 852229
Email	mail@thewhitecliffs.com
Web	www.thewhitecliffs.com

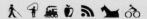

The Salutation

An enchanting house, utterly beguiling. You slip through a gate on the bustling quay, then there you are, peacefully ensconced behind ancient walls. The house, an absolute jaw-dropper, was built by Lutyens in 1911, but it's almost eclipsed by the Secret Gardens, some of the loveliest in England. Gorgeous bedrooms are dotted about in three beautifully restored cottages; two suites in Knightrider House look out across beds of rose and iris. All come with gorgeous sitting rooms, fancy kitchens and super dining rooms, making them perfect boltholes for families or a group of friends. Four rooms share bathrooms, but are only let to the same party, so if you come alone, you may get a whole cottage to yourself. Every conceivable luxury comes in abundance: rich fabrics, antique furnishings, gorgeous linen, French-style beds. There are fresh flowers, too, lots of books and a bar that's 'on the house.' Breakfast is served grandly in the big house; dinner can be arranged for groups over 10. Medieval Sandwich waits, as does Canterbury and its cathedral and the links at Royal St George's. Very special.

Price	£180–£215.
Rooms	9: Knightrider House: 2 doubles, 2 doubles sharing bath. Coach House: 2 doubles. Garden Cottage: 3 doubles sharing bath & shower. All with kitchens.
Meals	Restaurants 200m.
Closed	Rarely.
Directions	M2 east, A299 for Ramsgate, A256 south to Sandwich. Over bridge, left along river, then right into Knightrider Street. On left at end of lane.

Dominic & Stephanie Parker
Knightrider Street,
Sandwich CT13 9EW

Tel	+44 (0)1304 619919
Email	dominic@the-salutation.com
Web	www.the-salutation.com

Entry 149   Map 4

The Bell Hotel

Sandwich, a Cinque port, is England's best-preserved medieval town. It's tiny, dates to the 12th century, and timber-framed houses are found all over town. The Bell stands opposite the old toll gate, where the river Stour glides past on its way to the sea. You can follow it down to Sandwich Bay past the famous Royal St George's golf course. Back at the hotel, oak revolving doors propel you into an elegant world of golden hues, smouldering logs and vintage luggage piled up in a corner. Open-plan interiors flow from restaurant to conservatory to bar. All are smart and airy, with blond wood and halogen lighting giving a contemporary feel. Doors open onto a terrace in summer, while locally sourced seasonal food hits the spot perfectly. Bedrooms come in different sizes and mix comfort and style in equal measure. The bigger ones with river views are fabulous, but all have warm colours, sparkling bathrooms, digital radios and WiFi access. Canterbury is a 20-minute drive, Broadstairs, a pretty seaside town, is worth a peek. *Minimum two nights at weekends June-Sept.*

Price	£110-£165. Suites £190-£210. Singles from £95. Half-board from £80 p.p.
Rooms	37: 29 twins/doubles, 4 family rooms, 2 singles, 2 suites.
Meals	Lunch from £5. Dinner £15-£30. Sunday lunch £15.50.
Closed	Never.
Directions	A2, M2, A299, then A256 south. Follow signs into Sandwich. Over bridge, hotel on left by river.

Matt Collins
1 Upper Strand Street,
Sandwich CT13 9EF

Tel	+44 (0)1304 613388
Email	bellhotel@shepherd-neame.co.uk
Web	www.bellhotelsandwich.co.uk

The Royal Harbour Hotel

A delightfully quirky townhouse hotel that stands on a Georgian crescent with magnificent views of harbour and sea. Simplicity, elegance and eccentricity go hand in hand. The sitting room is wonderful with stripped floors, gorgeous armchairs, a crackling fire and an honesty bar. Beautiful things abound: a roll-top desk, super art, potted palms, a miniature orange tree bearing fruit. There are binoculars with which to scan the high seas (Ramsgate was home to the Commander of the Channel Fleet), books by the hundred for a good read (Dickens's Bleak House is up the road in Broadstairs) and a library of DVDs for the telly in your room. Bedrooms at the front are tiny, but have the view, those at the back are bigger and quieter. The suite has a coal fire and French windows that open onto tiny balconies. You get crisp linen, duck-down pillows and excellent shower rooms. Breakfast is a leisurely feast with cured hams from James's brother, a Rick Stein food hero; there's a barbecue in the courtyard garden that guests can use in summer. *Minimum two nights at weekends in high season.*

Price	£99–£139. Singles from £79. Suite £198.
Rooms	19: 14 doubles, 2 family rooms, 2 singles, 1 suite.
Meals	Restaurants in town.
Closed	Rarely.
Directions	M2, A299, then A256 into Ramsgate. Follow signs for town centre, pick up coast on right. On left as road drops down hill. Off-road parking.

James Thomas
10-11 Nelson Crescent,
Ramsgate CT11 9JF

Tel	+44 (0)1843 591514
Email	info@royalharbourhotel.co.uk
Web	www.royalharbourhotel.co.uk

The Ashton

The Ashton offers what most people want: a host who goes the extra mile and beautiful rooms you don't want to leave. No surprise, then, to discover it was recently voted Number One B&B in the land. James, once a TV set designer, has poured in love and money, making his boutique B&B much more than an overnight stop for those hurtling along the M6. The house, set back from a quiet road, stands in country on the edge of historic Lancaster. Outside chickens strut their stuff, providing eggs for breakfast, while inside classical and contemporary styles mix delightfully. There's a small sitting room with candles in the fireplace, a dining room in racing green for excellent breakfasts, then a treatment room for massage at weekends. Best of all are the bedrooms. Some are bigger than others, but all come with Hypnos beds, crisp white linen, flat-screen TVs and DVD players; you'll find white robes in seriously cool bathrooms, too. Excellent local restaurants wait: the Bay Horse at Forton and the Highwayman at Nether Burrow are both worth the drive. Morecambe Bay is close, the Dales a little further. Brilliant.

Price	£115–£165. Singles from £95.
Rooms	5 twins/doubles.
Meals	Restaurants within 1 mile.
Closed	Never.
Directions	M6 junc. 33, then A6 north into Lancaster. Thro' traffic lights at supermarket; 1st right; then right at mini roundabout. Right after 0.5 mile for Clitheroe. On right after 0.3 mile.

James Gray
Wyresdale Road,
Lancaster LA1 3JJ

Tel	+44 (0)1524 68460
Email	stay@theashtonlancaster.com
Web	www.theashtonlancaster.com

The Cartford Inn

Patrick and Julie know how to run a great little inn: whisk up some fabulous food, throw in a pinch of contemporary style, then add distinctly groovy rooms and serve informally. It's a recipe that's proved so popular they've had to expand: the restaurant now overlooks the river Wyre, while nine sizzling new bedrooms have been added above. Not that they've lost an ounce of the magic that makes this place so special. The front bar, with its whitewashed walls, roaring fire and friendly locals, is a great place to stop for a pint of local ale, though a courtyard garden will draw you out in good weather. In typically relaxed style you can eat whatever you want wherever you want: tuck into king prawns with fresh mango and chilli salsa; oxtail, beef and real ale pudding with green beans; glazed lemon tart and raspberry sorbet. Bedrooms are just as good – gilded sleigh beds, funky wallpaper, crisp white linen, river views. One has a claw-foot bath in the room, the penthouse suite has its own balcony. Pull yourself away and follow the river; a two-mile circular walk will spin you round. Fantastic.

Price	£100–£120. Family rooms £140–£160. Suite £200–£230. Singles from £65 (Sun-Thurs only).
Rooms	14: 10 doubles, 1 twin, 1 suite for 2-6, 2 family rooms for 3-4.
Meals	Lunch from £8.50. Dinner, 3 courses, £20–£30.
Closed	Christmas Day.
Directions	M6 junc. 32, M55 junc 3, then A585 north. Right at T-junction onto A586 for Garstang. Little Ecclestone signed left.

Patrick & Julie Beaume
Cartford Lane, Little Eccleston,
Preston PR3 0YP

Tel   +44 (0)1995 670166
Email   info@thecartfordinn.co.uk
Web   www.thecartfordinn.co.uk

The Inn at Whitewell

It is almost impossible to imagine a day when a better inn will grace the English landscape. Everything here is perfect. The inn sits just above the river Hodder with five-mile views across blistering parkland to rising fells, one of England's best kept secrets; doors in the bar lead onto a terrace where guests sit in a row and gaze upon it. Inside, fires roar, the papers wait, there are beams, sofas, maps and copies of Wisden. Bedrooms, some in the Coach House, are exemplary and come with real luxury, perhaps a peat fire, a lavish four-poster, a fabulous Victorian power shower. All have beautiful fabrics, top linen and gadgets galore; many have the view – you can fall asleep at night to the sound of the river. There's are bar meals for those who want to watch their weight and a restaurant for splendid food (the Queen once popped in for lunch), so dig into seared scallops, Bowland lamb, a plate of cheese or something sweet; the Whitewell fish pie is rightly famous. Elsewhere, a small vintners in reception, seven miles of private fishing and countryside as good as any in the land. Magnificent.

Price	£120-£208. Suite £210. Singles from £88.
Rooms	23: 9 twins/doubles, 13 four-posters, 1 suite.
Meals	Bar meals from £8. Dinner £25-£35.
Closed	Never.
Directions	M6 junc. 31A, B6243 east through Longridge, then follow signs to Whitewell for 9 miles.

Charles Bowman
Dunsop Road, Whitewell,
Clitheroe BB7 3AT

Tel	+44 (0)1200 448222
Email	reception@innatwhitewell.com
Web	www.innatwhitewell.com

The Spread Eagle

If you're on a budget, but want something special, you'll find it here. The Spread Eagle is one of those rare places that scores ten out of ten on all counts. Its position on the banks of the Ribble is dreamy; the pub itself is a pleasure dome for the senses; its fabulous bedrooms are an absolute steal. It's a predictably popular spot with locals and walkers coming for tasty food, well-kept ales, and happy staff who go the extra mile. Inside: Farrow & Ball colours, sofas and settles, roaring fires, flagstones and beams. The dining room comes with library wallpaper, but this is an informal place and you can eat whatever you want wherever you want, perhaps pressed duck terrine, steak and stilton pudding, pear tarte tatin with cider sorbet. Gorgeous bedrooms have colour and style, lavish linen, big beds and fat mattresses. Some have river views, all have fancy showers, one has a bathtub in the room. You're in the glorious Ribble valley, on the edge of the Yorkshire Dales: Malham is close for walking, Settle for antiques. To quote a reader: 'I couldn't fault anything.' Wonderful.

Price	£85-£105. Suite £135. Singles from £70.
Rooms	7: 4 doubles, 2 twins/doubles, 1 suite.
Meals	Lunch & bar meals from £8.95. Dinner from £9.95.
Closed	Never.
Directions	A59 north past Clitheroe. Sawley & Sawley Abbey signed left after 2 miles.

Kate & Gary Peill
Sawley,
Clitheroe BB7 4NH

Tel   +44 (0)1200 441202
Email spread.eagle@zen.co.uk
Web   www.spreadeaglesawley.co.uk

The William Cecil

Two minutes from the A1, yards from the gates of the magnificent Burghley estate, the William Cecil opened its doors in July 2011. Although more lavish than sister-pub the Bull and Swan just down the hill, the striking stone building still displays Hillbrooke Hotels' signature blend of quirkiness and splendour. A sweeping staircase leads to cosy country-house bedrooms, individually designed by Christine Boswell, with big comfy beds, bold fabrics, eclectic furnishings from Rajhasthan and fabulous bathrooms; the best have roll top tubs and vast walk-in showers. Extra touches include organic vodkas by the bed (!). Downstairs, informality reigns through lounges and wood-floored bar and dining room. The food is local, fresh and delicious, with seasonal delights that include game from the Burghley estate. You might find fried duck egg with girolle mushrooms, grilled sea bass with fenel and blood orange, then Yorkshire parkin with vanilla ice cream. Walk it all off with a stroll into Stamford or explore the vast estate: you can reach it via the garden gate. The jewel in Stamford's crown – and great value, too.

Price	From £125.
Rooms	27: 20 doubles, 7 twins/doubles.
Meals	Lunch from £6.50. Dinner from £12. Sunday lunch, 3 courses, £24.50.
Closed	Never.
Directions	Sent on booking.

Paul Brown
St Martins,
Stamford PE9 2LJ
Tel   +44 (0)1780 750070
Email   enquiries@thewilliamcecil.co.uk
Web   www.thewilliamcecil.co.uk

The Magpies Restaurant Horncastle

Scrumptious cream teas are freshly homemade by chef Andrew and charming Caroline in their sweet black-and-cream cottage in a typical Lincolnshire market town. Leave space for dinner: perhaps samphire-seared scallop, Lincoln red beef with rösti and wild fungi, honey crème brûlée with poached plums... The intimate restaurant is Horncastle's best, focused on seasonal, local produce served in a fire-warmed dining room strung with twinkling lights. Diners order their meals from the comfort of big sofas in the creamy-russet lounge, and you can also sit out on the rear courtyard. Bedrooms are romantic spaces in pink, purple and gold, with big sparkling showers replete with lotions and fluffy towels. Wake to Lincolnshire sausages or pancakes dripping in syrup and fresh fruit. A treat – as is this fine town, once host to a famous medieval horse fair, now popular for Christmas markets, the Viking Way, the Spilsby and Snipe Dales nature reserves, and trips to Lincoln or the coast 20 miles away. This is a very charming restaurant with rooms in a little-known corner of England and it's a huge treat to stay.

Price	£110–£130. Singles from £70.
Rooms	3: 2 doubles, 1 twin/double.
Meals	Lunch from £20. Dinner £36–£42. Not Mon, Tues or Sat lunch.
Closed	Rarely.
Directions	Sent on booking.

Caroline & Andrew Gilbert
71-73 East Street,
Horncastle LN9 6AA

Tel	+44 (0)1507 527004
Web	www.magpiesrestaurant.co.uk

SACO Holborn Serviced Apartments

Lamb's Conduit Street is cool, quirky and pedestrianised with a sprinkling of cafés and restaurants, including the mayor of London's favourite eaterie. A recent refurbishment has made these serviced apartments a great central base for people who want to look after themselves. You get the equivalent of a hotel suite and find super-cool kitchens thrown in for free. Sparkling top-floor apartments open onto vast decked terraces while those below have walls of glass overlooking the street. It's all a big surprise, given the utilitarian 60s exterior: the interiors have both space and style, with open-plan kitchen/sitting rooms, excellent bathrooms, comfy bedrooms and lots of appealing extras such as washing machines, dishwashers and flat-screen TVs. The building stands directly opposite Great Ormond Street Hospital and it's quiet at night, devoid of the crowds. It's also brilliantly central: you can walk to St Paul's, Oxford Street *and* the British Museum. Waitrose for shopping and Russell Square for the tube are both a step away. *Long-stay rates available.*

Price	£183–£275.
Rooms	32 apartments for 2, 4 or 6. 2 penthouse suites.
Meals	Self-catered. Restaurants nearby.
Closed	Never.
Directions	Train: Liverpool Street. Tube: Russell Square. Bus: 19, 38, 55, 243. Private parking from £15 a day.

Tim Ripman
Spens House, 72–84 Lamb's
Conduit Street, Holborn,
London WC1N 3LT

Tel	+44 (0)20 7269 9930
Email	london@sacoapartments.com
Web	london.sacoapartments.com

22 York Street

The Callis family live in a Regency townhouse in W1 – not your average London residence and one that defies all attempts to pigeonhole it. There may be 10 bedrooms, but you should still expect the feel of home: Michael is determined to keep things friendly and easy-going. This might explain the salsa dancing lessons that once broke out at breakfast, a meal of great conviviality taken communally around a curved wooden table in the big and bright kitchen/dining room. Here, a weeping ficus tree stands next to the piano, which, of course, you are welcome to play. There's always something to catch your eye, be it the red-lipped oil painting outside the dining room or the old boots on the landing. Wooden floors run throughout, and the house has a huge sitting room, with sofas, books and backgammon. Expect silk eiderdowns, good beds and lots of space in the bedrooms: all are spotless and very comfy. This is Sherlock Holmes country and Madame Tussauds, Regent's Park and Lord's are all close by, as are hundreds of restaurants. A very friendly place.

Price	£129. Singles £89-£109.
Rooms	10: 5 doubles, 2 twins, 3 singles.
Meals	Continental breakfast included. Pubs/restaurants nearby.
Closed	Never.
Directions	Train: Paddington (to Heathrow). Tube: Baker Street (2-minute walk). Bus: 2, 13, 30, 74, 82, 113, 139, 274. Parking: £25 a day, off-street.

Michael & Liz Callis
Marylebone,
London W1U 6PX
Tel   +44 (0)20 7224 2990
Email   mc@22yorkstreet.co.uk
Web   www.22yorkstreet.co.uk

Searcys Roof Garden Bedrooms

Only in old black-and-white films do you sidle straight from the pavement into an ancient lift, losing your pursuer with sublime ease, but that's how it goes at Searcys. Four floors up and you emerge into a quiet corridor with lovely bedrooms waiting and an office that serves as reception. It is altogether low-key and surprising, with no public area and nothing 'hotelly', only the rooms themselves and the charming staff who bring breakfast and drinks and whatever you need. You're in a quiet area behind busy Knightsbridge, 30 seconds from Harrods, close to Harvey Nicks, with Hyde Park and the King's Road both a short stroll. As for the rooms, a recent refurbishment has brought comfort and style back to the middle of London; much is splendid. Breakfasts arrive promptly and elegantly to your room; somehow you feel that you are inhabiting a private space far from the delightful madness of London. Sleep with windows open and be accosted by nobody. If you want to eat in, local restaurants will deliver. Discreet and comfortable, with touches of luxury – a survivor in its own category.

Price	£221-£258. Singles from £144. Suite £310-£399.
Rooms	11: 7 twins/doubles, 3 singles, 1 family suite.
Meals	Continental breakfast included. 24-hour room service (light meals). Restaurants nearby.
Closed	23-27 December.
Directions	Train: Victoria (to Gatwick). Tube: Knightsbridge (5-minute walk); Sloane Sq. (10-minute walk). Bus: 9, 10, 14, 19, 22, 137. Parking: £58 a day, off-street.

Neringa Zutautaite
30 Pavilion Road, Knightsbridge,
London SW1X 0HJ

Tel	+44 (0)20 7584 4921
Email	rgr@searcys.co.uk
Web	www.searcys.co.uk/30-pavilion-road/bed-breakfast

Lime Tree Hotel

You'll be hard pressed to find better value in the centre of town. The Lime Tree — two elegant Georgian townhouses — stands less than a mile from Buckingham Palace, with Westminster, Sloane Square and Piccadilly easy strolls. Add warm interiors, kind owners and one of the capital's loveliest pubs waiting round the corner and you've unearthed a London gem. There's Cole & Son wallpaper in the airy dining room, so dig into an excellent breakfast (included in the price), then drop into the tiny sitting room next door for guide books and a computer for guests to use. Rooms — one on the ground floor with doors onto the garden — are just the ticket: smart without being lavish; this is a great place for a night or a week. Expect warm colours, crisp linen, pretty wallpaper and excellent bathrooms (most have super showers). Those at the front on the first floor have high ceilings and fine windows, those at the top are cosy in the eaves. Charlotte and Matt are hands-on and will point you in the right direction. Don't miss the Thomas Cubitt pub (50 paces from the front door) for seriously good food.

Price	£150–£175. Triple £170–£195. Family room £210. Singles £95–£125.
Rooms	25: 14 doubles, 3 twins, 4 triples, 1 family room, 3 singles.
Meals	Restaurants nearby.
Closed	Never.
Directions	Train: Victoria (to Gatwick). Tube: Victoria or Sloane Square. Bus: 11, 24, 38, 52, 73, C1. Parking: £34 a day off-street.

Charlotte & Matt Goodsall
135 Ebury Street,
London SW1W 9QU

Tel	+44 (0)20 7730 8191
Email	info@limetreehotel.co.uk
Web	www.limetreehotel.co.uk

The Troubadour

Bob Dylan played here in the '60s, so did Jimi Hendrix, Joni Mitchell and the Rolling Stones. The Troubadour is a slice of old London cool, a quirky coffee house/bar in Earls Court with a magical garden and a small club in the basement where bands play most nights. Outside, pavement tables make the best of the weather; inside, rows of teapots elegantly adorn the windows, as they have done since the bar opened in 1954. The ceiling drips with musical instruments, you find tables and booths, the odd pew. The kitchen is open all day (if you wear a hat on Tuesday nights, pudding is free), so try deep-fried calamari, rib-eye steak, amaretto French toast with walnut butter; in summer, you can eat in the garden. Next door, above their fabulous wine shop, a lovely suite up in the eaves gives views of London rooftops. Expect big colour, a super bed, an alcoholic fridge, a sofa in front of a flat-screen TV. There's a kitchen, too; wake before 9am and make your own breakfast, or come down after for bacon and eggs served late into the afternoon. There's poetry every other Monday and yoga in the gallery. Brilliant.

Price	£175. Singles from £160.
Rooms	1 suite for 2-4.
Meals	Continental breakfast included; cooked extras from £4.50. Lunch & dinner £5-£25.
Closed	25 & 26 December; 1 January.
Directions	Tube: Earl's Court or West Brompton (both 5-minute walk). Bus: 74, 328, 430, C1, C3. Car parks £35 a day.

Simon & Susie Thornhill
263-267 Old Brompton Road,
London SW5 9JA

Tel	+44 (0)20 7370 1434
Email	susie@troubadour.co.uk
Web	www.troubadour.co.uk

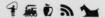

Temple Lodge Club

Temple Lodge, once home to the painter Sir Frank Brangwyn, is sandwiched between a courtyard and a lushly landscaped garden. The peace is remarkable making it a very restful place – simple yet human and warmly comfortable – an extremely nourishing experience. Michael and a small devoted team run it with quiet energy. You breakfast overlooking the garden, there are newspapers to browse, a library instead of TVs. Bedrooms make you smile and come with crisp linen, garden views, good books, excellent prints. They're surprisingly stylish – clean, uncluttered with a hint of country chic – and exceptional value for money (book well in advance!). Only two rooms have their own bathrooms and loo; if you don't mind that, you'll be delighted. The Thames passes by at the end of the road, the Riverside Studios are close for theatre and film, and the Gate Vegetarian Restaurant is ten paces across the courtyard. It's a well-known eatery and was Brangwyn's studio, hence the enormous artist's window. The house is a non-denominational Christian centre with two services a week, which you may take or leave as you choose.

Price	£88–£102. Singles £64–£69.
Rooms	10: 2 doubles, both en suite (1 with separate wc). 3 twins, 5 twins/singles all sharing 2 baths & 1 shower.
Meals	Continental breakfast included. Vegetarian restaurant across courtyard.
Closed	Never.
Directions	Tube: Hammersmith (5-minute walk). Bus: 9, 10, 27, 295.

Michael Beaumont
51 Queen Caroline Street, Hammersmith,
London W6 9QL

Tel	+44 (0)20 8748 8388
Email	templelodgeclub@btconnect.com
Web	www.templelodgeclub.com

MIC Hotel

Hotels in central London often cost a bomb, but rooms at MIC often buck that trend. It stands around the corner from Euston station in a pretty side street that's quiet at night. Tottenham Court Road, Camden Market and the British Museum are all close. The big surprise is a batch of good rooms that come with attractive prices. MIC itself is a social enterprise that supports a village in Kenya and pays for the education of overseas students who wouldn't be able to study without help. It funds this work with its bedrooms, conference suites and meeting rooms, all of which you can use when in town. Inside, you find a large central atrium: very informal, lots of colour. You can tap into free WiFi, order a coffee or a drink at the bar. There's food all day, the full English for breakfast (self-service style), paninis at lunch, perhaps rack of lamb or spicy salmon for dinner; there are loads of local restaurants, too. Rooms are modern, air-conditioned, comfortable and smart, with good bathrooms; become a member (from £100) for big discounts. Just round the corner is Eurostar.

Price	£159. Singles from £149.
Rooms	100: 79 doubles, 18 singles, 3 triples.
Meals	Lunch & dinner £5–£20. Pubs/restaurants nearby.
Closed	Never.
Directions	Train: Euston, St Pancras (Eurostar). Tube: Euston or Warren Street (both 5-min walk). Bus: 10, 18, 24, 29, 30, 59, 68, 73, 91, 134, 168. 253. Car parks £30 a day.

James Barr
81-103 Euston Street,
London NW1 2EZ

Tel	+44 (0)20 7380 0001
Email	reception@micentre.com
Web	www.micentre.com

Entry 164   Map 3

Gin Trap Inn

An actor and a lawyer run this old English Inn. Steve and Cindy left London for the quiet life and haven't stopped since, adding a bright airy conservatory dining room at the back and giving the garden a haircut. The Gin Trap dates to 1667, while the horse chestnut tree that shades the front took root in the 19th century; a conker championship is in the offing. A smart whitewashed exterior gives way to a beamed locals' bar with a crackling fire and the original dining room in Farrow & Ball hues. Upstairs, you find three delightful bedrooms in smart country style. Two have big bathrooms with claw-foot baths and separate showers, all come with timber frames, cushioned window seats, Jane Churchill fabrics and the odd chandelier; walkers will find great comfort here. Come down for delicious food: Thornham oysters, shoulder of lamb, a plate of local cheeses. (Breakfasts are just as good.) Ringstead – a pretty village lost in the country – is two miles inland from the coastal road, thus peaceful at night. You're on the Peddars Way, Sandringham is close and fabulous sandy beaches beckon.

Price	£78-£120. Singles from £39.
Rooms	3 doubles.
Meals	Lunch from £7. Dinner, 3 courses, £20-£25.
Closed	Rarely.
Directions	North from King's Lynn on A149. Ringstead signed right in Heacham. Pub on right in village.

Steve Knowles & Cindy Cook
6 High Street, Ringstead,
Hunstanton PE36 5JU

Tel	+44 (0)1485 525264
Email	thegintrap@hotmail.co.uk
Web	www.gintrapinn.co.uk

The White Horse

You strike gold at The White Horse. For a start, you get one of the best views on the North Norfolk coast – a long, cool sweep over tidal marshes to Scolt Head Island. But it's not just the proximity of the water that elates: the inn, its rooms and the delicious food all score top marks. Follow your nose and find a sunken garden at the front, a local's bar for billiards, a couple of sofas for a game of Scrabble, and a conservatory/dining room for the freshest fish. Best of all is the sun-trapping terrace; eat out here in summer. Walkers pass, sea birds swoop, sail boats glide off into the sunset. At high tide the water laps at the garden edge, at low tide fishermen harvest mussels and oysters from the bay. Inside, the feel is smart without being stuffy: stripped boards, open fires, seaside chic with sunny colours. Beautiful bedrooms in New England style come in duck-egg blue with spotless bathrooms. In the main building some have fabulous views, those in the garden open onto flower-filled terraces. The coastal path passes directly outside. *Minimum two nights at weekends.*

Price	£94–£180.
Rooms	15: 11 doubles, 4 twins.
Meals	Lunch & bar meals from £8.95. Dinner from £12.95.
Closed	Never.
Directions	Midway between Hunstanton & Wells-next-the-Sea on A149.

Cliff & James Nye
Brancaster Staithe,
King's Lynn PE31 8BY
Tel   +44 (0)1485 210262
Email   reception@whitehorsebrancaster.co.uk
Web   www.whitehorsebrancaster.co.uk

The Hoste Arms

Lord Nelson was once a local, now it's farmers, fishermen and film stars who jostle at the bar and roast in front of the fire. In its 300-year history the Hoste has been a court house, a livestock market, a gallery and a brothel; these days it's more a cosy social hub and even on a grey February morning buzzes with life – the locals in for coffee, the residents polishing off leisurely breakfasts. The place has a genius of its own with warm bold colours, armchairs to sink into, panelled walls, an art gallery plus a new beauty spa. Fancy food can be eaten anywhere and anytime, so dig into local oysters or mussels, braised pork cheeks with sautéed wild mushrooms and spiced sweet potato and vegetable cake with fenugreek sauce and bok choi. In summer, life spills out onto tables at the front or you can dine on the terrace in the garden at the back. Rooms are all different, the quietest away from the bar: a tartan four-poster, a swagged half-tester, leather sleigh beds in the Zulu Wing, luxury boutique rooms in Vine House, across the village green. The sandy beaches of the north Norfolk coast are on the doorstep.

Price	£137–£245. Half-board from £100 p.p.
Rooms	49 + 3: 34 twins/doubles & suites. Vine House: 7 doubles. Railway Inn: 7 doubles, 1 railway carriage for 2. 3 self-catering cottages.
Meals	Lunch from £5.50. Bar meals from £9.25. Dinner, 3 courses, from £25. Sunday lunch from £14.
Closed	Never.
Directions	On B1155 for Burnham Market. By green & church in village centre.

Emma Tagg
Market Place, Burnham Market,
King's Lynn PE31 8HD

Tel	+44 (0)1328 738777
Email	reception@hostearms.co.uk
Web	www.hostearms.co.uk

The Blakeney Hotel

The view here is imperious, a clean sweep across the salt marshes up to Blakeney Point. The estuary passes five paces from the front door and guests are prone to fall into graceful inertia and watch the boats slide by. There are plenty of places to do this from: a sun-trapping terrace; a convivial bar; a traditional restaurant for super food; a magnificent first-floor sitting room. Most of the bedrooms have recently been refurbished in warm contemporary style (cool creams, stylish fabrics, painted beams, fancy bathrooms), but the traditional rooms are pretty, too (soft chintz, yellows and reds, super beds, the crispest linen). You'll find the daily papers and an open fire in the sitting room; a snooker room; a super-cool indoor swimming pool with steam room and sauna attached. Outside, paths lead down to the marshes, there are seals to spot, birds to peer at, links golf at Sheringham and Cromer. Finally, delicious food awaits your return, perhaps local mussels in white wine, saddle of venison with a port sauce, roasted pineapple with rum and raisin ice cream.

Price	£182–£319. Singles from £91.
Rooms	63: 19 doubles, 36 twins/doubles, 8 singles.
Meals	Lunch from £9.50. Dinner, 3 courses, £29–£43.50.
Closed	Never.
Directions	A148 north from Fakenham, then B1156 north to Blakeney. In village on quay.

Michael Stannard
The Quay, Blakeney,
Holt NR25 7NE

Tel	+44 (0)1263 740797
Email	reception@blakeneyhotel.co.uk
Web	www.blakeneyhotel.co.uk

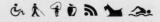

Cley Windmill

The setting here is magical with rushes fluttering in the salt marsh, raised paths leading off to the sea and a vast sky that seemingly starts at your feet. The windmill dates to 1713 and was converted into a house in the 1920s. Square rooms are bigger and suit those who prefer to shuffle, while round rooms in the tower are impossibly romantic (one is for mountaineers only). Six rooms are in the mill and you really want to go for these, though the cottage is set up for self-catering and visiting dogs. Inside, you find the loveliest drawing room – low ceiling, open fire, honesty bar, stripped floorboards… and a window seat to beat most others. Bedrooms come in country style with pretty pine, painted wood, colourful walls, super views. Rooms in the tower (with compact shower rooms) get smaller as you rise, but the view improves with every step; there's a viewing platform half way up for all. Meals are taken in a pretty dining room, so drop down for a big breakfast or book for dinner: homemade soups, local-fish pie, sinful puddings. There's a lovely walled garden for guests, too. *Minimum two nights at weekends.*

Price	£09–£189. Singles from £92. Cottage £275 first night, extra nights £85 (min. 3 nights).
Rooms	8 + 1: 6 doubles, 2 twins/doubles. 1 self-catering cottage.
Meals	Sunday lunch £21.30 (Nov-Apr). Dinner, 3 courses, £27.50-£32.50.
Closed	Christmas.
Directions	Head east through Cley on A149. Mill signed on left in village.

Charlotte Martin
The Quay, Cley,
Holt NR25 7RP

Tel	+44 (0)1263 740209
Email	info@cleywindmill.co.uk
Web	www.cleywindmill.co.uk

Entry 169   Map 7

The Wiveton Bell

A dreamy village one mile back from Norfolk's magical coast: you'll find a scattering of cottages, a brick-and-flint church and this super little inn on the village green. This is reclaimed land. 300 years ago the sea ran up to the church and eight trade ships sat in the harbour below; now idyllic views sweep across fields to Cley. As for the Bell, a recent refurbishment has planted it firmly back on the map. Airy interiors shine while old beams, timber frames and stripped boards give a warm rustic feel. You get bright whites, contemporary art and comfy armchairs in front of the wood-burner. Doors open back and front onto garden and green respectfully, though super-stylish bedrooms all have their own terrace. You also get fabulous bathrooms, flat-screen TVs and DVD players, then underfloor heating and iPod docks. Breakfast hampers are delivered to your door with a newspaper in the morning, so you can enjoy warm croissants leisurely in the summer sun. Great bistro-style food waits in the restaurant — fresh fish, local meat — while on a clear night shooting stars arch through the sky. *Minimum two nights at weekends.*

Price	£95–£140.
Rooms	4 doubles.
Meals	Lunch from £6.95. Dinner, 3 courses, around £30.
Closed	Christmas Day.
Directions	Wiveton signed south off A149 at Blakeney; pub on the green.

Berni Morritt & Sandy Butcher
Blakeney Road, Wiveton,
Holt NR25 7TL

Tel   +44 (0)1263 740101
Web   www.wivetonbell.com

Saracens Head

Lost in the lanes of deepest Norfolk, an English inn that's hard to beat. Outside, Georgian red-brick walls ripple around, encircling a beautiful courtyard where you can sit for sundowners in summer before slipping into the restaurant for a good meal. Tim and Janie came back from the Alps, unable to resist the allure of this inn. A sympathetic refurbishment has brightened things up, but the spirit remains the same: this is a country-house pub with lovely staff who go the extra mile. Downstairs the bar hums with happy locals who come for Norfolk ales and good French wines, while the food in the restaurant is as good as it ever was, perhaps Norfolk pigeon and pork terrine, wild sea bass, treacle tart and caramel ice cream. Upstairs you'll find a sitting room on the landing, where windows frame country views, and six pretty bedrooms. All have been redecorated and have smart carpets, blond wood furniture, comfy beds and sparkling bathrooms. Breakfast sets you up for the day, so explore the coast at Cromer, play golf on the cliffs at Sheringham, or visit Blickling Hall, a Jacobean pile. Blissful stuff.

Price	£100–£110. Singles £70.
Rooms	6: 5 twins/doubles, 1 family room.
Meals	Lunch from £6.50. Dinner, 3 courses, £25–£35. Not Mon; or Tues lunch Oct-June.
Closed	Christmas.
Directions	From Norwich A140 past Aylsham, then 3rd left for Erpingham. Right into Calthorpe, through village, straight out the other side (not right). On right after about 0.5 miles.

Tim & Janie Elwes
Wolterton,
Norwich NR11 7LZ

Tel	+44 (0)1263 768909
Email	info@saracenshead-norfolk.co.uk
Web	www.saracenshead-norfolk.co.uk

Strattons

There's nowhere quite like Strattons, a country-house bolthole that doubles as a contemporary art gallery. It's also one of Britain's greenest hotels (arrive by public transport and pay 10% less for your room), so substance and style go hand in hand. Wander about and find cowhide rugs on stripped wood floors, busts and murals by the dozen, art packed tight on the walls. Les and Vanessa met at art school and their Queen Anne villa overflows with beautiful things. Bedrooms are exquisite: a carved four-poster, a tented bathroom, Indian brocade, trompe l'œil panelling. You'll find vintage wallpaper, sofas by a log fire, new suites and apartments that spoil you rotten. Wonderful food in the candlelit restaurant (turn right by the chaise longue) is mostly organic, perhaps wild mushroom risotto, local pheasant, chocolate fondant with nougatine ice cream. Charlie talks you through the cheese board with great panache, and breakfast (smoked salmon, eggs from their own chickens, organic porridge) is equally divine. Don't miss the Brecks for cycle tracks through Thetford forest. *Minimum two nights at weekends.*

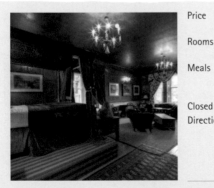

Price	£125–£180. Suites & apartments £165–£275. Singles from £100–£175.
Rooms	14: 6 doubles, 1 twin/double, 5 suites, 2 apartments.
Meals	Lunch in the deli from £6. À la carte dinner about £30. Sunday lunch £18–£25.
Closed	One week at Christmas.
Directions	Ash Close runs off north end of market place between W H Brown estate agents & fish & chip restaurant.

Vanessa & Les Scott
4 Ash Close,
Swaffham PE37 7NH

Tel	+44 (0)1760 723845
Email	enquiries@strattonshotel.com
Web	www.strattonshotel.com

The Mulberry Tree

Attleborough is ancient, mentioned in the Domesday Book. Its weekly market is 800 years old, its monastery suffered at the hands of Henry VIII and a fire swept through in 1559. These days it's a sleepy English country town with a good line in street names: Defunct Passage, Surrogate Precinct and Thieves Lane all bring a smile. It's also well-positioned for Norwich, Snetterton, Thetford Forest and Bury St Edmunds, making the Mulberry Tree a great little base for minor explorations. Airy interiors come in Farrow & Ball colours with stripped floors, big mirrors and contemporary art on the walls. There's a buzzing bar for local ales, a restaurant for super food and a garden that overlooks the bowling green. Best of all are excellent rooms that spoil you rotten: big beds, crisp linen, padded heads, flat-screen TVs. Willow twigs stand six feet high, mirrors lean against the wall, there are cushioned wicker chairs and fabulous tongue-and-groove bathrooms. Back downstairs in the bar, dig into Suffolk ham, free-range eggs and hand-cut chips, or slip into the restaurant for a three-course feast.

Price	£99.95. Singles £75.
Rooms	7: 6 doubles, 1 twin/double.
Meals	Lunch from £7. Dinner, 3 courses, £25–£30.
Closed	Christmas.
Directions	On one-way system around town centre at junction with Station Road.

Philip & Victoria Milligan
Station Road,
Attleborough NR17 2AS
Tel   +44 (0)1953 452124
Email relax@the-mulberry-tree.co.uk
Web   www.the-mulberry-tree.co.uk

The Pheasant Inn

A really super little inn, the kind you hope to chance upon. The Kershaws run it with great passion and an instinctive understanding of its traditions. The stone walls hold 100-year-old photos of the local community; from colliery to smithy, a vital record of its past. The bars are wonderful: brass beer taps glow, anything wooden – ceiling, beams, tables – has been polished to perfection and the clock above the fire keeps perfect time. The attention to detail is a delight, the house ales expertly kept: Timothy Taylor's and Northern Kite. Robin cooks with relish, again nothing too fancy, but more than enough to keep a smile on your face – cider-baked gammon, grilled sea bass with herb butter, wicked puddings, Northumbrian cheeses; as for Sunday lunch, *The Observer* voted it the best in the North. Bedrooms in the old hay barn are as you'd expect: simple and cosy, good value for money. You are in the glorious Northumberland National Park – no traffic jams, no rush. Hire bikes and cycle round the lake, canoe or sail on it, or saddle up and take to the hills. *Minimum two nights at weekends.*

Price	£90-£100. Singles £50-£65. Half-board from £70 p.p.
Rooms	8: 4 doubles, 3 twins, 1 family room.
Meals	Bar meals from £8.95. Dinner, 3 courses, £18-£22.
Closed	25-27 December. Mon & Tues (Nov-Mar).
Directions	From Bellingham follow signs west to Kielder Water & Falstone for 9 miles. Hotel on left, 1 mile short of Kielder Water.

Walter, Irene & Robin Kershaw
Stannersburn,
Hexham NE48 1DD

Tel	+44 (0)1434 240382
Email	stay@thepheasantinn.com
Web	www.thepheasantinn.com

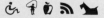

Hart's Nottingham

A small enclave of good things. You're on the smart side of town at the end of a cul-de-sac, thus remarkably quiet. You're also at the top of the hill and close to the castle with exceptional views that sweep south for ten miles; at night, a carpet of light sparkles. Inside, cool lines and travertine marble greet you in reception. Bedrooms are excellent, not huge, but perfectly adequate and extremely well designed. All come with wide-screen TVs, Bose sound systems, super little bathrooms and king-size beds wrapped in crisp white cotton. Those on the ground floor open onto a fine garden, each with a terrace where you can breakfast in good weather; rooms on higher floors have better views (six overlook the courtyard). A cool little bar, the hub of the hotel, is open for breakfast, lunch and dinner, but Hart's Restaurant across the courtyard offers fabulous food, perhaps pan-fried wood pigeon with blackberries, free-range chicken with wild garlic, tarte tatin with caramel ice cream. There's a private car park for hotel guests and a small gym for those who must.

Price	£125-£175. Suites £265.
Rooms	32: 29 doubles, 1 family room, 2 suites.
Meals	Continental breakfast £9, full English £14. Bar snacks from £3.50. Lunch from £14.95. Dinner, 3 courses, from £26.
Closed	Never.
Directions	M1 junc. 24, then follow signs for city centre and Nottingham Castle. Left into Park Row from Maid Marian Way. Hotel on left at top of hill. Parking £8.50/night.

Adam Worthington
Standard Hill, Park Row,
Nottingham NG1 6GN

Tel	+44 (0)115 988 1900
Email	reception@hartshotel.co.uk
Web	www.hartsnottingham.co.uk

Langar Hall

Langar Hall is one of the most engaging and delightful places in this book – reason enough to come to Nottinghamshire. Imogen's exquisite style and natural joie de vivre make this a mecca for those in search of a warm, country-house atmosphere. The house sits at the top of a hardly noticeable hill in glorious parkland, bang next door to the church. Imo's family came here over 150 years ago, building on the site of Admiral Lord Howe's burned-down home. Much of what fills the house arrived then and it's easy to feel intoxicated by beautiful things: statues and busts, a pillared dining room, ancient tomes in overflowing bookshelves, an eclectic collection of oil paintings. Bedrooms are wonderful, some resplendent with antiques, others with fabrics draped from beams or trompe l'œil panelling. Heavenly food, simply prepared for healthy eating, makes this almost a restaurant with rooms, so come for Langar lamb, fish from Brixham, game from Belvoir Castle and garden-grown vegetables. In the grounds: medieval fishponds, canals, a den-like adventure play area and, once a year, Shakespeare on the lawn.

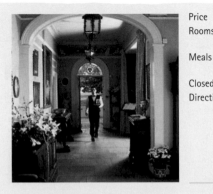

Price	£100–£199. Suite £199.
Rooms	12: 7 doubles, 2 twins, 1 four-poster, 1 suite, 1 chalet for 2.
Meals	Lunch from £18.50. Dinner, 3 courses, £25–£35.
Closed	Never.
Directions	From Nottingham A52 towards Grantham. Right, signed Cropwell Bishop, then straight on for 5 miles. House next to church on edge of village, signed.

Imogen Skirving
Church Lane, Langar,
Nottingham NG13 9HG

Tel	+44 (0)1949 860559
Email	info@langarhall.co.uk
Web	www.langarhall.com

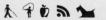

The Feathered Nest Country Inn

The village is tiny, the view is fantastic, the bar is lively, the rooms are a treat. This 300-year-old malthouse recently had a facelift and now shines. Interiors mix all the old originals – stone walls, timber frames, beamed ceilings, open fires – with a contemporary, rustic style. The net result is an extremely attractive country inn, one of the best in the south. Downstairs, one room flows into another. You get beautiful bay windows, roaring fires, saddled bar stools, green leather armchairs. Everywhere you go something lovely catches the eye, not least the view – the best in the Cotswolds; it will draw you to the terrace where your eyes drift off over quilted fields to a distant ridge. You get beds of lavender, swathes of lawn, a vegetable garden that serves the kitchen. Bedrooms upstairs are gorgeous. One is enormous, two have the view, beds are dressed in crisp linen. Most have power showers, one has a claw-foot bath, all have robes. There are coffee machines and iPod docks, too. Super food waits downstairs: Old Spot terrine, Fairford chicken, rhubarb and champagne jelly. *Minimum two nights at weekends.*

Price	£130–£165. Suite £180.
Rooms	4: 1 double, 1 twin, 1 family room, 1 suite.
Meals	Lunch & dinner £6.50–£30. Not Sun eve or Mon (except bank hols).
Closed	Rarely.
Directions	North from Burford on A424 for Stow-on-the-Wold. After 4 miles right for Nether Westcote. In village.

Tony & Amanda Timmer
Nether Westcote,
Chipping Norton OX7 6SD

Tel	+44 (0)1993 833030
Email	reservations@thefeatherednestinn.co.uk
Web	www.thefeatherednestinn.co.uk

The Kingham Plough

You don't expect to find locals clamouring for a table in a country pub on a cold Tuesday in February, but different rules apply at the Kingham Plough. Emily, once junior sous chef at the famous Fat Duck in Bray, is now doing her own thing and it would seem the locals approve. You eat in the tithe barn, now a splendid dining room, with ceilings open to ancient rafters and excellent art on the walls. Attentive staff bring sublime food. Dig into game broth with pheasant dumplings, fabulous lamb hotpot with crispy kale, and hot chocolate fondant with blood orange sorbet. Interiors elsewhere are equally pretty, all the result of a delightful refurbishment. There's a piano by the fire in the locals' bar, a terrace outside for summer dining, fruit trees, herbs and lavender in the garden. Bedrooms, three of which are small, have honest prices and come with super-comfy beds, flat-screen TVs, smart carpets, white linen, the odd beam; one has a claw-foot bath. Arrive by train, straight from London, to be met by a bus that delivers you to the front door. The Daylesford Organic farm shop/café is close.

Price	£90–£130. Singles from £75.
Rooms	7 twins/doubles.
Meals	Lunch from £15. Bar meals from £5. Dinner, 3 courses, about £30. Sunday lunch from £17.
Closed	Christmas Day.
Directions	In village, off B4450, between Chipping Norton & Stow-on-the-Wold.

Emily Watkins & Miles Lampson
The Green, Kingham,
Chipping Norton OX7 6YD

Tel	+44 (0)1608 658327
Email	book@thekinghamplough.co.uk
Web	www.thekinghamplough.co.uk

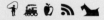

The Kings Head Inn

The sort of inn that defines this country: a 16th-century cider house made of ancient stone that sits on the green in a Cotswold village with free-range hens strutting their stuff and a family of ducks bathing in the pond. Inside, locals gather to chew the cud, scoff great food and wash it down with a cleansing ale. The fire burns all year, you get low ceilings, painted stone walls, country rugs on flagstone floors. Bedrooms, all different, are scattered about; all are well priced. Those in the main house have more character, those in the courtyard are bigger (and quieter). You'll find painted wood, lots of colour, pretty fabrics, spotless bathrooms; most have great views, too. Breakfast and supper are taken in a pretty dining room (exposed stone walls, pale wood tables), while you can lunch by the fire in the bar on Cornish scallops, steak and ale pie, then a plate of British cheeses. There are lovely unpompous touches like jugs of cow parsley in the loo, and loads to do: antiques in Stow, golf at Burford, walking and riding through gorgeous terrain. The front terrace teams with life in summer.

Price	£95-£125. Singles from £70.
Rooms	12: 10 doubles, 2 twins/doubles.
Meals	Lunch from £7.50. Bar meals from £5. Dinner from £9.50. Sunday lunch, 3 courses, £30.
Closed	Christmas Day & Boxing Day.
Directions	East out of Stow-on-the-Wold on A436, then right onto B4450 for Bledington. Pub in village on green.

Archie & Nicola Orr-Ewing
The Green, Bledington,
Chipping Norton OX7 6XQ

Tel	+44 (0)1608 658365
Email	info@kingsheadinn.net
Web	www.kingsheadinn.net

The Feathers Hotel

Woodstock is hard to beat, its golden cottages stitched together seamlessly. It's intrinsically linked to Blenheim Palace, one of Britain's finest houses, seat of the Dukes of Marlborough, birthplace of Winston Churchill. You can stroll up in five minutes, drop your jaw, then return to this wonderfully indulging hotel. It sits serenely on the high street with a carriage arch leading through to a stone courtyard where you sit in summer sipping your Pimms; just heavenly. Inside, a total refurbishment has poured in colour and style. You get old stone walls, parquet flooring, a roaring wood-burner, ancient windows that flood the place with light. Bedrooms are dreamy, big or small, with beautiful fabrics, lovely beds, mohair throws, delicious wallpapers. Some have sofas, all come with robes in gorgeous bathrooms. Back downstairs, the bar has over 100 varieties of gin – there's even a tasting menu with a different shot at each course. They'll help you wash down some wonderful food, perhaps scallop ravioli, slow-cooked Tamworth pork, passion fruit soufflé with its own sorbet. Oxford is close.

Price	£169–£229. Suites £259–£319. Singles from £129. Min. 2 nights at weekends in summer.
Rooms	21: 13 doubles, 3 twins/doubles, 5 suites.
Meals	Lunch from £5. Dinner £39.95–£49.95 (not Sunday eve).
Closed	Never.
Directions	North from Oxford on A44. In Woodstock left after traffic lights & hotel on left.

Luc Morel
Market Street,
Woodstock OX20 1SX

Tel	+44 (0)1993 812291
Email	enquiries@feathers.co.uk
Web	www.feathers.co.uk

Kings Arms Hotel

The Kings Arms stands in the middle of Woodstock, part inn, part chic hotel, part super little restaurant. The big draw here is Blenheim Palace – childhood home to Winston Churchill and one of the country's loveliest buildings. This brings a varied crowd to the bar, tourists from all over the world as well as die-hard locals, who come for the lovely food, the happy vibe and the half-price champagne on Wednesday nights. Inside, old and new combine as airy open-plan interiors drift from one room to another. Downstairs, you find boarded floors and an open fire in the bar, then an airy dining room with gilded mirrors and logs piled high in alcoves. Lovely, uncluttered bedrooms ramble about upstairs, all recently refurbished. Expect lime-white walls, mango wood beds, smart new carpets and lovely art. A couple are huge, most overlook the village, several have fancy new bathrooms. Equally up-to-date are the menus downstairs, so don't miss the irresistible food, perhaps crayfish cocktail, slow-roasted duck, lemon curd brûlée with honey shortbread. Bicester Village and Oxford are both close.

Price	£150. Singles from £80. Half-board from £100 p.p. No under 12s overnight.
Rooms	15 doubles.
Meals	Lunch from £8.75. Dinner, 3 courses, £20–£30.
Closed	Never.
Directions	In Woodstock on A44 at corner of Market Street in town centre.

David & Sara Sykes
19 Market Street,
Woodstock OX20 1SU

Tel	+44 (0)1993 813636
Email	stay@kingshotelwoodstock.co.uk
Web	www.kingshotelwoodstock.co.uk

The Swan

This ancient country pub sits in glorious country with the river Windrush passing yards from the front door and a cricket pitch waiting beyond. It started life as a water mill and stands on the Devonshire estate (the Duchess advised on its restoration). Outside, wisteria wanders along stone walls and creepers blush red in the autumn sun. Interiors come laden with period charm: beautiful windows, open fires, warm colours, the odd beam. Over the years thirsty feet have worn grooves into 400-year-old flagstones, so follow in their footsteps and stop for a pint of Hook Norton at the bar, then eat from a seasonal menu that brims with local produce: deep-fried Windrush goat's cheese, Foxbury Farm chargrilled steak, rich chocolate tart with orange sorbet. Fires roar in winter while doors in the conservatory restaurant open to a pretty garden in fine weather. Bedrooms in the old forge are the most recent addition. Expect 15th-century walls and 21st-century interior design. You get pastel colours to soak up the light, smart white linen on comfy beds and a pink chaise longue in the suite.

Price	£120–£130. Suite from £180. Singles from £70.
Rooms	6: 4 doubles, 1 twin, 1 suite.
Meals	Lunch & bar meals from £7.50. Dinner from £12. Sunday lunch, 3 courses, £30.
Closed	Christmas Day & Boxing Day.
Directions	West from Oxford on A40 for Cheltenham/Burford. Past Witney and village signed right at 1st r'bout.

Archie & Nicola Orr-Ewing
Swinbrook,
Burford OX18 4DY

Tel	+44 (0)1993 823339
Email	info@theswanswinbrook.co.uk
Web	www.theswanswinbrook.co.uk

Burford House

Burford was made rich by 14th-century mill owners. Its golden high street slips downhill to the river Windrush, where paths lead out into glorious country, passing a church that dates to Norman times; Cromwell held a band of Levellers here in 1649 and their murals survive inside. Halfway up the hill, this 17th-century timber-framed house stands bang in the middle of town. Interiors sweep you back to the soft elegance of old England: a couple of cosy sitting rooms, a whispering wood-burner, exposed stone walls, a courtyard for summer dining. Slip into the restaurant and find Farrow & Ball colours, freshly cut flowers, rugs on wood boards, theatre posters hanging on the wall. The food is delicious so come for ham hock terrine, a trio of Cotswold lamb, a plate of rhubarb puddings. Bedrooms are delightful, two across the courtyard in the coach house. Some have oak beams, others a claw-foot bath. All come with super beds, woollen blankets and robes in good bathrooms; those at the back have rooftop views. Wake on Sunday to the sound of pealing bells. *Minimum two nights at weekends.*

Price	£159–£199. Singles from £124.
Rooms	8: 3 doubles, 2 twins/doubles, 3 four-posters.
Meals	Light lunch from £4.95. Dinner (Wed-Sat) about £35.
Closed	Rarely.
Directions	In centre of Burford, halfway down hill. Free on-street parking, free public car park nearby.

Ian Hawkins & Stewart Dunkley
99 High Street,
Burford OX18 4QA

Tel	+44 (0)1993 823151
Email	stay@burfordhouse.co.uk
Web	www.burfordhouse.co.uk

The Plough at Clanfield

A country-house inn with a sitting-room bar, a great place to wash up for a couple of nights. It dates to 1550 and was once a wool merchant's house, but changed its colours to welcome travellers crossing the Thames at nearby Radcot Bridge. Outside, a lawn runs up to a smart terrace, where you sit in summer sipping something from the gin pantry with a plume of wisteria resplendent on the golden walls behind. Inside, you get all the old stuff – ancient beams, mullioned windows, stone floors – but Martin's eye for beautiful things has added oodles of style. You find sofas in front of a roaring fire, bold colours and country rugs, eclectic art crammed on the walls, games to be played in the sitting room. Bedrooms – some huge in an attractive extension, others smaller with wonky floors above the shop – are delightful and come with excellent bathrooms. What's more, they're free on Sunday nights if you spend £75 in the restaurant, a hugely popular ruse, so book early. As for the food, expect delicious country cooking: lots of game, fantastic seafood, irresistible puddings. Badbury Hill, an Iron Age hill fort, is close.

Price	£115–£160. Four-poster £150–£175. Singles from £89. Half-board from £82.50 p.p.
Rooms	11: 6 doubles, 2 twins/doubles, 3 four-posters.
Meals	Lunch & dinner £5–£35.
Closed	24–28 December.
Directions	North from Farringdon on A4095. In village on left.

Martin Agius
Bourton Road,
Clanfield OX18 2RB

Tel	+44 (0)1367 810222
Email	bookings@theploughclanfield.co.uk
Web	www.theploughclanfield.co.uk

The Trout at Tadpole Bridge

A 17th-century Cotswold inn on the banks of the Thames; pick up a pint, drift into the garden and watch life float by. Gareth and Helen bought The Trout after a two-year search and have cast their fairy dust into every corner: expect super bedrooms, oodles of style, delicious local food. The downstairs is open plan and timber-framed, with stone floors, gilt mirrors, wood-burners and logs piled high in alcoves. Bedrooms at the back are away from the crowd; three open onto a small courtyard where wild roses ramble on creamy stone – but you may prefer to stay put in your room and indulge in unabashed luxury. You get the best of everything: funky fabrics, trim carpets, monsoon showers (one room has a claw-foot bath), DVD players, flat-screen TVs, a library of films. Sleigh beds, brass beds, beautifully upholstered armchairs... one room even has a roof terrace. You can watch boats pass from the breakfast table, feast on local sausages, tuck into homemade marmalade courtesy of Helen's mum. Food is as local as possible, there are maps for walkers to keep you thin. *Minimum two nights at weekends May-October.*

Price	£130. Suite £160. Singles from £85.
Rooms	6: 2 doubles, 3 twins/doubles, 1 suite.
Meals	Lunch & dinner £10.95–£19. Sunday lunch from £11.95.
Closed	Christmas Day & Boxing Day.
Directions	A420 southwest from Oxford for Swindon. After 13 miles right for Tadpole Bridge. Pub on right by bridge.

Gareth & Helen Pugh
Buckland Marsh,
Faringdon SN7 8RF

Tel	+44 (0)1367 870382
Email	info@trout-inn.co.uk
Web	www.trout-inn.co.uk

Old Parsonage Hotel

A country house in the city, with a lively bar for a drop of champagne, a rooftop terrace for afternoon tea and a hidden garden where you can sit in the shade and listen to the bells of St Giles. Logs smoulder in the original stone fireplace, the daily papers wait by an ancient window and an extensive collection of exquisite art hangs on the walls. You feast in the restaurant on meat from the owner's Oxfordshire farm or fish from the Channel Islands, then retire to warm stylish bedrooms which are scattered all over the place – some at the front (where Oscar Wilde entertained lavishly when he was sent down), others at the back in a sympathetic extension where some suites have French windows onto tiny balconies and a couple of the less-expensive rooms open onto private terraces. Expect Vi-Spring mattresses, flat-screen TVs, crisp white linen, spotless bathrooms. Daily walking tours led by an art historian are 'on the house', while the hotel can book a punt on the Cherwell, then pack you a picnic, so glide effortlessly past spire and meadow before tying up for lunch. *Minimum two nights at weekends.*

Price	£132-£225. Suites £202-£295.
Rooms	30: 22 twins/doubles, 7 suites for 3, 1 for 4.
Meals	Breakfast £12.95-£14. Lunch & dinner £10-£45.
Closed	Never.
Directions	From A40 ring road, south onto Banbury Road; thro' Summertown and hotel on right just before St Giles Church.

	1 Banbury Road, Oxford OX2 6NN
Tel	+44 (0)1865 310210
Email	info@oldparsonage-hotel.co.uk
Web	www.oldparsonage-hotel.co.uk

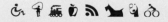

Old Bank Hotel

You're in the heart of old Oxford. Stroll south past Corpus Christi to Christ Church meadows, head north for the Radcliffe Camera and the Bodleian Library. Back at the Old Bank warm contemporary elegance comes with an important collection of modern art and photography. It adorns most walls, even in bedrooms, and catalogues can be perused. Downstairs the old tiller's hall is now a vibrant bar/brasserie with fine arched windows giving views onto the high street; come for cocktails before a convivial meal (fish from the Channel Islands, meat from the owner's farm). Bedrooms upstairs are exemplary, with fine beds, piles of cushions, Denon CD players, flat-screen TVs. Bigger rooms have sofas, you get robes in super bathrooms, there's free broadband access throughout. Service is friendly and serene: curtains are pleated, beds are turned down, the daily papers delivered to your door. There's room service, too. Breakfast is served in the tiller's hall or on the deck in the courtyard in summer. Off-street parking is priceless, daily walking tours led by an art historian are free for guests. *Minimum two nights at weekends.*

Price	£134-£390. Suite £305-£435.
Rooms	42: 12 twins/doubles, 29 doubles, 1 suite for 2-5.
Meals	Breakfast £31.50-£14.50. Lunch & dinner £10-£30.
Closed	Never.
Directions	Cross Magdalen Bridge for city centre. Straight through 1st set of lights, then left into Merton St. Follow road right; 1st right into Magpie Lane. Car park 2nd right.

Ben Truesdale
92-94 High Street,
Oxford OX1 4BJ

Tel	+44 (0)1865 799599
Email	info@oldbank-hotel.co.uk
Web	www.oldbank-hotel.co.uk

Hambleton Hall Hotel

A sublime country house, one of the loveliest in England. The position here is matchless. The house stands on a tiny peninsular that juts into Rutland Water. You can sail on it or cycle around it, then come back to the undisputed wonders of Hambleton: sofas by the fire in the panelled hall, a pillared bar in red for cocktails and a Michelin star in the dining room. French windows in the sitting room (beautiful art, fresh flowers, the daily papers) open onto idyllic gardens. Expect clipped lawns and gravel paths, a formal parterre garden that bursts with summer colour and a walled swimming pool with views over grazing parkland down to the water. Bedrooms are the very best. Hand-stitched Italian linen, mirrored armoires, fabulous marble bathrooms – and Stefa's eye for fabrics, some of which coat the walls, is faultless; the Croquet Pavilion, a supremely comfortable two-bedroom suite, has its own terrace. Polish the day off with incredible food, perhaps sautéed scallops with lemon grass, fallow venison with gin and tonic jelly, passion fruit soufflé with banana sorbet. *Minimum two nights at weekends.*

Price	£250–£420. Singles from £200. Pavilion £525–£625 for 4.
Rooms	17: 15 twins/doubles, 1 four-poster. Pavilion: 1 suite (1 four-poster, 1 twin/double) for 4.
Meals	Lunch, 2 courses, from £22. Dinner £38.50–£70.
Closed	Never.
Directions	From A1, A606 west towards Oakham for about 8 miles, then left, signed Hambleton. In village bear left and hotel signed right.

	Tim & Stefa Hart
	Ketton Road, Hambleton, Oakham LE15 8TH
Tel	+44 (0)1572 756991
Email	hotel@hambletonhall.com
Web	www.hambletonhall.com

The Olive Branch

A Michelin-starred pub in a sleepy Rutland village, where bridle paths lead out across peaceful fields. The inn dates to the 17th century and is built of Clipsham stone. Inside, a warm, informal rustic chic hits the spot perfectly; come for open fires, old beams, exposed stone walls and choir stalls in the bar. Chalk boards on tables in the restaurant reveal the names of the evening's diners, while the food – seared scallops with black pudding fritter, slow-roast pork belly with creamed leeks and apple sauce – elates. As do the hampers that you can whisk away for picnics in the country. Bedrooms in Beech House across the lane are impeccable. Three have terraces, one has a free-standing bath, all come with crisp linen, pretty beds, Roberts radios, real coffee. Super breakfasts – smoothies, boiled eggs and soldiers, the full cooked works – are served in a smartly renovated barn, with flames leaping in the wood-burner. The front garden fills in summer, the sloe gin comes from local berries, and Newark is close for the biggest antiques market in Europe. A total gem. *Ask about cookery demos.*

Price	£115–£195. Singles from £97.50.
Rooms	6: 5 doubles, 1 family suite.
Meals	Bar meals £10.50. Dinner from £14.50. Sunday lunch £24.95.
Closed	Rarely.
Directions	A1 five miles north of Stamford, then exit onto B668. Right and right again for Clipsham. In village (Beech House across the road from The Olive Branch).

	Ben Jones & Sean Hope
	Main Street, Clipsham,
	Oakham LE15 7SH
Tel	+44 (0)1780 410355
Email	info@theolivebranchpub.com
Web	www.theolivebranchpub.com

Soulton Hall

There's been a house on this land since 1066, but Soulton goes back to 1430, a fortified house that was home to the first Protestant mayor of London. It stands magnificently in 500 acres of pasture and woodland, yours to roam. It's a family affair: John farms, Ann looks after the house. Climb the steps, slip through a spectacular stone doorway, arrive in the hall, sink in a sofa in front of a fire. Potter about and find an attractive dining room and a cosy bar, but it's the bedrooms in the main house that leave the big impression. You'll find them up an old oak staircase (and you glimpse a section of original wattle and daub on your way up). Four grand country-house bedrooms wait. They come with timber frames, mullioned windows, the odd panelled wall and polished floors; three have fancy bathrooms. It's all splendidly regal, and while simpler bedrooms are also available, it's worth bagging one of these. Back downstairs, you eat in style, perhaps carrot and coriander soup, lemon sorbet with sparkling wine, chicken cooked with hazelnuts and cream, sticky toffee pudding.

Price	£110–£150.
Rooms	7: 3 doubles, 1 twin/double. Carriage House: 2 doubles. Garden room: 1 four-poster.
Meals	Dinner, 4 courses, £38.50.
Closed	Rarely.
Directions	North from Shrewsbury on A49. Left in Prees Green onto B5065 for Wem. House on left after two miles.

Ann & John Ashton
Shrewsbury SY4 5RS

Tel	+44 (0)1939 232786
Email	enquiries@soultonhall.co.uk
Web	www.soultonhall.co.uk

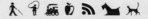

Sebastian's

This lovely little restaurant with rooms occupies an old merchant's house that dates from 1640. Michelle and Mark have been at the helm for 23 years cooking up a fine reputation – not only for their delicious food, but for the quirky, old-world interiors in which they serve it. Step off the street to find huge beams, timber frames, half panelling and stripped floors. In between you get smartly clothed tables, fairy lights and candles, exotic screens and fresh flowers. Old posters of the Orient Express hang on the walls (Mark supplies the train with canapés and desserts). Back in the restaurant there are sofas in front of a cavernous fire that smoulders from morning to night in winter. Here you drool over the menu before digging into fabulous food, perhaps scallop ravioli with lemon grass and ginger, loin of lamb with a goat's cheese tart, limoncello mousse. Six delightful rooms wait, two in the main house (timber frames, lots of colour), four off the courtyard (comfy sofas, lovely bathrooms). Montgomery, the prettiest town in Wales, is close.

Price	£75. Singles £65.
Rooms	6: 5 doubles, 1 twin/double.
Meals	Continental breakfast £6.95, full English £11.95. Dinner £19.95–£39.50.
Closed	Rarely.
Directions	Sent on booking.

Michelle & Mark Sebastian Fisher
45 Willow Street, Oswestry SY11 1AQ
Tel   +44 (0)1691 655444
Email   sebastians.rest@virgin.net
Web   www.sebastians-hotel.com

Pen-y-Dyffryn Country Hotel

In a blissful valley lost to the world, this small, traditional country house sparkles on the side of a peaceful hill. To the front, beyond the stone terraces that drip with aubretia, fields tumble down to a stream that marks the border with Wales. Outside, daffodils erupt in spring, the lawns are scattered with deckchairs in summer, paths lead onto the hill for excellent walks. Inside, colourful interiors are warmly attractive: Laura Ashley wallpaper and an open fire in the quirky bar; shuttered windows and super food in the yellow restaurant; the daily papers and a good collection of art in the sitting room. Bedrooms are stylish without being grand. Most have great views, one has a French sleigh bed, good bathrooms come with fluffy towels. Four rooms are dog-friendly and have their own patios, you get crisp white linen, silky curtains, padded bedheads. There's plenty of space, ideal for a gathering, and super food to help you celebrate, perhaps Shetland mussels, Welsh beef, a plate of local cheese; the smoked haddock at breakfast is divine. Offa's Dyke and Powys Castle are close. *Minimum two nights at weekends.*

Price	£114–£166. Singles £86.
Rooms	12: 8 doubles, 4 twins.
Meals	Light lunch (for residents) by arrangement. Dinner £30–£37.
Closed	Rarely.
Directions	From A5 head to Oswestry. Leave town on B4580, signed Llansilin. Hotel 3 miles up. Approach Rhydycroesau, left at town sign, first right.

Miles & Audrey Hunter
Rhydycroesau, Oswestry SY10 7JD

Tel	+44 (0)1691 653700
Email	stay@peny.co.uk
Web	www.peny.co.uk

The Castle Hotel

This thriving medieval market town sits amid some of the loveliest country in the land, a launch pad for walkers and cyclists, with Offa's Dyke, Long Mynd and the Kerry Ridgeway all close. After a day in the hills what better than to roll back down to this quirky hotel for a night of genteel carousing. You'll find heaps of country comforts: hearty food, an impeccable pint, cosy rooms with honest prices. Downstairs, there's a coal fire in the pretty snug, oak panelling in the breakfast room, and Millie the short-haired dachshund who patrols the corridors with aplomb. Spotless bedrooms upstairs have good beds, warm colours, flat-screen TVs, an armchair if there's room. Some are up in the eaves, several have views of the Shropshire hills. Back downstairs you find the sort of food you hanker for after a day in the open air, perhaps broccoli and stilton soup, beef and ale pie, sticky toffee pudding (all for a song). Don't miss the hugely popular real ale festival in July, the beer drinker's equivalent of Glastonbury. There's a lovely garden, too, perfect for sundowners in summer.

Price	£85–£105. Singles from £60. Half-board from £67.50 p.p.
Rooms	8: 5 doubles, 1 twin, 2 family rooms.
Meals	Lunch from £4.50. Dinner, 3 courses, about £25.
Closed	Christmas Day.
Directions	At top of hill in town, off A488.

	Henry Hunter
	Bishops Castle SY9 5BN
Tel	+44 (0)1588 638403
Email	stay@thecastlehotelbishopscastle.co.uk
Web	www.thecastlehotelbishopscastle.co.uk

The Lion at Leintwardine

The position here is lovely with the river Teme streaming under a packhorse bridge and long views shooting west across water meadows. Lawns run down to the water, so sit with a glass of Pimm's in summer and watch the swans glide by. Inside, you find the fruits of an attractive renovation. There are sofas in the hall, a wood-burner in the bar, lime greens and timber frames in the pretty restaurant. An airy, open-plan feel runs throughout. The odd chandelier dangles from the ceiling, while walls everywhere host a fantastic collection of black-and white photos, a hundred years of village life on display; just magical. Super bedrooms upstairs aren't huge, but nor are their prices and they don't stint on style. Expect sleigh beds, a wall of paper, pretty fabrics, crisp linen; bathrooms are equally good. Outside, there's lots to do: Offa's Dyke, Ludlow and its castle, you can even hire bikes and take to the hills. Back at the inn, delicious food waits, perhaps crab and lemongrass mousse, local duck with Pear William confit, spiced pineapple with elderflower sorbet.

Price	£100–£120. Singles from £85.
Rooms	8: 6 doubles, 1 twin, 1 single.
Meals	Lunch from £6.95. Dinner, 3 courses, about £30. Sunday lunch from £13.95.
Closed	Christmas Day.
Directions	West from Ludlow on A4113. On left in village by bridge.

Jessica Griffiths
Leintwardine,
Craven Arms SY7 0JZ

Tel   +44 (0)1547 540203
Email   enquiries@thelionleintwardine.co.uk
Web   www.thelionleintwardine.co.uk

The Swan

The Swan is gorgeous, a contemporary take on a village local. It's part of a new wave of cool little pubs that open all day and do so much more than serve a good pint. The locals love it. They come for breakfast, pop in to buy a loaf of bread, then return for afternoon tea and raid the cake stands. It's set back from the road, with a sprinkling of tables and chairs on the pavement in French-café style. Interiors mix old and new brilliantly. You get Farrow & Ball colours and cool lamps hanging above the bar, then lovely old rugs on boarded floors and a wood-burner to keep things toasty. Push inland and find an airy restaurant open to the rafters that overlooks the garden. Here you dig into Tom Blake's fabulous food (he's ex-River Cottage), anything from a Cornish crab sandwich with lemon mayo to a three-course feast, maybe Wye valley asparagus, Wedmore lamb chops, bitter chocolate mousse with chocolate cookies. Bedrooms are lovely. Two have fancy baths in the room, you get vintage French furniture, iPod docks, colourful throws and walk-in power showers. Glastonbury is close, as are the Mendips.

Price	£85–£110.
Rooms	6: 4 doubles, 2 twins/doubles.
Meals	Lunch from £5. Dinner, 3 courses, about £25. Sunday lunch from £14. Bar meals only Sun night.
Closed	Rarely.
Directions	M5, junc. 22, then B3139 to Wedmore. In village.

Cassia Stevens
Cheddar Road,
Wedmore BS28 4EQ

Tel	+44 (0)1934 710337
Email	info@theswanwedmore.com
Web	www.theswanwedmore.com

At The Chapel

Every now and then you walk into a small hotel and immediately know you've struck gold. That's what happens here. You cross the threshold and suddenly your pleasure receptors erupt in delight. At the front, you find an intoxicating wine shop on one side, then an irresistible bakery on the other (if you stay, they leave freshly baked croissants outside your room in the morning, a pre-breakfast snack). Back downstairs your eyes draw you through to an enormous room. This is an old Baptist chapel that Catherine and Ahmed bought ten years ago; the chapel itself, now a restaurant/café/art gallery/theatre was once their sitting room. You get white walls, vast windows, contemporary art and a rather cool bar. The food is perfect, nothing too posh, just seriously tasty stuff: fabulous pizza, fish from Lyme Bay, an ambrosial baked aubergine with parmesan and basil. Below, outside, a gorgeous terrace looks out over the town to green hills; above, fabulous bedrooms come with flawless white marble bathrooms. We've run out of space, so come to see for yourself; expect something very special.

Price	£100–£150. Suite £250.
Rooms	5: 4 doubles, 1 suite.
Meals	Breakfast from £2.50. Lunch & dinner £5–£35.
Closed	Rarely.
Directions	Bruton is 5 miles north of the A303 at Wincanton. On high street.

Catherine Butler & Ahmed Sidki
High Street,
Bruton BA10 0AE

Tel	+44 (0)1749 814070
Email	mail@atthechapel.co.uk
Web	www.atthechapel.co.uk

The Pilgrims Restaurant

Medieval pilgrims in search of King Arthur's tomb would stop here for sustenance before heading out across the marshes on their way to Glastonbury abbey. These days, the food, the welcome and the rooms are all so lovely you're more likely to suffer a crisis of faith and stay put. Jools is to blame – his food is far too good to miss, good enough to alter the DNA of these walls – the Pilgrims has recently morphed into a restaurant with rooms by popular demand. All the lovely old stuff survives – stone walls, timber frames, panelled walls and a couple of sofas in front of the fire. Tables in the restaurant are nicely spaced apart, the lighting is subtle, the service hits the spot. As for the food, expect local ingredients cooked to perfection, perhaps Lyme Bay scallops, rack of local lamb, Somerset rhubarb crumble. Five lovely bedrooms wait in the old skittle alley. Three have cathedral ceilings, all come with exposed stone walls, flat-screen TVs and crisp linen on good beds. As for the bathrooms, expect double-ended baths, separate power showers, fluffy robes. Wells and Glastonbury are close.

Price	£80-£120.
Rooms	5: 4 doubles, 1 twin/double.
Meals	Lunch from £8. Dinner, 3 courses, about £30. Sunday lunch £19. Not Monday.
Closed	Rarely.
Directions	On B3153 between Castle Cary & Somerton. In village by traffic lights.

Julian & Sally Mitchison
Lovington,
Castle Cary BA7 7PT

Tel   +44 (0)1963 240597
Email   jools@thepilgrimsatlovington.co.uk
Web   www.thepilgrimsatlovington.co.uk

The Queen's Arms

Stride across rolling fields, feast on Corton Denham lamb, retire to a perfect room. Buried down several Dorset/Somerset border lanes, Gordon and Jeanette Reid's 18th-century stone pub has an elegant exterior – more country gentleman's house than pub. The bar, with its rug-strewn flagstones and bare boards, pew benches, deep sofas and crackling fire, is most charming. In the dining room – big mirrors on terracotta walls, new china on old tables – robust British dishes are distinguished by fresh ingredients from local suppliers. Try pheasant, pigeon and black pudding terrine, followed by monkfish with chive velouté... then make room for a comforting crumble. Bedrooms are beautifully designed in soothing colours, and all have lovely views over the village and surrounding hills. New coach house rooms are super, too: underfloor heating, crisp linen and down duvets, brass and sleigh beds, iPod docks and immaculate wet rooms. Expect Moor Queen's Revival on tap, homemade pork pies on the bar, Black Spot bacon at breakfast, and stunning walks from the front door. Dogs are very welcome.

Price	£85-£120. Singles from £75. Dogs welcome in ground floor bedroom.
Rooms	8: 5 doubles, 1 twin, 1 twin/double, 1 four-poster.
Meals	Lunch from £6.50. Dinner, 3 courses £25-£30.
Closed	Never.
Directions	From A303 take Chapel Cross turning. Through South Cadbury, then next left & follow signs to Corton Denham. Pub at end of village on right.

Gordon & Jeanette Reid
Corton Denham,
Sherborne DT9 4LR
Tel   +44 (0)1963 220317
Email   relax@thequeensarms.com
Web   www.thequeensarms.com

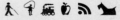

Little Barwick House

A dreamy restaurant with rooms lost in the hills three miles south of Yeovil. Tim and Emma rolled west ten years ago and have gathered a legion of fans who come to feast on their ambrosial food. The stage is this small Georgian country house which stands in three acres of peace. A curtain of trees shields it from the outside world, horses graze in the paddock below and afternoon tea is served in the garden in summer, so sip your Earl Grey accompanied by birdsong. Inside, graceful interiors flood with light courtesy of fine windows that run along the front. There's an open fire in the cosy bar, eclectic reading in the pretty sitting room, and hessian-style carpets in the high-ceilinged dining room. Upstairs, super bedrooms hit the spot with warm colours, silk curtains and a country-house feel. But dinner is the main event, heaven in three courses. Everything is home-made and cooked by Tim and Emma, an equal partnership in the kitchen. Try twice-baked cheese soufflé, pan-fried fillet of Cornish sea bass, apple strudel with calvados ice cream. A treat. *One-night weekend bookings occasionally refused.*

Price	Half-board £105–£130 p.p.
Rooms	6: 4 doubles, 2 twins.
Meals	Lunch £23.95–£27.95 (not Mon/Tues). Dinner included; non-residents, £43.95 (not Sun/Mon).
Closed	Sundays & Mondays. 2 weeks in January.
Directions	From Yeovil A37 south for Dorchester; left at 1st r'bout. Down hill, past church, left in village and house on left after 200 yds.

Emma & Tim Ford
Rexes Hollow Lane, Barwick,
Yeovil BA22 9TD

Tel	+44 (0)1935 423902
Email	reservations@barwick7.fsnet.co.uk
Web	www.littlebarwickhouse.co.uk

Lord Poulett Arms

In a ravishing village, an idyllic inn, French at heart and quietly groovy. Part pub, part country house, with walls painted in reds and greens and old rugs covering flagged floors, the Lord Poulett gives a glimpse of a 21st-century dream local, where classical design fuses with earthy rusticity. A fire burns on both sides of the chimney in the dining room; on one side you can sink into leather armchairs, on the other you can eat under beams at antique oak tables while candles flicker. Take refuge with the daily papers on the sofa in the locals' bar or head past a pile of logs at the back door and discover an informal French garden of box and bay trees, with a piste for boules and a creeper-shaded terrace. Bedrooms upstairs come in funky country-house style, with fancy flock wallpaper, perhaps crushed velvet curtains, a small chandelier or a carved-wood bed. Two rooms have slipper baths behind screens in the room; two have claw-foot baths in bathrooms one step across the landing; Roberts radios add to the fun. Delicious food includes summer barbecues, Sunday roasts and the full works at breakfast.

Price	£85–£95. Singles £60–£65.
Rooms	4: 2 doubles, both en suite. 2 doubles, each with separate bath.
Meals	Lunch & dinner £10–£25.
Closed	Never.
Directions	A303, then A356 south for Crewkerne. Right for West Chinnock. Through village, 1st left for Hinton St George. Pub on right in village.

Steve & Michelle Hill
High Street,
Hinton St George TA17 8SE

Tel	+44 (0)1460 73149
Email	reservations@lordpoulettarms.com
Web	www.lordpoulettarms.com

The Devonshire Arms

A lively English village with a well-kept green; the old school house stands to the south, the church to the east and the post office to the west. The inn (due north) is over 400 years old and was once a hunting lodge for the Dukes of Devonshire; a rather smart pillared porch survives at the front. These days open-plan interiors are warmly contemporary with high ceilings, shiny blond floorboards and fresh flowers everywhere. Hop onto brown leather stools at the bar and order a pint of Moor Revival, or sink into sofas in front of the fire and crack open a bottle of wine. In summer, life spills onto the terrace at the front, the courtyard at the back and the lawned garden beyond. Super bedrooms run along at the front; all are a good size, but those at each end are huge. You get fresh light rooms, natural flooring, crisp white linen and freeview TV. Two have free-standing baths, some have compact showers. Delicious food is on tap in the restaurant – chargrilled scallops, slow-cooked lamb, passion fruit crème brûlée – so take to the nearby Somerset levels and walk off your indulgence in style.

Price	£87.50–£135. Singles from £75.
Rooms	9: 8 doubles, 1 twin.
Meals	Lunch from £6.95. Dinner £11.50–£18.95.
Closed	Rarely.
Directions	A303, then north on B3165, through Martock to Long Sutton. On village green.

Philip & Sheila Mepham
Long Sutton,
Langport TA10 9LP

Tel	+44 (0)1458 241271
Email	mail@thedevonshirearms.com
Web	www.thedevonshirearms.com

Farmers Arms

A lovely inn lost in peaceful hills on the Somerset Levels – a great base for a night or two of affordable luxury. Outside, cockerels crow, cows graze and glorious views from the beer garden drift downhill for a couple of miles – a perfect spot for a pint in summer. Inside, you'll find friendly natives, sofas in front of an open fire and a timber-framed bar, where one airy room rolls into another giving a sense of space and light. There are beamed ceilings, tongue-and-groove panelling, logs piled high in the alcoves. Bedrooms – some big, some huge – are just the ticket. They come with whitewashed walls, cast-iron beds, varnished floors, power showers or double-ended baths. One has a daybed, others have sofas, another has a private courtyard. Delicious food flies from the kitchen, perhaps half a pint of Atlantic prawns, West Country lamb with dauphinoise potatoes, orange and mango cheesecake; in summer you can eat in a courtyard garden. There are local stables if you want to ride and great walking, so bring your boots. Five berths for camper vans wait above the beer garden, too.

Price	£95–£125. Singles from £85.
Rooms	5: 4 doubles, 1 twin/double.
Meals	Lunch & dinner £5–£35.
Closed	Never.
Directions	M5 junc. 25, then south on A358. On dual carriageway, right, signed West Hatch. Follow signs to RSPCA centre up hill for two miles. Signed on left.

Nick Millard
West Hatch,
Taunton TA3 5RS

Tel	+44 (0)1823 480980
Email	info@fawh.co.uk
Web	www.farmersarmssomerset.co.uk

The Castle at Taunton

A Saxon castle took root on this land 1,300 years ago. Its fortunes fluctuated with the centuries and it fell into disrepair, but when the hotel came along, in 1830, it was crenellated in keeping with the old battlements around it (now the museum). The best spot to take it all in is the garden, once the Norman keep. Spin through the revolving doors and you find the sort of place that befits this gracious county town. At times it's as if you've entered a gentleman's club, but it manages to bridge the spirit of the past with the needs of the present, hence the the ever-busy brasserie, a cool little bar for a pre-dinner snifter, a grand function room for private parties and nooks and crannies in which to hide away in. Best of all is the music. Five weekends a year are given over to chamber music with musicians from all over the world flying in to perform: stupendous stuff. Country-house bedrooms are sprinkled about and come with pretty fabrics, the odd antique, huge beds dressed in white linen. The cricket ground is a short stroll, the best of the West Country is on your doorstep.

Price	£180. Garden rooms £240. Singles from £120.
Rooms	44: 27 twins/doubles, 12 singles, 5 garden rooms.
Meals	Lunch & dinner £15-£45.
Closed	Never.
Directions	M5 junc. 25 or 26, then centre of town. In town, pick up brown signs to hotel and follow them in.

Kit Chapman
Castle Green,
Taunton TA1 1NF

Tel	+44 (0)1823 272671
Email	reception@the-castle-hotel.com
Web	www.the-castle-hotel.com

Combe House Hotel

A country lane winds up to this hotel, which basks peacefully in the first folds of the Quantocks. Woodlands rise, a stream pours past and paths lead out for uplifting walks, though with the recent addition of a couple of treatments rooms and a hot tub, you might want to stay put. The hotel, an old mill, dates back to the 17th century and couldn't be in better hands; Gareth and Catherine came to look after the place and have done just that. Outside, free-range chickens stroll around a very productive kitchen garden, while inside you find airy interiors, smart carpets, a wood-burner in the inglenook, the odd exposed wall. Sofas take the strain in the sitting room, armchairs do the job in the bar and you eat under beams in the restaurant, where seriously good local food does the trick: seared scallops with cauliflower purée, Exmoor lamb with dauphinoise potatoes, passion fruit brûlée with mango sorbet. Bedrooms have all been refurbished. Expect a contemporary country style with warm colours, silky throws, flat-screen TVs, and robes in super new bathrooms. There are deer on the hill, too.

Price	£125–£150. Suites £175. Singles from £65. Half-board from £80 p.p.
Rooms	15: 11 twins/doubles, 2 singles, 2 suites.
Meals	Lunch from £5.50. Sunday lunch from £16. Dinner, 3 courses, about £30.
Closed	Never.
Directions	From Bridgwater A39 to Minehead. At Holford left at Plough Inn; follow lane thro' village. Bear left at fork signed Holford Combe; on right.

Gareth & Catherine Weed
Holford,
Bridgwater TA5 1RZ

Tel	+44 (0)1278 741382
Email	enquiries@combehouse.co.uk
Web	www.combehouse.co.uk

Marston Lodge

Marston Lodge is an antidote to all things bland and beige. It is the private fiefdom of Alex, an old-school adventurer, who rode across Australia on a horse before embarking on a career as a deep-sea diver. These days he's back on dry land, stamping his larger-than-life personality over his quirky hotel. It stands in leafy splendour, high on the hill, next to the church, with views of beach and moor. Inside, eccentricity abounds. There's a pretty sitting room with an open fire, a simple dining room with views over town, then a distinctly retro bar that opens onto a terrace. Upstairs, bedrooms come in bold colours with oak furniture, pretty fabrics and super bathrooms. Those at the front have big views, so try to bag one of these; if you don't 450 pieces of art scattered about the house will compensate. Outside, a terraced garden climbs up past a chicken coop (home-laid eggs for breakfast) to a small lawn and vegetable garden, where you can fall asleep in a hammock. Don't miss Dunster, the moors or the coastal paths for excellent walking. There are stables, too, if you want to ride.

Price	£100. Singles £75. Minimum 2 nights.
Rooms	10: 8 doubles, 2 twins.
Meals	Restaurants within 0.5 miles.
Closed	January.
Directions	See website (try not to use Sat-Nav!).

	Alex Mendoza
	St Michael's Road,
	Minehead TA24 5JP
Tel	+44 (0)1643 702510
Email	marstonlodge@aol.com
Web	www.marstonlodgehotel.co.uk

The Oaks Hotel

Another old-school charmer. This Edwardian house sits above the village, a winning position on the side of the hill. A beautiful garden wraps around you; views to the front shoot out to sea, those to the side skim over rooftops and land on Exmoor hills. Tim and Anne do it all themselves and practice the art of old-fashioned hospitality with great flair: they stop to chat, carry bags, ply you with tea and cake on arrival. Logs smoulder on the fire in the hall, hot coals glow in the sitting room. There's a snug bar, parquet flooring, floral fabrics, masses of books. Spotless bedrooms, all with sea views, are lovely; deeply comfy, lots of colour, great value for money. You get bowls of fruit, crisp white linen, fluffy bathrobes and Roberts radios; most have sofas, while beds are turned down every evening. As for dinner, Anne whisks up a four-course feast, perhaps smoked duck and almond salad, Cornish crab cakes with lime and ginger, Somerset pork with prunes and sherry, hot treacle tart with marmalade ice cream. Exmoor, the coast and Dunster Castle all wait.

Price	Half-board £110 p.p.
Rooms	7: 6 twins/doubles, 1 double.
Meals	Dinner, 4 courses, included; non-residents, £37.50.
Closed	November-April.
Directions	A39 west to Porlock. Keep left down hill into village and hotel on left after 200m.

Anne & Tim Riley
Porlock TA24 8ES

Tel	+44 (0)1643 862265
Email	info@oakshotel.co.uk
Web	www.oakshotel.co.uk

Netherstowe House

This quirky hotel is full of surprises, not least its wonderful bedrooms that are an absolute steal, but also for its peculiar location on the edge of a 1970s housing estate. If the latter puts you off, don't let it – the house is hidden by fine beech hedging and once up the drive you forget the outside world. Inside you fall immediately under the spell of some rather eccentric interiors that mix country-house style with 19th-century colonial overtones. You'll find varnished wood floors, roaring fires, tropical plants erupting with style, the odd chandelier. Gorgeous bedrooms are great value for money and come in an elegant clean style: beautiful beds, cool colours, old armoires. Bathrooms are fabulous. If you want something more contemporary, nip across the courtyard to the serviced apartments. They come with fancy kitchens but breakfast is included and the hotel is yours to roam. As for the food, it's served in a couple of smart dining rooms, perhaps wild mushroom risotto, slow-cooked spicy pork belly, roast pineapple with mango salsa. There are good steaks in the colourful cellar bistro, too.

Price	£85-£125. Apartments £115.
Rooms	17: 8 twins/doubles, 1 four-poster. Garden: 8 apartments (with kitchens) for 2.
Meals	Lunch from £14.95. Dinner, 3 courses, about £30.
Closed	26 December-2 January.
Directions	Sent on booking.

Ben Heathcote
Netherstowe Lane, Lichfield WS13 6AY

Tel	+44 (0)1543 254270
Email	info@netherstowehouse.com
Web	www.netherstowehouse.com

Ounce House

Bury St Edmunds, an ancient English town, is a dream; if you've never been, don't delay. The Romans were here, the barons hatched plans for Magna Carta within the now-crumbled walls of its monastery, and its Norman abbey attracted pilgrims by the cartload. The town was made rich by the wool trade in the 1700s and highlights include the cathedral (its exquisite new tower looks hundreds of years old) and the magnificent Abbey Gardens, perfect for summer picnics. Just around the corner Ounce House, a handsome 1870 red-brick townhouse, overflows with creature comforts, so slump into leather armchairs in front of a carved fireplace and gaze at walls of art. You'll also find a snug library, a lawned garden and homely bedrooms packed with books, mahogany furniture and fresh flowers. Princely breakfasts are served on blue-and-white Spode china at one vast table. This is B&B in a grand-ish home and ever-cheerful Simon and Jenny will pick you up from the station or book a table at a local restaurant. Try The Fox (around the corner) or Maison Bleue (excellent seafood). Don't miss the May arts festival.

Price	£125–£135. Singles £85–£95.
Rooms	5: 4 doubles, 1 twin.
Meals	Restaurants 5-minute walk.
Closed	Rarely.
Directions	A14 north, then central junction for Bury, following signs to historic centre. At 1st r'bout left into Northgate St. On right at top of hill.

Simon & Jenny Pott
13-14 Northgate Street,
Bury St Edmunds IP33 1HP

Tel	+44 (0)1284 761779
Email	enquiries@ouncehouse.co.uk
Web	www.ouncehouse.co.uk

The Swan at Lavenham

The Swan is ancient, 600 years old, a spectacular tangle of medieval timber and sagging beams. Recently refurbished in epic style, you get the impression it has never looked better. Inside, fires roar, ceilings soar and the loveliest staff weave through the mix delivering sinful plates of afternoon tea or cocktails before supper. Potter about and find a minstrel's gallery in the vaulted dining room, a fabulous old bar that was a favourite haunt of WWII airmen, then a lawned courtyard garden, where you can stop for a glass of Pimm's in summer. Bedrooms are lovely, some vast with four-posters and timber-framed walls, others more contemporary with cool colours and good sofas. All have super-comfy beds, crisp white linen, sparkling bathrooms and fluffy robes; bowls of fruit come as standard, beds are turned down during dinner. Elsewhere, there's a 14th-century hall for private dinners and weddings, and you can eat in an open-plan brasserie if you want something lighter. Finally, medieval Lavenham is a sight to behold; don't miss it. *Some on-site parking. Ask about special offers.*

Price	£195–£250. Suites & four-posters £290–£350. Single from £105. Half-board from £122.50 p.p. Min. 2 nights at weekends.
Rooms	45: 32 twins/doubles, 10 suites, 2 four-posters, 1 single.
Meals	Lunch, 2 courses, from £16.95. Dinner, 3 courses £35.95. Brasserie, 2 courses, from £16.
Closed	Never.
Directions	On high street in village.

	Ingo Wiangke
	High Street,
	Lavenham CO10 9QA
Tel	+44 (0)1787 247477
Email	info@theswanatlavenham.co.uk
Web	www.theswanatlavenham.co.uk

The Great House

Lavenham is a Suffolk gem, a medieval wool town trapped in aspic. The Great House stands across the market place from the Guildhall, its Georgian façade giving way to airy 15th-century interiors, where timber frames and old beams mix with contemporary colours and varnished wood floors. The poet Stephen Spender once lived here and the house became a meeting place for artists, but these days it's the ambrosial food that draws the crowd. It's French to its core – the cheese board must qualify as one of the best in Britain – so dig into something delicious, perhaps venison, pistachio and sultana terrine, sea bass served with olives and white wine, then tarte tatin with cinnamon ice cream. Fabulous bedrooms – all recently refurbished in lavish style – come with fabulous bed linen, suede sofas, coffee machines, and robes in magnificent bathrooms. Four are huge, but even the tiniest is a dream. One has a regal four-poster, another has a 14th-century fireplace in its bathroom. All come with an array of gadgets: hi-fis, surround-sound, flat-screen TVs. *Minimum two nights at weekends.*

Price	£95-£175. Suites £155-£225. Half-board from £112.50 p.p.
Rooms	5: 4 doubles, 1 twin/double.
Meals	Continental breakfast £10, full English £15. Lunch from £17.50 (not Mon/Tues). Dinner £31.95 (not Sun/Mon).
Closed	First 3 weeks in January; 2 weeks in July.
Directions	A1141 to Lavenham. At High Street 1st right after The Swan or up Lady Street into Market Place. On-site parking.

Régis & Martine Crépy
Market Place, Lavenham,
Sudbury CO10 9QZ

Tel	+44 (0)1787 247431
Email	info@greathouse.co.uk
Web	www.greathouse.co.uk

The Crown

Everything here is good: a lovely country pub, a very pretty village, a sublime position in Constable country. The Crown dates back to 1560 and has old beams, timber frames and roaring fires, but the warm country interiors have youthful good looks – tongue-and-groove bars, terracotta-tiled floors, a fancy wine cellar that stands behind a wall of glass. Also: rugs and settles, the daily papers, leather armchairs in front of a wood-burner. Four ales wait at the bar, 30 wines come by the glass and seasonal rustic food has a big local following; try buck rarebit with fried quail's eggs, confit of Blythburgh pork with honey and apricots, steamed marmalade pudding with custard. In summer you can eat on the terrace. Airy bedrooms – peacefully hidden away at the bottom of the garden – are exemplary, with bathrooms as good as any you'll find. There are excellent beds, lovely linen, underfloor heating, a dash of colour. All have armchairs or sofas, three have French windows that open onto private terraces. Outside, fields stretch off to a distant ridge, birds soar high in the sky. A great place to eat, sleep and potter.

Price	£120–£200. Suite £175–£220. Singles from £90.
Rooms	11: 10 doubles, 1 suite.
Meals	Lunch & dinner £5–£25.
Closed	Rarely.
Directions	North from Colchester on A134, then B1087 east into Stoke-by-Nayland. Right at T-junction; pub on left.

Richard Sunderland
Park Street, Stoke-by-Nayland,
Colchester CO6 4SE

Tel	+44 (0)1206 262001
Email	enquiries@crowninn.net
Web	www.crowninn.net

Kesgrave Hall

This Georgian mansion sits in 38 acres of woodland with a sweeping drive that cuts through the trees. It was built for an MP in 1812, served as home to US airmen during WWII, then became a prep school; recently refurbished, it shines in contemporary splendour. Despite its county-house good looks, it is more a restaurant with rooms, and its emphasis on good food served informally is a big hit with locals; the place was crammed on a February afternoon. Inside, find Wellington boots lined up in the entrance, high ceilings in the huge sitting room, stripped boards in the humming bistro and doors onto a terrace that is used all summer. Excellent bedrooms have attractive prices. One is huge and comes with a little bling (faux-leopard skin sofa, free-standing bath), but all are lovely, some in the eaves, others overlooking the lawn. Expect warm colours, crisp linen, super bathrooms. Back downstairs you can watch the cooks at work in the restaurant, so dig into something tasty, perhaps crab linguine, steak and kidney pudding, treacle tart with clotted cream ice cream. Suffolk's magical coast is close.

Price	£125–£230. Suites £275–£300. Singles from £115.
Rooms	23: 10 doubles, 7 twins/doubles, 6 suites.
Meals	Breakfast £9–£15. Lunch & dinner, 3 courses, £25–£30.
Closed	Never.
Directions	Skirt Ipswich to the south on A14, then head north on A12. Left at 4th r'bout; signed right after 0.25 miles.

Oliver Richards
Hall Road, Kesgrave,
Ipswich IP5 2PU

Tel	+44 (0)1473 333741
Email	reception@kesgravehall.com
Web	www.milsomhotels.com

The Crown at Woodbridge

Woodbridge's long wait for a classy inn with great food, urbane bedrooms and a cosmopolitan air is over. The 400-year-old Crown emerged from the shadows in 2009 and it's the talk of the town. Everyone loves the new Crown, from its pastel façade to its cool laid-back interiors and humorous touches: beneath a glass roof a wooden skiff is suspended above a long granite-topped bar. In intimate dining rooms, chef-patron Stephen David's menu trawls Europe for inspiration and draws on Suffolk's natural larder. Look forward to hearty dishes full of flavour and some amazing taste combinations: Cromer crab cakes with pickled ginger; braised shin of beef in chocolate beer; Brancaster mussels; blueberry and almond tart. Wash it all down with Adnams or Meantime beers or delve into the impressive list of wines. Cosseting bedrooms decorated in simple, Nantucket style and themed in white and grey are a further attraction. There are big beds, quirky touches and a host of extras, from fruit, fresh coffee and homemade shortbread to soft bathrobes and heated bathroom floors. A chic Suffolk bolthole – unmissable!

Price	£125–£180. Singles from £95.
Rooms	10: 8 twins/doubles, 2 family rooms.
Meals	Lunch & dinner £9.50–£30. Sunday lunch from £12.50.
Closed	Rarely.
Directions	A12 north from Ipswich, then B1438 into town. Pass station and left into Quay St. On right.

Stephen David
Thoroughfare,
Woodbridge IP12 1AD
Tel   +44 (0)1394 384242
Email   info@thecrownatwoodbridge.co.uk
Web   www.thecrownatwoodbridge.co.uk

The Crown & Castle

The road runs out at sleepy Orford, so saddle up and head into the forest; cycle tracks and bridle paths sweep you in and you can return to the splendour of the Crown, a red-brick inn that stands close to a 12th-century castle. Today the feel is warm and airy with stripped wood floors, open fires, big colours and eclectic art: this is a very comfortable hotel. Beautiful bedrooms come with pretty fabrics, light colours, Vi-Spring beds and super bathrooms. Four in the main house have watery views, the suite is gorgeous and the garden rooms (dull on the outside, lovely within) are big and airy, with padded headboards, seagrass matting and doors onto a communal garden. All have crisp white linen, TVs, DVDs, digital radios. Wellington boots wait at the back door, so pull on a pair and discover Suffolk, or hop on a boat and chug over to Orfordness. Then return for some seriously good food, perhaps half a dozen oysters with shallot and thyme vinegar, rump of Suffolk lamb with spiced barberry and pistachio pilaf, a flourless bitter chocolate cake with cream. A treat. *Ask about events. Children over eight welcome.*

Price	£130–£190. Suite £245. Half-board from £98 p.p.
Rooms	19: 16 doubles, 2 twins, 1 suite.
Meals	Lunch from £7.50. À la carte dinner around £30.
Closed	Never.
Directions	A12 north from Ipswich, A1152 east to Woodbridge, then B1084 into Orford. Right in square for castle. On left.

David & Ruth Watson
Orford,
Woodbridge IP12 2LJ
Tel   +44 (0)1394 450205
Email   info@crownandcastle.co.uk
Web   www.crownandcastle.co.uk

The Old Rectory

An old country rectory with contemporary interiors; what would the rector think? You get stripped floors in the dining room, a 21st-century orange chaise longue by the honesty bar and windows dressed in fabulous fabrics. Michael and Sally swapped Hong Kong for Suffolk and the odd souvenir came with them: wood carvings from the Orient and framed Burmese chanting bibles. In winter, a fire smoulders at breakfast; in summer, you feast in a huge stone-flagged conservatory where doors open onto two acres of orchard and lawns. A warm country-house informality flows within, so help yourself to a drink, sink into a sofa or spin onto the terrace in search of sun and birdsong. Smart bedrooms are warmly decorated; one is up in the eaves, one overlooks the church, another has a claw-foot bath. Delicious food includes veg from the garden, eggs from the hens and homemade jams; for dinner perhaps parsnip soup and roast loin of Suffolk pork, then almond and lemon tart. Sutton Hoo is close as is Snape Maltings (opera singers occasionally stay and warm up for work in the bedrooms). A happy house. *Min. two nights at weekends Apr-Oct.*

Price	£95–£140. Singles from £75.
Rooms	7: 5 doubles, 1 twin/double, 1 four-poster.
Meals	Dinner, 3 courses, £28. Mon, Wed & Fri only (except for parties of 8 or more).
Closed	Occasionally.
Directions	North from Woodbridge on A12 for 8 miles, then right onto B1078. In village, over railway line; house on right just before church.

Michael & Sally Ball
Station Road, Campsea Ashe,
Woodbridge IP13 0PU

Tel	+44 (0)1728 746524
Email	mail@theoldrectorysuffolk.com
Web	www.theoldrectorysuffolk.com

Wentworth Hotel

The Wentworth has the loveliest position in town, the beach, quite literally, a pebble's throw from the garden, the sea rolling east under a vast sky. Inside, fires smoulder, clocks chime and seaside elegance abounds. It's all terrifically English, with Zoffany wallpapers, kind local staff and an elegant bar that opens onto a terrace garden. The restaurant looks out to sea, comes in Georgian red and spills onto the sunken terrace in summer for views of passing boats. What's more, it serves up delicious English fare, perhaps stilton soup, confit of pork, then lemon tart. The hotel has been in the same family since 1920 and old-fashioned values mix harmoniously with new-fangled necessities. Bedrooms are extremely comfortable, those at the front have huge sea views (and binoculars). Expect warm colours, wicker armchairs, padded headboards and comfortable beds. Bathrooms, all refurbished, are excellent. Sofas galore wait in the sitting room, but you may want to spurn them to walk by the sea. Joyce Grenfell was a regular. The Snape Maltings are close. *Minimum two nights at weekends.*

Price	£145-£191. Singles from £85. Half-board £70-£105 p.p.
Rooms	35: 24 twins/doubles, 4 singles. Darfield House: 7 doubles.
Meals	Bar meals from £5. Lunch from £12. Dinner, 3 courses, £25.
Closed	Never.
Directions	A12 north from Ipswich, then A1094 for Aldeburgh. Past church, down hill, left at x-roads; hotel on right.

Michael Pritt
Wentworth Road,
Aldeburgh IP15 5BD

Tel	+44 (0)1728 452312
Email	stay@wentworth-aldeburgh.com
Web	www.wentworth-aldeburgh.com

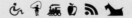

The Brudenell Hotel

The Brudenell stands bang on the beach in one of England's loveliest seaside towns. It makes the most of its view. A dining terrace at the front runs the length of the building; a glass-fronted restaurant swims in light; an elegant sitting room looks the right way. The hotel mixes a contemporary style and an informal feel to great effect: find coastal art, sunny colours, driftwood sculptures on display. Beautiful bedrooms come in different shapes and sizes. Those at the back look onto open country and river marsh, those at the front have hypnotic views of sea and sky. A chic style runs throughout: cool colours, fabulous fabrics, blond wood furniture, sofas if there's room; bathrooms are predictably divine. Back downstairs the open-plan brasserie is the hub of the hotel. There's a cocktail bar where you can wash back oysters with a glass of champagne, then booths and tables for super food, perhaps Parma ham with pan-fried langoustine, Sutton Hoo chicken with tarragon mash, banoffee pie and banana ice cream. As for gorgeous Aldeburgh, you can walk, sail, swim, or shop. *Minimum two nights at weekends.*

Price	£150–£325. Singles from £80.
Rooms	44: 30 twins/doubles, 12 doubles, 2 singles.
Meals	Lunch from £10.25. Dinner, 3 courses, about £30.
Closed	Never.
Directions	A1094 into Aldeburgh. Right at T-junction, down high street, last left in village before car park & yacht club.

Garth Wray
The Parade,
Aldeburgh IP15 5BU

Tel	+44 (0)1728 452071
Email	info@brudenellhotel.co.uk
Web	www.brudenellhotel.co.uk

The Dolphin Inn

Thorpeness is a one-off, the perfect antidote to the 21st century. The village was brainchild of G S Ogilvie, who set out to create a holiday resort for children, free of piers and promenades, with safety assured. His master stroke is the Meare – a 64-acre lake, never more than three feet deep, which was inspired by his friend, J M Barrie, creator of *Peter Pan*. Children can row, canoe or sail up creeks and discover islands that may have a lurking (wooden) crocodile round the corner. The Dolphin – bang in the middle of the village – is a great little inn with three cute bedrooms that come in smart cottage style; expect old pine furniture, soft colours and spotless bathrooms. Downstairs, two lively bars come with open fires and wooden floors, while doors open onto a vast garden for barbecues, hog roasts and al fresco dinners (the pub heaves in summer). No-nonsense food hits the spot, perhaps grilled sardines with basil pesto, chargrilled steak with chunky chips, a plate of local cheeses. There's a great golf course, an unspoilt beach, and the birdwatching centre at Minsmere is close.

Price	£75–£110. Singles from £55.
Rooms	3 doubles.
Meals	Lunch & dinner £5–£30.
Closed	Never.
Directions	From A12 at Farnham, A1094 to Aldeburgh seafront. Left & follow coast road for 2 miles into Thorpeness. Inn on right, signed.

David James
Peace Place, Thorpeness,
Aldeburgh IP16 4EF

Tel	+44 (0)1728 454994
Email	info@thorpenessdolphin.com
Web	www.thorpenessdolphin.com

The Westleton Crown

This is one of England's oldest coaching inns, with 800 years of continuous service under its belt. It stands in a village two miles inland from the sea at Dunwich, with Westleton Heath running east towards Minsmere Bird Sanctuary. Inside, you find the best of old and new. A recent refurbishment has introduced Farrow & Ball colours, leather sofas and a tongue-and-groove bar, and they mix harmoniously with panelled walls, stripped floors and ancient beams. Weave around and find nooks and crannies in which to hide, flames flickering in an open fire, a huge map on the wall for walkers. You can eat wherever you want, and a conservatory/breakfast room opens onto a terraced garden for summer barbecues. Fish comes straight off the boats at Lowestoft, local butchers provide local meat. Bedrooms are scattered about – between the inn and the car park annexe – and come in cool lime white with comfy beds, crisp linen, flat-screen TVs. Super bathrooms are fitted out in Fired Earth, and some have claw-foot baths. Aldeburgh and Southwold are close by. *Minimum two nights at weekends.*

Price	£90–£180. Suites £170–£215. Singles from £80.
Rooms	34: 26 doubles, 2 twins, 2 family rooms, 3 suites, 1 single.
Meals	Lunch & bar meals from £5.50. Dinner from £11.95. Sunday lunch £26.
Closed	Never.
Directions	A12 north from Ipswich. Right at Yoxford onto B1122, then left for Westleton on B1125. On right in village.

Gareth Clarke
The Street, Westleton,
Saxmundham IP17 3AD

Tel	+44 (0)1728 648777
Email	info@westletoncrown.co.uk
Web	www.westletoncrown.co.uk

The Anchor

The Anchor is one of those wonderful places that has resisted the urge to be precious. This is a cool little seaside inn where relaxed informality reigns; kids are welcome, staff are lovely, dogs fall asleep in the bar. You're 500m back from the sea with a vast sky hovering above and waves breaking in the distance. Outside, a big terrace fills with happy locals in summer, while a lawned garden stretches off towards the water. Inside, a beautiful simplicity abounds – Cape Cod meets English country local. You'll find books everywhere, wonderful art, then roaring fires, scrubbed pine tables, old leather benches and painted tongue and groove. Sophie's ambrosial local food is the big draw, perhaps cheese soufflé with caramelised onions, roast cod with lentils and chorizo, then banana fritters with toffee sauce. Bedrooms are great value; those in the house are simpler, while the fabulous garden chalet suites have just been superbly refurbished. They're big, airy and open onto terraces that overlook the garden. Mark's menu of bottled beers is exceptional, as is the night sky. Unmissable.

Price	£110–£140. Singles from £95.
Rooms	10: 4 doubles, 6 garden suites.
Meals	Lunch from £6. Dinner, 3 courses, £25-£30.
Closed	Never.
Directions	On right in village by sea.

Mark & Sophie Dorber
Main Street,
Walberswick IP18 6UA
Tel   +44 (0)1502 722112
Email   info@anchoratwalberswick.com
Web   www.anchoratwalberswick.com

Park House hotel & spa

A blissful pocket of rural Sussex. Park House sits in 12 acres of glorious English gardens with quilted fields circling the grounds and the South Downs rising beyond. Potter about outside and find a croquet lawn, a grass tennis court and a six-hole golf course that slips into the country. Fine shrubberies burst with colour while Wellington boots wait at the front door for long country walks. You may prefer to stay put; the most recent addition to the Park House empire is its fabulous spa. It comes with a very swanky indoor pool to go with its outside partner, four treatment rooms, a sauna and steam room, then a proper gym and a terraced bar for lazy afternoons. As for the house, it's just as good. Beautiful interiors abound mixing country-house style with contemporary colours. The pavilion bar overlooks the gardens, you breakfast in the conservatory or out on the terrace, there are flagstones in reception, the daily papers in the sitting room, great food in the dining room. Gorgeous bedrooms are the final luxury: heavenly beds, big country views, fancy bathrooms, iMac TVs. Exceptional. *Special rates for Goodwood.*

Price	£160–£224. Family suites & cottage £230–£360.
Rooms	20 + 1: 10 twins/doubles, 6 doubles, 4 family suites. Self-catering cottage for 2-4.
Meals	Lunch, 2 courses, from £20.95. Afternoon tea £19.95. Dinner, 3 courses, £37.50.
Closed	Rarely.
Directions	South from Midhurst on A286. At sharp left bend, right (straight ahead), signed Bepton. Hotel on left after 2 miles.

	Rebecca Coonan
	Bepton,
	Midhurst GU29 0JB
Tel	+44 (0)1730 819000
Email	reservations@parkhousehotel.com
Web	www.parkhousehotel.com

The Royal Oak Inn

This extremely attractive inn sits in a sleepy Sussex village with the South Downs rising above and the coast at Chichester waiting below. Inside, a modern, rustic feel prevails: stripped floors, exposed brickwork and the odd racing print (the inn was once part of the Goodwood estate). There's a small bar for a pint in front of an open fire, but these days this is a pretty much a dining pub and the restaurant spreads itself far and wide, through the conservatory and out onto the terrace. A small army of chefs conjure up irresistible food, perhaps shallot and goat's cheese tarte tatin, Sussex pork with calvados cream, then glazed lemon tart. Elegant bedrooms are sprinkled about, some in cottages, others upstairs at the back of the pub. All come in elegant, contemporary style with good fabrics, leather armchairs, big comfy beds and fancy bathrooms; CD players, plasma screens, and DVD libraries keep you amused. Staff are attentive, complimentary newspapers arrive with breakfast, a secret garden looks out over cornfields. Chichester Theatre, Bosham and Goodwood are close. *Minimum two nights at weekends.*

Price	£110-£185. Cottage rooms £180-£260. Singles from £90.
Rooms	8: 4 doubles, 1 twin, 3 cottage rooms for 2-4.
Meals	Lunch from £6.25. Dinner, 3 courses, £30-£35.
Closed	Rarely.
Directions	From Chichester A286 for Midhurst. First right at first mini roundabout into E. Lavant. Down hill, past village green, over bridge, pub 200 yds on left. Car park opposite.

Charles Ullmann
Pook Lane, East Lavant,
Chichester PO18 0AX

Tel	+44 (0)1243 527434
Email	rooms@royaloakeastlavant.co.uk
Web	www.royaloakeastlavant.co.uk

The Crab & Lobster

This tiny arrowhead of land south of Chichester is something of a time warp, more 1940s than 21st century. The Crab & Lobster is older still – 350 years at last count. It sits on Pagham Harbour, a tidal marsh that teems with preening birds. Outside, you find a smart whitewashed exterior and a small garden for dreamy views across grazing fields to the water. Inside, a glittering refurbishment comes in contemporary style with Farrow & Ball colours, flagstone floors, blond wood furniture, suede armchairs and a smouldering fire. Big mirrors reflect the light, candles flicker in the evening. Upstairs, four super rooms come in duck-egg blue with crisp white linen, flat-screen TVs and gorgeous little bathrooms. Three have views of the water, one is up in the eaves and has a telescope to scan the high seas. There's much to explore: Bosham, where King Canute tried to turn back the waves; Fishbourne, for its imperious Roman palace; the Witterings, for sand dunes and miles of beach. Don't forget dinner, perhaps fresh calamari, Barbary duck, marmalade bread and butter pudding. *Minimum two nights at weekends.*

Price	From £140. Cottage from £220.
Rooms	4 + 1: 4 doubles. Self-catering cottage for 4.
Meals	Lunch from £10.50. Bar meals from £6.50. Dinner from £16.95. Sunday lunch, 2-3 courses, £24-£35.
Closed	Rarely.
Directions	Mill Lane is off B2145 Chichester to Selsey road, just south of Sidlesham. Pub close to Pagham Harbour.

Sam Bakose
Mill Lane, Sidlesham,
Chichester PO20 7NB

Tel	+44 (0)1243 641233
Email	enquiries@crab-lobster.co.uk
Web	www.crab-lobster.co.uk

Arundel House

Arundel is a dream, old England at the foot of a Norman castle. Below, the Arun runs off to sea; above, a cathedral soars towards heaven. Arundel House – a listed Georgian merchant's house close to the quay – stands on the tiny high street, opposite the Tudor post office, around the corner from the market place, where castle turrets rise above rippling red roofs. Inside, warm contemporary interiors have light wood floors, red and cream walls, candles on modern dining tables and a relaxed atmosphere. Spotless compact bedrooms have the lot: wooden beds, crisp white linen, flat-screen TVs, and coffee machines; there are swanky bathrooms, too. The best, the suite, is on two floors. Head down for delicious food, maybe chicken livers on toasted brioche, roast salmon with crab risotto, summer pudding with red berry sauce. Breakfast (organic porridge with honey; local sausages and free range eggs) is equally sinful and will set you up for the day. Come by train, bring your boots, follow the river, take to the hills. There's an August arts festival and the castle opens April to November.

Price	£85-£95. Suite £110-£120. Singles from £75. Half-board from £62.50 p.p.
Rooms	5: 4 doubles, 1 suite.
Meals	Lunch (not Mon) & dinner (not Sun/Mon) from £12.50.
Closed	Sunday nights & Mondays.
Directions	A27 to Arundel, then one-way system into town. Through market square (castle on left) and opp. post office.

11 High Street,
Arundel BN18 9AD

Tel	+44 (0)1903 882136
Email	info@arundelhousearundel.co.uk
Web	www.arundelhousearundel.co.uk

Burpham Country House & Brasserie

Come for old England in the foothills of the South Downs. Woodpeckers and warblers live in the woods, the church was built in 1167 and when you potter south to Arundel, its magnificent castle looms across the fields. The road runs out in the village and the house stands quietly, with colour tumbling from stone walls and a lawned terrace in front of a Victorian veranda. Originally a Georgian hunting lodge, it served as a vicarage to Tickner Edwardes, the great apiarist, who fought in Gallipoli; John Ruskin knew the house, too. Inside, warmly comfortable interiors are stylish without being style-led. There's an airy sitting-room bar, a panelled restaurant for local food and a brick-and-flint conservatory that opens onto a croquet lawn. Spotless bedrooms are good value for money, some big, some smaller, all with crisp linen, airy colours and flat-screen TVs; most have country views. Collared doves nest in the garden, swans winter on the Arundel wetlands and Alfred the Great extended this ridge 1,200 years ago to defend England from the Vikings. There's cricket in summer, too. *Minimum two nights at weekends April-October.*

Price	£80–£140.
Rooms	9: 5 doubles, 4 twins/doubles.
Meals	Dinner, 3 courses, £25–£27 (plus 10% service). Not Sun or Mon.
Closed	Rarely.
Directions	A27 east from Arundel, past station, then left for Burpham. Straight ahead for 2.5 miles; on left.

Jacqueline & Steve Penticost
Burpham,
Arundel BN18 9RJ

Tel	+44 (0)1903 882160
Email	info@burphamcountryhouse.com
Web	www.burphamcountryhouse.com

Windfalls

On the Crabbet Park Estate – ten minutes from Gatwick – a sanctuary run by Margarita. Past the neighbouring Gatwick Worth Hotel, ignoring the hum of the M23, you approach the gates that promise serenity and calm. Buddhas perch on gateposts, the black and glass entrance is enticing, and the lofty marble entrance hall leads to an oasis of calm: dark wood slatted blinds and great comfy sofas, pillar candles, big lilies, and a delicious waft of the orient. Generous ground-floor bedrooms speak of the east: who would not fall for the opulent quilts, the dark muslin-draped four-posters, the walk-in rain showers? If you fancy a proper soak, go for the smaller room tucked under the eaves, with whitewashed beams and a shabby chic charm. Margarita, passionate about her first private enterprise, does it all: cleans immaculately, greets beautifully and cooks like an angel. A buddha overlooks breakfasts at the long wooden table, there are well-priced drinks behind the bar and delectable, complimentary cream teas. Pillows and duvets are goosedown, mattresses are deep, honeymooners may never want to leave.

Price	£110–£210.
Rooms	4 doubles.
Meals	Restaurants 5-10 minute drive.
Closed	Rarely.
Directions	Sent on booking.

Margarita Courtenay
Turners Hill Road, Worth,
Crawley RH10 4SS
Tel +44 (0)1293 889598
Email info@windfalls.co.uk
Web www.windfalls.co.uk

The Bull

Stepping into The Bull is like travelling back in time to Dickensian England; little seems to have changed in 200 years. OK, so electricity has been introduced, but even that is rationed on aesthetic grounds; as a result, light plays beautifully amid old timbers. Elsewhere, fires roar, beams sag, candles twinkle, tankards dangle. You might call it 'nostalgic interior design', but whatever it is, the locals love it; the place was packed on a Sunday afternoon in late January. Well-kept ales are on tap in the bar, excellent food flies from the kitchen, perhaps caramelised parsnip and apple soup, a magnificent plate of rare roast beef, then chilled white chocolate and vanilla fondue. Upstairs, four pretty rooms await (two are larger, two are above the bar) and more are planned. You may find timber-framed walls, leather sleigh beds or statues of eastern deities, while representation from the 21st century includes digital radios, contemporary art and very good compact bathrooms. Bring walking boots or mountain bikes and take to the high trails on the South Downs National Park, which rise beyond the village. Brighton is close.

Price	£80–£120.
Rooms	4: 3 doubles, 1 twin/double.
Meals	Lunch & dinner from £10.
Closed	Never.
Directions	Leave A23 just north of Brighton for Pyecombe. North on A273, then west for Ditchling on B2112. In centre of village at crossroads.

Dominic Worrall
2 High Street, Ditchling,
Hassocks BN6 8TA
Tel   +44 (0)1273 843147
Email   info@thebullditchling.com
Web   www.thebullditchling.com

The Griffin Inn

A proper inn, one of the best, a community local that draws a well-heeled and devoted crowd. The occasional touch of scruffiness makes it almost perfect; fancy designers need not apply. The Pullan family run it with huge passion. You get cosy open fires, 400-year-old beams, oak panelling, settles, red carpets, prints on the walls... this inn has aged beautifully. There's a lively bar, a small club room for racing on Saturdays and two cricket teams play in summer. Bedrooms are tremendous value for money and full of uncluttered country-inn elegance: uneven floors, lovely old furniture, soft coloured walls, free-standing Victorian baths, huge shower heads, crisp linen, fluffy bathrobes, handmade soaps. Rooms in the coach house are quieter, those in next-door Griffin House quieter still. Smart seasonal menus include fresh fish from Rye and Fletching lamb. On Sundays in summer they lay on a spit-roast barbecue in the garden, with ten-mile views stretching across Pooh Bear's Ashdown Forest to Sheffield Park. Not to be missed. *Minimum two nights bank holiday weekends.*

Price	£85–£145. Singles £60–£80 (Sun–Thurs).
Rooms	13: 6 doubles, 7 four-posters.
Meals	Bar meals from £11. Dinner, 3 courses, £30–£40.
Closed	Never.
Directions	From East Grinstead A22 south, right at Nutley for Fletching. On for 2 miles into village.

Nigel & James Pullan
Fletching,
Uckfield TN22 3SS

Tel	+44 (0)1825 722890
Email	info@thegriffininn.co.uk
Web	www.thegriffininn.co.uk

Newick Park Hotel & Country Estate

A heavenly country house that thrills at every turn. The setting – 255 acres of parkland, river, lake and gardens – is spectacular; come in winter and you may wake to find a ribbon of mist entangled in a distant ridge of trees. Inside, majestic interiors elate, be it sagging bookshelves in a panelled study, Doric columns in a glittering drawing room or roaring fires in a sofa-strewn hall. You get all the aristocratic fixtures and fittings – grand pianos, plaster mouldings, a bar that sits in an elegant alcove – while views from the terrace run down to a lake. Oils hang on walls, chandeliers dangle above. Country-house bedrooms fit the bill: lush linen, thick floral fabrics, marble bathrooms with robes and lotions, views to the front of nothing but country; some are the size of a London flat. A two-acre walled garden provides much for the table, so don't miss exceptional food, perhaps a hen's egg with Serrano ham, pheasant from the woods around you, Earl Grey tea parfait. Peacocks roam outside, the Ashdown Forest is close for pooh sticks. *Minimum two nights at weekends during Glyndebourne.*

Price	£165–£285. Singles from £125.
Rooms	16 twins/doubles.
Meals	Lunch from £17.50. Dinner about £35.
Closed	New Year's Eve & New Year's Day.
Directions	From Newick village turn off the green & follow signs to Newick Park for 1 mile until T-junction. Turn left; after 300 yds, entrance on right.

Michael & Virginia Childs
Newick,
Lewes BN8 4SB

Tel	+44 (0)1825 723633
Email	bookings@newickpark.co.uk
Web	www.newickpark.co.uk

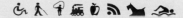

Chilverbridge House

Nick and Nina's stunning 17th-century house stands in seven lovely acres overlooking the South Downs; you'll find sweeping lawns, an iris-fringed pond, a tennis court, a swimming pool and access to Arlington Reservoir Nature Reserve. As for the once-dilapidated Old Granary and Coach House, a magical renovation has produced four gorgeous bedrooms – a big hit with the Glyndebourne set. They come in grand style with balconies or private patios onto the garden. You get beautiful beds, goose down duvets and plump pillows, then Colefax & Fowler fabrics, delicious antiques and lots of high-tech gadgetry. Bathrooms are the best; all have baths, walk-in showers and thick bathrobes; book Sackville for the slipper bath with soothing garden views. In summer, you breakfast like a king on the terrace with views of the Wilmington Long Man; at other times, you eat at linen-clothed tables by the fire in the beamed dining room. Magical local walking waits, but the view from the sunloungers flanking the swimming pool may encourage a certain laziness. A brilliant bolthole with good restaurants waiting closer by.

Price	£120–£160. Singles £100–£140.
Rooms	4: 2 suites, 2 doubles.
Meals	Restaurants within 1 mile. Dinner, 3 courses, £35 by arrangement.
Closed	Never.
Directions	Sent on booking.

Nick & Nina Keats
Chilver Bridge Road,
Arlington BN26 6SB
Tel   +44 (0)7748 395327
Email   chilverbridge@chilverbridgehouse.com
Web   www.chilverbridgehouse.com

Wingrove House

A beautiful house at the end of Alfriston High Street with delightful terraces that give the feel of Provence. A vine runs along an old stone wall, colour bursts from well-kept beds, olive trees shimmer in the sun. In good weather you can breakfast here with the daily papers, so dig into scrambled eggs and croissants, then wash it all down with freshly squeezed orange juice. This is the last house in a pretty red-brick village with the South Downs Way passing directly to the south; strike out across the fields to the cliffs of Beachy Head. Return to find an extremely attractive house: stripped floors, an open fire and leather sofas in the sitting roomthat opens onto the upper terrace; an airy restaurant for super food. You can eat al fresco in summer, on carpaccio of Sussex beef with truffle oil, confit belly of pork with salsa verde, warm chocolate pudding. Big bedrooms are just as good. Those at the front open onto the veranda, those at the side overlook the village church and green. All come in a smart, clipped style: big mirrors, light colours, crisp linen, pretty furniture.

Price	£95–£185.
Rooms	5: 4 doubles, 1 twin.
Meals	Lunch from £10. Dinner, 3 courses, £28–£32.
Closed	Rarely.
Directions	M23, A23, then A27 east from Brighton. Past Berwick, then south at r'bout for Alfriston. In village on left.

Nicholas Denyer
High Street, Alfriston,
Polegate BN26 5TD

Tel   +44 (0)1323 870276
Email   info@wingrovehousealfriston.com
Web   www.wingrovehousealfriston.com

Belle Tout Lighthouse

On top of a white cliff, a fabulous lighthouse with rather good views. To your left, Beachy Head, to your right, Birling Gap – it's a magical position with the South Downs rolling into the English Channel. As for the lighthouse, it dates to 1832, was recently moved backwards 57 feet to stop it crumbling into the sea and featured prominently in the BBC's production of *The Life and Loves of a She-Devil*. It re-opened in 2010 after a splendid renovation as a lovely little B&B hotel. Bedrooms are rather wonderful: not huge, but most with double-aspect windows that bring the outside in. You find white walls to soak up the light, fantastic views of rolling hills, pretty fabrics, lovely linen, the odd exposed brick wall; shower rooms are small but sweet, and one room has a bath. Ian's legendary breakfasts are served on high with views of sea and cliff. There's a fabulous sitting room up here, too, where guests gather each night before climbing up to explore the lantern room. You'll eat well in the village pub, though a local deli will bring picnics in summer. Magnificent walking waits.

Price	£138–£231. Singles from £97. Minimum stay 2 nights.
Rooms	6 doubles.
Meals	Pub/restaurant within 1 mile.
Closed	Christmas & New Year.
Directions	Sent on booking.

Ian Noall
Beachy Head Road, Beachy Head,
Eastbourne BN20 0AE

Tel	+44 (0)1323 423185
Email	info@belletout.co.uk
Web	www.belletout.co.uk

The Tiger Inn

The Tiger sits on a village green that has hardly changed in 50 years and in summer life spills onto the terrace to soak up an English sun. It's all part of a large estate that hugs the coast from Beachy Head to Cuckmere Haven with Birling Gap in between; some of the best coastal walking in the south lies on your doorstep. Back at the inn a fabulous renovation has breathed new life into old bones. Downstairs has bags of character with low beams, stone floors, ancient settles and a roaring fire. Beer brewed on the estate pours from the tap, so try a pint of Legless Rambler before digging into hearty food – Beachy Head beer battered catch of the day, sausage and mash with a sweet onion gravy, treacle tart with vanilla ice cream. Five country-house bedrooms are the big surprise. Find beautiful fabrics, padded bedheads, funky bathrooms, the odd beam. Beds are dressed with lambs' wool throws, warm colours hang on the walls. Back outside, white cliffs wait, as do the South Downs. Finally, Arthur Conan Doyle knew the village and a blue plaque on one of the cottages suggests Sherlock Holmes retired here.

Price	£95.
Rooms	5: 4 doubles, 1 twin.
Meals	Lunch from £8.95. Dinner from £8.95. Sunday lunch, 3 courses, around £20.
Closed	Never.
Directions	West from Eastbourne on A259. Left in village. Parking on right near village hall.

Jacques Pienaar
The Green, East Dean,
Eastbourne BN20 0DA

Tel   +44 (0)1323 423209
Email   info@beachyhead.org.uk
Web   www.beachyhead.org.uk

Strand House

Strand House was built in 1425 and originally stood on Winchelsea harbour, though the sea was reclaimed long ago and marshland now runs off to the coast. You can walk down after breakfast, a great way to atone for your bacon and eggs. Back at the house, cosy interiors come with low ceilings, timber frames and ancient beams, all of which give an intimate feel. You'll find warm reds and yellows, sofas galore, a wood-burner in the sitting room and an honesty bar where you help yourself. It's a homespun affair: Hugh cooks breakfast, Mary conjures up delicious dinners… maybe grilled goat's cheese with red onion marmalade, Dover sole with a lemon butter, rhubarb and ginger crumble. Attractive bedrooms are warm and colourful and a couple are small; one has an ancient four-poster, some have wonky floors, all have beamed ceilings, good linen, comfy beds. Tall people are better off with ground-floor rooms as low ceilings are de rigueur on upper floors; all rooms have compact bathrooms. The house, once a workhouse, was painted by Turner and Millais. A short walk through the woods leads up to the village.

Price	£70–£180. Singles from £60.
Rooms	13: 8 doubles, 2 triples, 1 twin/double, 1 twin, 1 suite.
Meals	Dinner, 3 courses, £32.50.
Closed	Occasionally.
Directions	A259 west from Rye for 2 miles. House on the left at foot of hill, opposite Bridge Inn pub.

Mary Sullivan & Hugh Davie
Tanyards Lane, Winchelsea,
Rye TN36 4JT

Tel	+44 (0)1797 226276
Email	info@thestrandhouse.co.uk
Web	www.thestrandhouse.co.uk

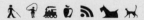

The Gallivant Hotel

A boutique hotel down by the sea – friendly, stylish, very well priced. Across the road, enormous dunes tumble down to Camber Sands for five miles of uninterrupted beach, so watch the kite-surfing or walk up to the river Rother and follow it into Rye (three miles). Back at The Gallivant charming interiors have a warm seaside feel: comfy bedrooms come in light colours, you get crisp linen and colourful cushions on big driftwood beds, feather pillows, a cookie jar from the kitchen; spotless bathrooms provide for a good soak after a hard day on the beach. The airy bistro opens onto a dining veranda in summer, where you dig into local food, with plaice and mackerel fresh from the market. Try Rye Bay scallops, Romney Marsh Lamb, then Sussex Pond pudding – or, if the weather's right, barbecues in the beach marquee – a good spot after a day on the sand. There's a good DVD library at reception and a cookery course for budding chefs. Kite-surfing, golf and bird-watching can all be arranged. Port Lympne Safari Park is close, as is Dungeness; Derek Jarman's Prospect Cottage is worth a look. *Minimum two nights at weekends.*

Price	£115–£195.
Rooms	18: 12 doubles, 5 suites, 1 beach hut room.
Meals	Lunch from £12.50. Dinner, 3 courses, about £30.
Closed	Rarely.
Directions	A259 east from Rye, then B2075 for Camber & Lydd. On left after 2 miles.

Harry Cragoe
New Lydd Road, Camber,
Rye TN31 7RB

Tel	+44 (0)1797 225057
Email	enquiries@thegallivanthotel.com
Web	www.thegallivanthotel.com

Jeake's House

Rye is utterly gorgeous, one of those lovely English country towns that's been around for centuries, but has never lost its looks. The same is true of Jeake's House. It's spent 300 years on this peaceful cobbled street in the old town accruing a colourful past as a wool store, a school, and the home of American poet Conrad Potter Aiken. Inside, you get all the trimmings: timber frames, ancient beams and smartly carpeted corridors that weave along to cosy bedrooms, the latter being generously furnished, deeply comfortable and excellent value for money. Some have four-posters, all have rich fabrics, one has a telly concealed in the wood-burner. The galleried dining room – once an old Baptist chapel, now painted deep red – is full of busts, books, clocks and mirrors – a fine setting for a full English breakfast. There's also a lovely cosy honesty bar, where a fire burns in winter. Outside, you'll find art galleries, antiques shops, old churches and river walks. All this would be blossom in the wind without Jenny, whose natural friendliness has created a winning atmosphere. Don't miss it. *Children over eight welcome.*

Price	£90–£138. Singles £79.
Rooms	11: 7 twins/doubles, 3 four-poster suites, all en suite. 1 double with separate bath.
Meals	Restaurants within walking distance.
Closed	Never.
Directions	From centre of Rye on A268, left off High St onto West St, then 1st right into Mermaid St. House on left. Private car park, £3 a day for guests.

Jenny Hadfield
Mermaid Street,
Rye TN31 7ET

Tel	+44 (0)1797 222828
Email	stay@jeakeshouse.com
Web	www.jeakeshouse.com

The George in Rye

Ancient Rye has a big history. It's a reclaimed island, a Cinque Port which held its own army. Henry James lived here, too, and the oldest church clock in England chimes at the top of the hill. As for The George, it stands serenely on the cobbled high street. Built in 1575 from reclaimed ships' timbers, its exposed beams and panelled walls remain on display. Inside, beautiful interiors mix contemporary and classical styles to great effect – expect Jane Austen in the 21st century. There's a roaring fire in the bar, screen prints of the Beatles on the walls in reception, a first-floor ballroom with a minstrels' gallery. Gorgeous bedrooms come in all shapes and sizes, but chic fabrics, Frette linen and Vi-Spring mattresses are standard, as are cashmere covers on hot water bottles. Finally, excellent brasserie-style food waits in the lovely new restaurant – perhaps Spanish charcuterie, half a lobster, treacle tart and stem ginger ice cream; you can wash it all back with delicious wines, some English. Festivals abound: scallops in February, art in September. Exceptional.

Price	£135–£195. Suites £295. Singles from £95.
Rooms	34: 8 doubles, 21 twins/doubles, 5 suites.
Meals	Lunch & dinner from £12.95.
Closed	Never.
Directions	Follow signs up hill into town centre. Through arch; hotel on left, below church. 24-hour parking 5 minutes down hill.

Alex & Katie Clarke
98 High Street,
Rye TN31 7JT

Tel	+44 (0)1797 222114
Email	stay@thegeorgeinrye.com
Web	www.thegeorgeinrye.com

Prawles Court

Everything here is wonderful: house, gardens, owners, rooms. This is a magnificent country house, a B&B that thrills, as good as any hotel. It stands in 27 acres of peace, lost to the world in idyllic country (you can walk across fields to Bodiam Castle). It started out as an Elizabethan farmhouse, but was remodelled by Nathaniel Lloyd in Arts & Crafts style in the 1920s; on completion, it featured in *Country Life*. These days, after a fine refurbishment, it must qualify as one of the loveliest places to stay in Sussex. Potter about and find half-panelling in an exquisite drawing room, timber frames in the gorgeous dining room, an honesty bar stashed away in an elegant armoire. Bedrooms upstairs are divine: wonderful beds, beautiful fabrics, super colours, bowls of fruit. Two are huge, all have robes in exceptional bathrooms. You breakfast in the orangery on home-laid eggs and local bacon washed down with Sussex apple juice; at night, the vegetable garden provides much for dinner, served grandly in the dining room. Magical Sussex is all around. *Minimum two nights at weekends in summer.*

Price	£130–£160. Singles from £100.
Rooms	4: 1 double, 3 twins/doubles.
Meals	Dinner, by arrangement, from £35.
Closed	Christmas & New Year.
Directions	A21 south thro' Hurst Green, then left, opp. pub, for Bodiam. Over x-roads, through Bodiam, over steam railway, then 2nd left into Shoreham Lane. 2nd drive on right.

Candida & Rob Machin
Shoreham Lane, Ewhurst Green,
Robertsbridge TN32 5RG

Tel	+44 (0)1580 830136
Email	info@prawlescourt.com
Web	www.prawlescourt.com

The Howard Arms

The Howard stands on Ilmington Green, seven miles south of Stratford-upon-Avon; it was built at roughly the same time as Shakespeare wrote *King Lear*. Little has changed since and it's a fabulous country inn, one of the best. All the old fixtures and fittings remain – polished flagstones, heavy beams, mellow stone walls – as logs crackle contentedly on a vast open fire and a blackboard menu scales the wall above. Toast your toes while you take your pick, then dig into grilled sardines, beef, ale and mustard pie, spicy pear and apple crumble. Elsewhere, you find oils on walls, books on shelves, settles in alcoves, beautiful bay windows. An elegant dining room floods with light, courtesy of fine arched windows that overlook the green. Three gorgeous bedrooms in the main house mix period style with modern luxury, while five new garden rooms come in elegant contemporary style with fancy bathrooms. There are maps for walkers, so follow paths through village and field. The church dates back to the 11th century (there are Thompson mice within) and Simon de Montfort owned this land in 1469.

Price	£100-£145. Singles £75.
Rooms	8: 5 doubles, 3 twins/doubles.
Meals	Lunch from £4.50. Dinner from £10.50.
Closed	Never.
Directions	From south take A429 Fosse Way through Moreton-in-Marsh. After 5 miles left to Ilmington.

Emma O'Connell
Lower Green, Ilmington,
Shipston-on-Stour CV36 4LT

Tel	+44 (0)1608 682226
Email	info@howardarms.com
Web	www.howardarms.com

Lucknam Park Hotel & Spa

It's like a Merchant Ivory film: a one-mile drive that sweeps you up an avenue of beech trees, cutting through a 500-acre estate before delivering you into the arms of this magnificent 1720 mansion. Inside, find a panelled library with a roaring fire, a golden drawing room that opens onto a terrace and a Michelin-starred restaurant for ambrosial food; but follow your nose through a beautiful courtyard and you wash up at an ultra-cool spa. A fire runs along one side of the swimming pool, there's a saltwater plunge pool, a steam room and sauna, treatment rooms galore. Stop at the brasserie for a spot of lunch, then explore the grounds; you can walk for an hour without leaving the estate. There are mountain bikes to spin you round, you'll pass floodlit tennis courts, an arboretum, there's even an equestrian centre with a ring for jumping or dressage and a cross-country course that cuts through the park. Bedrooms match the mood. Those in the main house are magnificently grand, those around the courtyard are a little more contemporary. All come with robes in fine bathrooms and Anne Semonin toiletries.

Price	£330–£520. Suites £725–£1,115.
Rooms	42: 29 twins/doubles, 13 suites.
Meals	Breakfast £16–£22. Brasserie lunch & dinner £19–£40. Restaurant (not Sun eve or Mon) dinner £70; tasting menu £90; Sunday lunch £39.
Closed	Never.
Directions	M4 junc. 17, then A350 south to Chippenham & A420 west for Bristol. Left in Box, through village. Hotel signed right after 2 miles.

Claire Randal
Colerne,
Bath SN14 8AZ

Tel	+44 (0)1225 742777
Email	reservations@lucknampark.co.uk
Web	www.lucknampark.co.uk

Guyers House

This fine old country house stands in six acres of sublime English gardens, reason enough to visit. You'll find an orchard and a kitchen garden that provide much for your dinner, a croquet lawn flanked by rambling roses, then a smart sweep down to a flourishing pond. The best place to drink in the view is the gravelled terrace at the back of the house, perfect for afternoon tea in summer. As for Guyers, it started life in 1671, a small farmhouse that has grown grandly over the years. These days you find an open fire in reception, a small ballroom, a pretty sitting room and a quirky bar in the old stables that opens onto an attractive courtyard. Best of all is the restaurant, where you dig into fabulous food, perhaps watercress soup with a soft poached hen's egg, loin of venison with a sage and rosemary jus, then caramelised banana with honeycomb ice cream. Pretty bedrooms are scattered about, some in the main house, others in garden rooms. None are enormous, but nor is their price, and all come with warm colours, crisp linen and lovely garden views. Bath, Highgrove and Dyrham Park are all close.

Price	£116–£126. Singles from £92.
Rooms	38: 9 doubles, 1 twin, 5 singles, 1 four-poster. Garden House: 3 twins, 18 doubles, 1 single.
Meals	Lunch from £12.50. Dinner £18.50–£23.50. À la carte from £33.
Closed	Never.
Directions	West from Chippenham on A4 for Bath. Past Corsham turn off, through Pickwick, signed right after 800m.

Neil Glasspool
Pickwick,
Corsham SN13 0PS

Tel	+44 (0)1249 713399
Email	enquiries@guyershouse.com
Web	www.guyershouse.com

Methuen Arms Hotel

Built around the remains of a 14th-century nunnery, converted into a brewery and coaching inn in 1608, and with an impressive Georgian façade, the Methuen has history in spades. Restyled as a boutique inn following a sympathetic restoration, its doors swung open in November 2010 to reveal a stunning interior. From a grand tiled hallway a sweeping staircase leads to a dozen ultra-stylish rooms, those in the former nunnery oozing character with wonky beams and other fascinating features. All have colourful headboards on big beds, wonderfully upholstered armchairs, funky colourful rugs and some rather swish bathrooms, the best with roll top tubs and walk-in showers. Back downstairs are rugs on stone and wood floors, crackling logs in old stone fireplaces, glowing candles on tables and vintage photos of Corsham; the traditional bar and informal dining rooms are truly inviting. A seasonal modern British menu is a further enticement, so tuck into pasta with game ragu, fish pie, or lamb marinated in oregano and garlic. This grand almost Tardis-like inn promises more rooms in 2012.

Price	£130–£170. Singles from £90.
Rooms	12: 10 doubles, 1 twin/double, 1 family room.
Meals	Lunch from £5.95. Dinner, 3 courses, about £30. Sunday lunch £17.95–£21.95.
Closed	Never.
Directions	M4 junc. 17, then A350 south & A4 west. B3353 south into Corsham. On left.

Martin & Debbie Still
2 High Street, Corsham SN13 0HB
Tel   +44 (0)1249 717060
Email   info@themethuenarms.com
Web   www.themethuenarms.com

King's Arms

In 1125 Cluniac monks founded a monastery in the village; this venerable old building was their sleeping quarters. It turned into an alehouse in the 19th-century to satisfy an army of miners, who dug Bath stone from under these hills. These days, it's one of the loveliest inns you could hope to chance upon, with an ancient stone courtyard at the front and a small garden overlooking the farm behind. Inside, find painted panelling, cool colours, vintage wallpaper and thick curtains drawn across doorways. A vast inglenook, piled high with logs, was discovered during recent excavations in the restaurant, while the bar plays host to a colourful cast of farmers and shoot parties, who come for a good pint and some great food. Bedrooms above the shop are seriously spoiling. You get the full works: crisp white linen on low-slung beds, claw-foot baths, iPod docks, robes and Zoffany fabrics; one room is enormous and has its own fire. Unpretentious country food waits below, perhaps rabbit terrine, steak frites, sticky toffee pudding. There's a DVD library, playing cards and games. Bath is close.

Price	£95–£135. Suites £175–£225. Singles from £85.	
Rooms	5: 2 doubles, 3 suites.	
Meals	Lunch from £4.50. Dinner, 3 courses, about £25.	
Closed	Never.	
Directions	M4 junction 18, then A46/A4 to Bathford. South on A363 for two miles, then left for Monkton Farleigh. Left at x-roads and on left.	

Joe Holden
Monkton Farleigh BA15 2QH

Tel	+44 (0)1225 858705
Email	thekingsarmsbath@gmail.com
Web	www.kingsarms-bath.co.uk

The Lamb at Hindon

The Lamb has been serving ale on Hindon's high street for 800 years. It is a yard of England's finest cloth, a place where shooting parties come for lunch, where farmers meet to chew the cud. Step inside and find huge oak settles, heavy old beams, then deep red walls and roaring fires. A clipped Georgian country elegance lingers; you almost expect Mr Darcy to walk in, give a tormented sigh, then turn on his heels and vanish. There are flagstone floors and stripped wooden boards, window seats and gilded mirrors; old oils entwined in willow hang on the walls, a bookshelf is stuffed with aged tomes of poetry. At night, candles come out, as do some serious whiskies, and in the restaurant you can feast on ham hock and foie gras ballotine, game pie or Dover sole, then local cheeses. Revamped bedrooms come with mahogany furniture, rich colours, tartan throws, the odd four-poster, and some rather smart bathrooms. Splash out and stay in one of the cosy new rooms in the converted coach house. Fishing can be arranged, or you can shoot off to Stonehenge, Stourhead, Salisbury or Bath.

Price	From £75. Four-posters from £85. Suites from £100.
Rooms	19: 10 doubles, 2 twins/doubles, 4 four-posters, 3 suites.
Meals	Lunch & dinner £5–£25.
Closed	Never.
Directions	M3, A303 & signed left at bottom of steep hill two miles east of junction with A350.

Bernice Gallagher
High Street, Hindon,
Salisbury SP3 6DP

Tel	+44 (0)1747 820573
Email	reservations@lambathindon.co.uk
Web	www.lambathindon.co.uk

The Beckford Arms

You arrive in style: a fine sweep though the Fonthill estate and under the Triumphal Arch. Wash up at this country-house inn and expect to be seduced; after a severe fire it has risen, phoenix-like, from the ashes. Outside, a half-acre garden is ridiculously pretty – hammocks in the trees, parasols on the terrace, church spire soaring to the heavens; – but this Georgian house is equally sublime, an inn for all seasons. Inside: a drawing room where facing sofas are warmed by a roaring fire; a restaurant with a wall of glass that opens onto the terrace; a bar with parquet flooring for an excellent local pint. Follow your nose and chance upon the odd chandelier, roaming wisteria, logs piled high inside and out and a rather grand mahogany table in the private dining room. Bedrooms are small but perfectly formed with prices to match: white walls, the best linen, sisal matting, super bathrooms. As for the food, there's much to please, perhaps marrow fritters with lemon mayo, local partridge with bread sauce, chocolate bread and butter pudding. There are film nights most Sundays, the cricket team comes to celebrate.

Price	£95-£120.
Rooms	8: 7 doubles, 1 twin/double.
Meals	Main courses £9.95-£13.75.
Closed	Never.
Directions	On the road between Tisbury and Hindon, three miles south of A303 (Fonthill exit).

Daniel Brod & Charlie Luxton
Fonthill Gifford, Tisbury,
Salisbury SP3 6PX

Tel	+44 (0)1747 870385
Email	info@beckfordarms.com
Web	www.beckfordarms.com

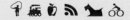

Howard's House

A gorgeous English village, a wormhole back in time. The building, Grade-II listed, dates from 1623 and comes with fine gardens, beyond which fields sweep uphill to a ridge of old oak. You can walk straight out, so bring your boots. Inside, airy country-house interiors come with exquisite arched windows, flagstones in reception and the odd beam. Deep sofas, fresh flowers and the morning papers wait in the sitting room, where a fire crackles on cold days; when the sun shines, doors open onto a very pretty terrace, where you can breakfast in good weather. Elegant bedrooms mix old and new to great effect. They're not overly plush, but deeply comfortable nonetheless with warm colours, mullioned windows, bowls of fruit and a sofa if there's room. Expect oak headboards, pretty fabrics, robes in good bathrooms. Spin downstairs for dinner – perhaps fillet of sea bass with parsnip purée, Scottish beef with roasted shallots, apple crème caramel with a calvados jelly – then climb back up to find your bed turned down. Salisbury, Stonehenge and the gardens at Stourhead are all close.

Price	£190. Four-poster £210. Singles from £120.
Rooms	9: 6 doubles, 1 twin/double, 1 four-poster, 1 family room.
Meals	Lunch £28.50. Dinner £29.50; à la carte around £45.
Closed	Rarely.
Directions	A30 from Salisbury, B3089 west to Teffont. There, left at sharp right-hand bend following brown hotel sign. Entrance on right after 0.5 miles.

Noele Thompson
Teffont Evias,
Salisbury SP3 5RJ

Tel	+44 (0)1722 716392
Email	enq@howardshousehotel.co.uk
Web	www.howardshousehotel.co.uk

The Compasses Inn

In the middle of a lovely village of thatched and timber-framed cottages, this inn seems so content with its lot it could almost be a figment of your imagination. Over the years, 14th-century foundations have gradually sunk into the ground. Its thatched roof is like a sombrero, shielding bedroom windows that peer sleepily over the lawn. Duck instinctively into the sudden darkness of the bar and experience a wave of nostalgia as your eyes adjust to a long wooden room, with flagstones and cosy booths divided by farmyard salvage: a cartwheel here, some horse tack there; at one end is a piano, at the other, a brick hearth. The pub crackles with Alan and Susie's enthusiasm and their hospitality is a big draw. People come for the food as well: Lyme Bay scallops on black pudding with crispy bacon, or Wiltshire venison steak, dauphinoise potatoes and red wine and juniper jus. Bedrooms are at the top of stone stairs outside the front door and have the same effortless charm; thick walls, wonky windows, spotless bathrooms. And the sweet serenity of Wiltshire lies just down the lane. *Minimum two nights at weekends in summer.*

Price	£85. Singles from £65. Cottage £100–£130.
Rooms	4 + 1: 3 doubles, 1 twin/double. Self-catering cottage for 4.
Meals	Lunch from £5.50. Dinner from £15.
Closed	Christmas Day & Boxing Day.
Directions	From Salisbury A30 west. 3rd right after Fovant, signed Lower Chicksgrove, then 1st left down single track lane to village.

Alan & Susie Stoneham
Lower Chicksgrove, Tisbury,
Salisbury SP3 6NB

Tel	+44 (0)1722 714318
Email	thecompasses@aol.com
Web	www.thecompassesinn.com

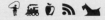

The Cottage in the Wood & Outlook Restaurant

A nine-mile ridge runs above the hotel, from where fabulous walks lead through light-dappled trees. There's a terrace for afternoon tea, too, so sip your Earl Grey amid 30-mile views that stretch off to distant Cotswold hills. And while the view is utterly magical, so is this hugely welcoming hotel. The décor is not cutting-edge contemporary, but nor would you want it to be; here is a hotel where old-fashioned values win out. Service is charming, the sort you only get with a passionate family at the helm and a battalion of long-standing staff to back them up. Add to that fabulous food in a restaurant that drinks in the view, and you have a winning combination for those who seek solid comforts rather than fly-by-night fashion. Rooms are split between the main house (simple, traditional), the cottage (cosy low ceilings, warm and snug) and the Pinnacles (hugely pleasing, nice and spacious, super bathrooms, the odd balcony). All have crisp linen and woollen blankets, floral fabrics, flat-screen TVs and DVD players; ask for a four-poster if you'd like one. A pretty garden adds the colour.

Price	£99–£198. Singles £79–£121. Half-board £66–£126 p.p. (min. 2 nights).
Rooms	30: 24 doubles, 5 twins/doubles, 1 four-poster.
Meals	Lunch from £5.45. Sunday lunch £23.95. Dinner, 3 courses, £25–£40. Packed lunch £8.95.
Closed	Never.
Directions	M5 junc. 7, then A449 through Gt Malvern. In Malvern Wells 3rd right after Railway pub. Signed.

John & Sue Pattin
Holywell Road,
Malvern WR14 4LG
Tel   +44 (0)1684 588860
Email   reception@cottageinthewood.co.uk
Web   www.cottageinthewood.co.uk

Estbek House

A super find on the Whitby coast. This is a quietly elegant restaurant with rooms ten paces from the beach at Sandsend. It's small, intimate and very welcoming. Tim cooks brilliantly, David talks you through his exceptional wine list and passes on the local news. Cliffs rise to the north, the beach runs away to the south, East Beck river passes directly opposite, ducks waddle across the road. There's a terrace at the front for drinks in summer and a small bar on the lower ground, where you can watch Tim at work in his kitchen. Upstairs, two airy dining rooms swim in seaside light and come with stripped floors, old radiators and crisp white tablecloths. Grab a window seat for watery views and dig into fresh Whitby crab with avocado and mango salad, local lamb with rhubarb compote, apricot tarte tatin. Bedrooms – bigger on the first floor, small on the second – have painted panelling, crisp white linen, colourful throws and shuttered windows. Breakfast is delicious – David's mum makes the marmalade. There are cliff walks, the moors to discover and you can follow the river upstream to Mulgrave Castle.

Price	£120–£150. Singles from £80.
Rooms	6: 5 doubles, 1 twin/double.
Meals	Dinner, 3 courses, about £35.
Closed	Occasionally.
Directions	North from Whitby on A174 to Sandsend. On left in village by bridge.

David Cross & Tim Lawrence
Eastrow, Sandsend,
Whitby YO21 3SU

Tel	+44 (0)1947 893424
Email	info@estbekhouse.co.uk
Web	www.estbekhouse.co.uk

Harry's Bar & Brasserie

Bang smack in the middle of Whitby, a fancy little bar where you can watch the world pass by. Tables and chairs line up smartly on the pavement, while walls of glass protect against the weather. Cool tunes float about, you can sip champagne at the mirrored bar, dip into some tapas for a spot of lunch, or simply order a coffee and read the daily papers. A flight of stairs leads up past a gallery of famous Hollywood faces to a neat restaurant, where views stretch over the water to St Mary's Church. Here you dig into more substantial fare, such as Whitby langoustine, pan-fried halibut, homemade chocolate brownie. Seafood and fish come straight off local boats, as fresh as can be. Most surprising of all are three delicious bedrooms above the shop. All have the view, none are small, and the suite has an entire floor to itself; take your pick knowing all are lovely. They come with comfy beds dressed in crisp linen, lots of colour, coffee machines, and robes in fabulous travertine shower rooms. Armchairs look the right way, though Whitby will draw you out. Brilliant.
Minimum two nights at weekends.

Price	£100–£135. Suite £150–£165.
Rooms	3: 2 doubles, 1 suite.
Meals	Tapas lunch/dinner from £6.95. À la carte about £25–£35.
Closed	Never.
Directions	Drop down to the sea front and keep left before the bridge, ignoring the no-entry signs. On left after 0.25 miles, opposite fish market.

Julie Tuby
10-11 Pier Road,
Whitby YO21 3PU

Tel	+44 (0)1947 601909
Email	info@harrysloungebar.co.uk
Web	www.harrysloungebar.co.uk

The White Swan Inn

A dreamy old inn that stands on Market Place, where farmers set up shop on the first Thursday of the month. The exterior is 16th century and flower baskets hang from its mellow stone walls. Inside, discover a seriously pretty world: stripped floors, open fires, a tiny bar, beautiful windows. The restaurant is at the back – the heart and soul of the inn – with delicious food flying from the kitchen, perhaps Whitby fishcakes, rack of spring lamb, glazed lemon tart with blood-orange sorbet. Excellent bedrooms are scattered about. Those in the main house have padded bedheads, delicious linen, Osborne & Little fabrics and flat-screen TV/DVDs; bathrooms have robes and Bath House oils. Rooms in the courtyard tend to be bigger and come in crisp contemporary style with black-and-white screen prints, mohair blankets and York stone bathrooms. You'll also find a cool little residents' sitting room here, with a huge open fire, an honesty bar, a purple pool table and cathedral ceilings. The moors are all around: fabulous walking, Castle Howard and Whitby wait. *Pets £12.50. Minimum two nights some weekends.*

Price	£150–£200. Suites £220–£270. Singles from £120.
Rooms	21: 14 doubles, 4 twins/doubles, 3 suites.
Meals	Lunch from £5.25. Dinner £25–£45. Sunday lunch £22.50.
Closed	Never.
Directions	From North A170 to Pickering. Entering town left at traffic lights, then 1st right into Market Place. On left.

Victor & Marion Buchanan
Market Place,
Pickering YO18 7AA
Tel   +44 (0)1751 472288
Email   welcome@white-swan.co.uk
Web   www.white-swan.co.uk

The Pheasant

Jacquie's eye for interior design has recently turned the Pheasant into a small-scale pleasure dome. It sits above the village pond with a terrace for drinks in the sun, but the drawing room is utterly gorgeous, so you may well choose to hole up inside. You'll find elegant sofas, walls of books, an open fire, flowers everywhere. Cool, earthy tones run throughout, there's a smart bar, padded window seats, candles flickering at night. Outside, a converted stone barn is home to a pretty swimming pool and you can potter across in bathrobes for a dip. Beautiful bedrooms are scattered about. There's a suite in the garden with a decked terrace, then a couple of lovely family rooms with bunk beds for kids. Those in the main house are no less beautiful: cool colours, chic fabrics, the odd four-poster, padded bedheads. Best of all is the food, perhaps hand-dived scallops with Yorkshire rhubarb, roasted wood pigeon with wild garlic risotto, lime tart with banana sorbet. Castle Howard for Brideshead fans and the Moors for walkers both wait. You can self-cater in three gorgeous cottages, too.

Price	£155. Suite £200. Singles from £78. Half-board from £110 p.p. Cottages £700 per week (or from £150 B&B per night).
Rooms	15 + 3: 11 doubles, 1 single, 2 family rooms, 1 suite. 3 self-catering cottages.
Meals	Light lunches from £6. Dinner, 3 courses, about £40. 7-course tasting menu £65.
Closed	Never.
Directions	Leave Helmsley to the east on A170. First right for Harome and hotel in village.

Jacquie Pern & Peter Neville
Harome,
Helmsley YO62 5JG

Tel	+44 (0)1439 771241
Email	reservations@thepheasanthotel.com
Web	www.thepheasanthotel.com

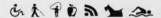

The White Bear Hotel

At five o'clock on a Friday evening there's only one place to be in town: the tap room at the White Bear, spiritual home of Theakston's beer. The great and the good gather to mark the end of the week, the odd pint is sunk, the air is thick with gossip. Interior design is strictly 19th century – red leather, polished brass, a crackling fire. Elsewhere. a country-house dining room in salmon pink; a handsome public bar with stripped floorboards and the odd beam; a flower-festooned terrace for lunch in the sun. Twenty-first century luxury comes courtesy of excellent bedrooms. They occupy the old Lightfoot brewery, but don't expect nostalgia here. The style is contemporary, with beautiful fabrics, warm colours, sumptuous beds and cutting-edge bathrooms; some have views across town and the vast penthouse is open to the rafters. There's a courtyard for guests, a sitting room, too; staff will bring drinks if you want privacy and peace. As for dinner, delicious comfort food waits in the restaurant: smoked salmon, steak and ale pie, treacle sponge pudding. The Dales are all around.

Price	£103.50. Suite £195.
Rooms	14: 13 twins/doubles, 1 suite.
Meals	Lunch from £4.95. Dinner, 3 courses, about £30.
Closed	Never.
Directions	North from Ripon on A6108. In Masham up hill (for Leyburn). Right at crest of hill. Signed.

Sue Thomas
Wellgarth, Masham,
Ripon HG4 4EN

Tel	+44 (0)1765 689319
Email	sue@whitebearmasham.co.uk
Web	www.thewhitebearhotel.co.uk

Swinton Park

Swinton is utterly glorious, a fabulous old pile that flaunts its beauty with rash abandon. It stands in 200 acres of parkland, part of a 20,000-acre estate. You get the full aristocratic works: five lakes and a huge kitchen garden outside, then stately interiors at every turn within. Expect marble pillars, varnished wood floors, vast arched windows, roaring fires. The drawing room is stupendous, a little like the salon of 17th-century French château, but the dining room is equally impressive, its magnificent ceiling worth the trip alone. The main corridor is an art gallery, there's a bar in the old chapel, a hugely popular cookery school in the old stables, then a small spa, too. Bedrooms come in grand style: plush fabrics, huge beds, marble bathrooms, decanters of complimentary gin and whisky. One of the suites occupies the turret, some rooms have sublime views over Home Lake, a couple interconnect, so perfect for families. As for the food, game from the estate and vegetables from the garden are plentiful, while hampers can be left in bothies for walkers wanting a rather good lunch. Magnificent.

Price	£185–£300. Suites £310–£380. Half-board from £127.50 p.p.
Rooms	31: 25 twins/doubles, 6 suites.
Meals	Lunch from £21.50. Dinner £52. Tasting menu £60.
Closed	Never.
Directions	A1(M), Junc. 50, follow signs to Masham on road that runs parallel to motorway. After 3 miles, left onto B6267 to Masham. Hotel signed in village, 1 mile south-west, past golf course.

Mark & Felicity Cunliffe-Lister
Swinton,
Ripon HG4 4JH

Tel	+44 (0)1765 680900
Email	reservations@swintonpark.com
Web	www.swintonpark.com

The Burgoyne Hotel

The Burgoyne is one of the loveliest places to stay in the Dales. The view from the front is imperious, a smooth sweep three miles south off to Swaledale; half a dozen benches on the village green look the right way. Inside, the past lives on: an elegant drawing room with a crackling fire where you gather for drinks before dinner; a restaurant in racing green where you feast on delicious food – perhaps smoked salmon with prawns and lemon, roast lamb with red-wine gravy, pan-fried pineapple with espresso ice cream. Julia and Mo – fabulous new owners – are here to keep the traditions alive, while updating as they go. Bedrooms come in country-house style: colourful fabrics, excellent beds, thick white linen, a sofa if there's room. A four-poster occupies the old snooker room, all but one room has the view. There are maps for walkers, fishing can be arranged, Durham and Hadrian's Wall are close. As for Reeth, it's a gorgeous old traditional village, mentioned in the Domesday Book, with a market every Friday and the best grouse moors in Britain. Dogs very welcome.

Price	£127.95–£160.95. Four-poster £182. Suite £192.50. Singles from £110.
Rooms	8: 3 doubles, 1 four-poster, 1 suite, 1 twin, all en suite. 2 twins with separate bathrooms.
Meals	Dinner, 4 courses, £39.
Closed	Midweek in January (Mon-Thurs).
Directions	From Richmond A6108, then B6270 to Reeth. Hotel on north side of village green.

Julia & Mo Usman
Reeth,
Richmond DL11 6SN

Tel	+44 (0)1748 884292
Email	enquiries@theburgoyne.co.uk
Web	www.theburgoyne.co.uk

Yorebridge House

Every century Yorebridge House reinvents itself. It started life in 1850 as a headmaster's house, only to be snapped up by the Yorkshire Dales National Park to act as their HQ. With the advent of the 21st century, it aptly evolved into a super-cool hotel and those who like an excess of style will find it here. The house stands in five acres on the banks of two rivers, with fishing rights if you want to try your luck. Interiors sparkle, the result of a total renovation. You find leather sofas in the sitting room, where 1920s school photos adorn the walls; there are stripped floors and a slab of granite in the funky bar, and banks of windows in the restaurant. Gaze out on Nappa Scar while feasting on serious food, perhaps Whitby crab and shellfish consommé, Yoredale lamb with fennel purée, coconut panna cotta and pineapple sorbet. Bedrooms are exceptional, some with hot tubs on terraces, others with double-ended baths. All come with fabulous fabrics, beautiful colours, Bang & Olufsen TVs, magnificent bathrooms. Kayaking can be arranged. There are jazz nights, too.

Price	£200–£240. Suite £250.
Rooms	11: 8 doubles, 2 twins/doubles, 1 suite.
Meals	Lunch from £5.95. Dinner, 3 courses, £44.50. Bar meals from £12.95.
Closed	Never.
Directions	East from Hawes on A684. In Bainbridge bear left at Rose & Crown for Askrig. On right after 400m.

David & Charlotte Reilly
Bainbridge DL8 3EE
Tel　　+44 (0)1969 652060
Email　enquiries@yorebridgehouse.co.uk
Web　　www.yorebridgehouse.co.uk

Entry 256　Map 6

The Traddock

This family-run hotel is decidedly pretty and sits on southern fringes of the Yorkshire Dales; those looking for a friendly base will find it here. You enter through a wonderful drawing room – crackling fire, pretty art, the daily papers, cavernous sofas – but follow your nose and find polished wood in the dining room, panelled walls in the breakfast room and William Morris wallpaper in the sitting-room bar, where you can sip a pint of Skipton ale while indulging in a game of Scrabble. Bedrooms are just the ticket, some seriously swanky in contemporary style, others deliciously traditional with family antiques, quilted beds, perhaps a claw-foot bath. Those on the second floor have a cosy attic feel, all have fresh fruit, flat-screen TVs, homemade shortbread and Dales views. Elsewhere, a white-washed sitting room that opens onto the garden and fabulous local food in the rug-strewn restaurant, perhaps poached asparagus, fell-bred lamb, apple and butterscotch crumble. Three Peaks are at the door, so come to walk. Don't miss the caves at Ingleborough or Settle for antiques. *Minimum two nights at weekends March-October.*

Price	£95–£190. Singles from £85.
Rooms	12: 8 doubles, 1 twin/double, 2 family rooms, 1 single.
Meals	Lunch from £9.50. Dinner, 3 courses, around £30.
Closed	Never.
Directions	0.75 miles off the A65, midway between Kirkby Lonsdale & Skipton, 4 miles north-west of Settle.

Paul Reynolds
Austwick, Settle LA2 8BY

Tel	+44 (0)1524 251224
Email	info@austwicktraddock.co.uk
Web	www.thetraddock.co.uk

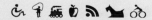

The Tempest Arms

A 16th-century, award-winning ale house three miles west of Skipton with great prices, friendly staff and an easy style. Inside you find stone walls and open fires, six ales on tap at the bar and a smart beamed restaurant. An airy open-plan feel runs throughout with sofas and armchairs strategically placed in front of a fire that burns on both sides. Delicious traditional food is a big draw – the inn was packed for dinner on a Wednesday in April. You can eat wherever you want, so grab a seat and dig into Yorkshire puddings with a rich onion gravy, cottage pie with a Wensleydale crust, treacle tart with pink grapefruit sorbet. Bedrooms are just as good. Those in the main house are simpler, those next door in two newly built stone houses are rather indulging. You get crisp linen, neutral colours, slate bathrooms and flat-screen TVs. Some have views of the fells, the suites are large and worth the money, a couple have decks with hot tubs to soak in. The Dales are on your doorstep, this is a great place for walkers. Skipton, a proper Yorkshire market town, is worth a look. Hard to fault for the price.

Price	£85. Suites £100–£140. Singles from £62.50.
Rooms	21: 9 twins/doubles, 12 suites.
Meals	Lunch & bar meals from £8.95. Dinner from £14.95.
Closed	Never.
Directions	A56 west from Skipton. Signed left after two miles.

Martin & Veronica Clarkson
Elslack,
Skipton BD23 3AY

Tel	+44 (0)1282 842450
Email	info@tempestarms.co.uk
Web	www.tempestarms.co.uk

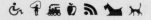

Devonshire Fell Hotel

You're high on the hill with huge views of Wharfdale: mountains rise, the river roars and in summer you can watch the cricket team toil on the pitch below. Up at this rather cool hotel there's a plant-festooned terrace and a trim lawn for sunbathing (people do). Inside, funky interiors are the order of the day. A lilac bar comes with halogen lighting and leather sofas; wander on and find stripped floors, Designers Guild fabrics and a wood-burner to keep you warm. There's a sense of space, too, with one room flowing into another, the bar, restaurant and conservatory united by an open-plan feel. Expect splashes of colour, padded bedheads and beautiful upholstery in the bedrooms; those at the front have stupendous views. You get big TVs, DVD players, a sofa if there's room; tongue-and-groove bathrooms come with robes and fluffy towels. Back downstairs, delicious food is served informally in the bar, perhaps a haddock burger with tartare sauce and crushed peas. In the restaurant try Lishman black pudding; honey roast duck; vanilla crème brûlée with strawberries. There are movie nights and the walking is heavenly.

Price	£129–£259.
Rooms	12: 6 doubles, 4 twins, 2 suites.
Meals	Lunch from £13.95. Dinner £26–£32.
Closed	Never.
Directions	From Harrogate A59 west for 15 miles, then right onto B6160, signed Burnsall & Bolton Abbey. Hotel on the edge of the village.

Stephane Leyreloup
Burnsall,
Skipton BD23 6BT

Tel	+44 (0)1756 729000
Email	res@devonshirehotels.co.uk
Web	www.devonshirefell.co.uk

The Bijou

Great prices, an easy style and ever-present owners are the hallmarks of this smart B&B hotel close to the centre of town. Outside, a small, manicured garden leads up to a Victorian stone townhouse; inside, a clean contemporary feel runs throughout. Gill and Stephen (he's ex-Hotel du Vin) renovated completely; out with the woodchip and swirly carpets, in with stripped boards and faux-zebra-skin rugs. There's a cool little sitting room with an open fire, a computer for guests to use, and an honesty bar on tap all day. Bedrooms mix leather bedheads, airy colours, Cole & Son wallpaper and orange stools. Excellent bathrooms, most compact, have smart creamy ceramics, you get waffle robes, hot water bottles, flat-screen TVs and double glazing (the house is set back from the road). Two rooms in the coach house are good for small groups. Breakfast is a leisurely feast: freshly squeezed orange juice, eggs and bacon from a local farm, homemade breads and muesli. Don't miss the Stray (the vast common that wraps up the town) or Betty's for afternoon tea. Good restaurants wait, too.

Price	£85–£110. Singles from £65.
Rooms	10: 8 doubles, 1 twin, 1 single.
Meals	Restaurants within walking distance.
Closed	23–30 December.
Directions	A61 north into town, following signs for Ripon. Past Betty's Teashop, down hill, back up, past Cairn Hotel. Signed on left.

Stephen & Gill Watson
17 Ripon Road,
Harrogate HG1 2JL
Tel   +44 (0)1423 567974
Email info@thebijou.co.uk
Web   www.thebijou.co.uk

Gallon House

A bespoke B&B that clings to the side of an impossibly steep hill with a medieval castle tottering on one side, a grand Victorian railway bridge passing on the other and the serene river sparkling below. Ancient steps lead gently down, you can follow the Nidd into the country or hire a boat and mess about on it. Climb back up to this magical house, where walls of glass bring in the view. There's Lloyd Loom wicker in the small conservatory, an open fire in the panelled sitting room, stripped floors and delicious communal breakfasts in the dining room. Best of all is the sun terrace for one of Yorkshire's best views, with parasols and pots of colour, and deckchairs to take the strain. Bedrooms are warmly stylish, not too big, but spoiling nonetheless, with bathrobes and white towels, crisp linen and soft colours, videos and CD players. Two have the view, two have showers in the actual room. As for dinner, Rick, a chef, is a maestro in the kitchen, so come down for something tasty, perhaps salmon fish cakes, rack of lamb, pear and almond tart. A great little place. *No credit cards.*

Price	£120. Singles £85.
Rooms	3: 2 doubles, 1 twin.
Meals	Dinner, 3 courses, £40, by arrangement.
Closed	Christmas & New Year.
Directions	A1(M) junc. 47, A59 west for 3 miles. Climb hill into Knaresborough. Left into Market Place at Barclays bank; 1st right into Kirkgate; on left.

	Sue & Rick Hodgson
	47 Kirkgate,
	Knaresborough HG5 8BZ
Tel	+44 (0)1423 862102
Email	gallon-house@ntlworld.com
Web	www.gallon-house.co.uk

The Black Swan at Oldstead

In glorious isolation, a sparkling country inn. Outside, a grass terrace shaded by cherry trees gives views of field and ridge, a perfect spot for a pint in summer. Inside is a bar of matchless elegance: a fire primed for combustion, 400-year-old flagstones, a couple of gorgeous bay windows, candelabra hanging from the ceiling. The inn is built into the side of a hill with stairs that lead up to a country-house restaurant, where smart rugs cover golden floorboards and cream walls make the most of the light. But the food is what you've come for. The Banks family has farmed here for generations and much of what you eat comes straight from local fields. It's serious stuff, immaculately presented, perhaps game terrine and toasted brioche, haunch of venison with grain mustard risotto, an irresistible pear tarte tatin. Four sublime bedrooms wait in a low stone building next door. Expect a very pretty country style: beautiful beds, white linen, oak armoires, fabulous bathrooms (one has a copper bath). Each room opens to a peaceful terrace and they'll bring you a whisky before dinner.

Price	Half-board £135–£165 p.p.
Rooms	4: 2 doubles, 2 four-posters.
Meals	Lunch from £8.95. Set lunch, 2-3 courses, £20-£25. Dinner, 3 courses, included; non-residents, £37.50-£47. Tasting menu £60. No lunch Mon-Wed.
Closed	First 2 weeks in January.
Directions	A19 from Thirsk; left to Thirkleby & Coxwold, then left for Byland Abbey; follow signs left for Oldstead.

The Banks Family
Oldstead,
York YO61 4BL

Tel	+44 (0)1347 868387
Email	enquiries@blackswanoldstead.co.uk
Web	www.blackswanoldstead.co.uk

The Grange Hotel

York Minster is imperious, the oldest Gothic cathedral in northern Europe. It stands less than half a mile from the front door of this extremely comfortable Regency townhouse – a five-minute stroll after bacon and eggs. The streets around it give the feel of Dickensian London and a Roman column stands outside the West Door, but the interior astounds; the Great East Window is the largest piece of medieval stained glass in the world. Back at the hotel, a country-house elegance runs throughout: marble pillars in a flagged entrance hall, an open fire in the cosy Morning Room and a first-floor Drawing Room that opens onto a small balcony. Bedrooms come in different shapes and sizes, with smart florals, mahogany dressers, period colours, good bathrooms. The more expensive rooms are seriously plush with high beds and swathes of silky curtain. York racecourse brings in a crowd, there are deep red walls and leather chairs in the super-smart Ivy Brasserie; you can also eat downstairs in the vaulted New York grill where steaks are the order of the day. *Minimum two nights at weekends.*

Price	£137-£208. Four-poster £235. Suite £284. Singles from £123.
Rooms	36: 11 doubles, 18 twins/doubles, 3 four-posters, 3 singles, 1 suite.
Meals	Lunch from £10. Dinner, 3 courses, £30-£35 (early bird discount).
Closed	Never.
Directions	South into York from ring road on A19. On right after two miles, 500 yards north of York Minster.

George Briffa
1 Clifton,
York YO30 6AA

Tel	+44 (0)1904 644744
Email	info@grangehotel.co.uk
Web	www.grangehotel.co.uk

Channel Islands

The Georgian House

Holly's family have been holidaying in Alderney for more than 30 years, now she's come back to take over this treasure of an hotel. Along with her charming young team, they've turned it into the beating heart of the island. Step off the cobbled high street straight into a traditional, cosy bar; grab a bite here or something more extravagant in the light-strewn dining room that opens out to the pretty garden. Vegetables and salad come from their own allotment, the butter is vivid yellow and meat and fish is as local as can be: try the divine head-to-toe pork dish (great for sharing) or a zingy chilli squid. Upstairs three quaint bedrooms, all en suite, are pretty and pristine with locally made soaps and views to the town. The 100-seater cinema opposite shows arthouse films on reels, during the interval you wander over to The Georgian for a drink. The hotel is packed with locals and visitors alike, and rightly so; there are barbecues, bands, taster evenings, and a blissful atmosphere. Old forts and stunning beaches wait, so hire bikes and explore the island. And book early.

Price	£70-90. Singles from £55.
Rooms	3: 1 double, 2 twins/doubles.
Meals	Light lunch from £6. Dinner, 3 courses, £25-£30.
Closed	Mid-January to mid-March.
Directions	Sent on booking. Airport pick-ups.

Holly Fisher
Victoria Street,
Alderney GY9 3UF

Tel	+44 (0)1481 822471
Email	holly@georgianalderney.com
Web	www.georgianalderney.com

White House Hotel

Herm is unique, a tiny island run benignly by the 40 souls lucky enough to live on it. They keep things blissfully simple: no cars, no TVs, just a magical world of field and sky, a perfect place to escape the city. A coastal path rings the island; you'll find high cliffs to the south, sandy beaches to the north, cattle grazing the hills between. You get fabulous views at every turn – shimmering islands, pristine waters, yachts and ferries zipping about. There are beach cafés, succulent gardens, an ancient church, even a tavern. Kids love it, so do parents, and the self-catering cottages are extremely popular. As for the hotel, it lingers happily in an elegant past, a great base from which to enjoy the island. You'll find open fires, delicious four-course dinners, a tennis court with watery views, a pool to keep you cool. Spotless bedrooms are scattered about, some in the village's colour-washed cottages, others with balconies in the hotel. Several come in contemporary style with fancy bathrooms, but most are warmly traditional as befits the setting. Expect pretty colours, padded headboards and watery views.

Price	Half-board £95-£146 p.p. Self-catering cottages £273-£1,288 per week.
Rooms	40 + 20: 12 twins/doubles, 5 family rooms. Cottage rooms: 16 twins/doubles, 5 family rooms, 2 singles. 20 cottages for 2-6.
Meals	Lunch from £5. Dinner included; non-residents, £27.50.
Closed	November-Easter.
Directions	Via Guernsey. Trident ferries leave from the harbour at St Peter Port 8 times a day in summer (£11 return).

Siôn Dobson Jones
Herm Island GY1 3HR
Tel   +44 (0)1481 750075
Email   jonathanwatson@herm.com
Web   www.herm.com

Scotland

Darroch Learg Hotel

The country here is glorious – river, forest, mountain, sky – so walk by Loch Muick, climb Lochnagar, fish the Dee or drop down to Braemar for the Highland Games. Swing back to Darroch Learg and find nothing but good things. This is a smart family-run hotel firmly rooted in a graceful past, an old country house with roaring fires, polished brass, Zoffany wallpaper and ambrosial food in a much-admired restaurant. Ever-present Nigel and Fiona look after guests with great aplomb and many return year after year. Everything is just as it should be: tartan fabrics on the walls in the hall, Canadian pitch pine windows and doors, fabulous views sweeping south across Balmoral forest. Bedrooms upstairs come in different shapes and sizes; all have warmth and comfort in spades. Big grand rooms at the front thrill with padded window seats, wallpapered bathrooms, old oak furniture, perhaps a four-poster bed. Spotlessly cosy rooms in the eaves are equally lovely, just not quite as big. You get warm colours, pretty furniture, crisp white linen and bathrobes to pad about in. A perfect highland retreat.

Price	£150-£250. Half-board (obligatory at weekends) £105-£160 p.p.
Rooms	12: 10 twins/doubles, 2 four-posters.
Meals	Sunday lunch £24. Dinner £45; tasting menu, £55, on request.
Closed	Christmas & last 3 weeks in Jan.
Directions	From Perth A93 north to Ballater. Entering village hotel 1st building on left above road.

Nigel & Fiona Franks
56 Braemar Road,
Ballater AB35 5UX

Tel	+44 (0)1339 755443
Email	enquiries@darrochlearg.co.uk
Web	www.darrochlearg.co.uk

The Kilberry Inn

It's a little like *Local Hero*, a patch of heaven in the middle of nowhere with vast skies, forested hills and the Sound of Jura pouring past. As for the Kilberry, it stands on the road in this tiny village (cars pass at the rate of one an hour). Outside, the phone box is soon to become the smallest whisky bar in the world. Inside, oodles of rustic charm, with Farrow & Ball colours, exposed stone walls and an open fire that burns most nights. Half-bottles of champagne wait at the bar, as do local ales and excellent malts. In summer life spills onto the roadside for lunch in the sun. And the food here is the big draw. Clare's cooking is some of the best on the west coast, perhaps mussels and surf clams cooked in white wine, rack of hill lamb marinated in honey, then mocha brûlée with coffee ice cream. Spotless bedrooms have pretty colours, comfy beds, robes in compact shower rooms. Two are bigger; one has a sitting room, the other a hot tub on a private terrace. Elsewhere, sandy beaches, standing stones and golf at Machrihanish. Worth the detour. *Min. two nights at weekends July / Aug.*

Price	Half-board £100 p.p. Suite £107.50 p.p.
Rooms	5: 1 suite, 4 doubles.
Meals	Lunch from £15. 3-course, à la carte dinner included; non-residents, about £35.
Closed	Mondays. January & February. Sunday-Thursday in November & December.
Directions	A83 south from Lochgilphead for 3 miles, then right onto B8024 for 16 miles. In village on left.

Clare Johnson & David Wilson
Kilberry,
Tarbert PA29 6YD

Tel	+44 (0)1880 770223
Email	relax@kilberryinn.com
Web	www.kilberryinn.com

The Colonsay

Another fabulous Hebridean island, a perfect place to escape the world. Wander at will and find wild flowers in the machair, a golf course tended by sheep and huge sandy beaches across which cows roam. Wildlife is ever present, from a small colony of wild goats to a rich migratory bird population; the odd golden eagle soars overhead, too. At low tide the sands of the south give access to Oronsay. The island's 14th-century priory was one of Scotland's finest and amid impressive ruins its ornate stone cross still stands. As for the hotel, it's a splendid base and brims with an easy style – airy interiors, stripped floors, fires everywhere, friendly staff. There's a locals' bar for a pint (and a brewery on the island), a pretty sitting room packed with books, a dining room for super food, a decked terrace for drinks in the sun. Bedrooms have local art, warm colours, lovely fabrics and the best beds; some have sea views, all have good bathrooms. Spin around on bikes, search for standing stones, lie in the sun and stare at the sky. There's a festival in May for all things Colonsay. Wonderful.

Price	£85–£145. Singles from £70.
Rooms	9: 4 doubles, 3 twins, 1 single, 1 family room.
Meals	Lunch from £3.50. Packed lunch £7. Bar meals from £10.50. Dinner, 3 courses, about £25.
Closed	November, January (after New Year) & February.
Directions	Calmac ferries from Oban or Kennacraig (not Tues) or Hebridean Airways (Tues & Thurs). Hotel on right, half a mile up road from jetty.

Lorne Smith
Scalasaig,
Isle of Colonsay PA61 7YP

Tel	+44 (0)1951 200316
Email	hotel@colonsayestate.co.uk
Web	www.colonsayestate.co.uk

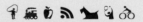

The Creggans Inn

The real James Bond once owned this hotel – Sir Fitzroy MacLean was one of a cast of characters on whom Ian Fleming modelled his hero; the fact the Royal Navy regularly send their big ships into Loch Fyne on exercise is purely coincidental. These days, life at the inn is decidedly restful. Views from the front stretch for miles, the loch eventually giving way to the distant peaks of the Kintyre peninsular. Inside, an airy elegance has spread far and wide. Downstairs, sofas and armchairs are liberally scattered about, there's a locals bar which doubles as the clubhouse for the village shinty team, then picture windows in the smart restaurant, where you dig into super local fare – perhaps grilled goats cheese, breast of guinea fowl, chocolate and hazelnut parfait – while watching the sun set over the hills. Traditional country-house bedrooms are lovely: warm colours, pretty fabrics, delicate wallpapers, padded bedheads; most have loch views. There's lots to do: castles and gardens, boat trips and golf, hills for cyclists and walkers. All this an hour and a half from hip Glasgow.

Price	£120–£180. Suite £160–£220. Singles from £85. Half-board from £80 p.p.
Rooms	14: 1 suite, 4 doubles, 9 twins/doubles.
Meals	Bar: lunch & dinner from £4.25. Restaurant: 4-course table d'hôte menu £37.
Closed	Never.
Directions	From Glasgow, A82 to Tarbert, A83 towards Inverary for 13 miles, then left on A815 to Strachur (10 miles). Hotel on left before village.

Archie & Gillian MacLellan
Loch Fyne, Strachur,
Cairndow PA27 8BX

Tel	+44 (0)1369 860279
Email	info@creggans-inn.co.uk
Web	www.creggans-inn.co.uk

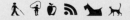

Ardanaiseig

You're lost to the world, ten miles down a track that winds past giant rhododendrons before petering out at this baronial mansion. Beyond, Loch Awe rules supreme, 30 miles of deep blue water on which to sail or fish. In one of the loveliest hotel drawing rooms you are ever likely to see – gold leaf panelling, cherubs in alcoves, Doric columns rising gleefully – an enormous window frames the view and a single sofa waits for those lucky enough to have it. Elsewhere, Wellington boots are on parade in the hall, fires roar wherever you go, eccentric art hangs on the dining room wall and a lawned terrace runs down to the loch. You're in 200 acres of private grounds; in May bluebells run riot. Country-house bedrooms are the real thing (old armoires, feather boa lamp shades, the odd four-poster), while the boat house has been converted into a funky suite with a wall of glass that opens onto a decked terrace. Dinner is a seven-course feast, as one might expect of this rather flamboyant hotel. Also, snooker, tennis and boats on which to row over to an island. Off-season breaks are a steal.

Price	£173–£363.
Rooms	18: 8 twins/doubles, 7 doubles, 2 four-posters, 1 boat house suite.
Meals	Light lunch from £6. Dinner, 7 courses, £50.
Closed	Rarely.
Directions	A85 to Taynuilt. Left onto B845 for Kilchrenan. Then left at Kilchrenan pub; down track for 4 miles.

Peter Webster
Kilchrenan,
Taynuilt PA35 1HE
Tel   +44 (0)1866 833333
Email   info@ardanaiseig.com
Web   www.ardanaiseig.com

Lerags House

You arrive in style, a spectacular sweep down a single-track road that tumbles over pretty hills to this lovely house by the water; hard to believe you're only four miles from Oban. Built in 1697, it once held all the land in the glen. Now it only has an acre, but it's a pretty one at that with lawns that roll down to tidal mud flats. You can watch the ebb and flow from the dining room while digging into Richard's lovely food, perhaps hand-dived Mull scallops with slow-roasted pork belly, Argyll lamb with spiced ginger sweetbreads, lemon cream with poached rhubarb. Airy interiors mix natural colours with comfy sofas, fresh flowers and lots of books. Richard and Nicola give guests exactly what they want: lots of style, great service, delicious food. Bedrooms are lovely: off-whites to soak up the light, big beds, crisp linen, padded bedheads. The suite has views to the loch and its own sitting area; bathrooms do the trick. At the end of the road you find the beach where Gavin Maxwell lived and wrote *Ring of Bright Water*. Day trips to Mull, Crinan and Kintyre are easy. A great base.

Price	£130. Suite £150. Singles from £110. Half-board £95-£105 p.p.
Rooms	5: 3 doubles, 1 twin/double, 1 suite.
Meals	Packed lunch £8. Dinner, 3 courses, £30.
Closed	Christmas.
Directions	From Oban, south on A816 for 2 miles, then right, signed Lerags for 2.5 miles. House on left, signed.

Richard & Nicola Fowler
Lerags,
Oban PA34 4SE
Tel   +44 (0)1631 563381
Email   leragshouse@yahoo.com
Web   www.leragshouse.com

The Manor House

A 1780 dower house for the Dukes of Argyll — their cottage by the sea — built of local stone, high on the hill, with long views over Oban harbour to the Isle of Mull. A smart and proper place, not one to bow to the fads of fashion: sea views from the lawn, cherry trees in the courtyard garden, a fire roaring in the drawing room, a beautiful tiled floor in the entrance hall and an elegant bay window in the dining room that catches the eye. Bedrooms tend to be small, but they're also rather pretty and come in warm colours — blues, reds, yellows, greens — with fresh flowers, crisp linen, bowls of fruit and piles of towels in good bathrooms; those that look seaward have binoculars with which to scour the horizon. Try Loch Fyne kippers for breakfast, salmon for lunch and, if you've room, rack of lamb for supper; there's excellent home baking, too. Ferries leave for the islands from the bottom of the hill — see them depart from the hotel garden. At the top, overlooking Oban, watch the day's close from McCaig's Folly; sunsets here are really special. *Children over 12 welcome.*

Price	£115–£225. Half-board £87.50–£147.50 p.p.
Rooms	11: 9 doubles, 2 twins.
Meals	Lunch from £8.50. Dinner £39.
Closed	Christmas.
Directions	In Oban follow signs to ferry. Hotel on right 0.5 miles after ferry turn-off, signed.

Gregor MacKinnon
Gallanach Road,
Oban PA34 4LS

Tel	+44 (0)1631 562087
Email	info@manorhouseoban.com
Web	www.manorhouseoban.com

The Airds Hotel & Restaurant

Ambrosial food, glittering interiors and faultless service make this one of Scotland's loveliest country-house hotels. Views from the front slide down to Loch Linnhe, sweep over Lismore Island and cross to the mountains of Ardnamurchan. A small conservatory, candlelit at night, frames the view perfectly, but in good weather you can slip across the lane to a colourful garden decked out with tables and parasols. Pre-dinner drinks are taken in the sitting rooms – open fires, elegant sofas, fresh flowers, lots of books – after which you're whisked off to the dining room, where delicious food is served on Limoges china. Whatever can be is homemade, so expect the best, perhaps goats cheese tart with leeks and wild garlic, cream of cauliflower and mustard soup, twice-cooked pork belly with tarragon butter, hot chocolate fondant with pistachio ice cream. Bedrooms elate. Some have terraces, others give loch views. Expect Frette linen, warm colours, mountains of pillows on fabulous beds, Italian robes in sparkling bathrooms and Bulgari toiletries. There's pink grapefruit and campari sorbet for breakfast. Unbeatable.

Price	Half-board £130-£230 p.p. Singles from £194. Cottage from £640 per week (high season) including breakfast.
Rooms	11 + 1: 8 twins/doubles, 3 suites. Self-catering cottage for 2.
Meals	Lunch £5-£25. Dinner, 5 courses, included; non-residents, £53.
Closed	Nov-Jan: 2 days midweek.
Directions	A82 north for Fort William, then A828 south for Oban. Right for Port Appin after 12 miles. On left after 2 miles.

Shaun & Jenny McKivragan
Port Appin,
Appin PA38 4DF

Tel	+44 (0)1631 730236
Email	airds@airds-hotel.com
Web	www.airds-hotel.com

Glengorm Castle

Few places defy overstatement, but Glengorm does so with ease. It stands in 5,000 acres at the top of Mull with views that stretch across miles of water to Coll and the Uists, Barra and Rhum. Directly in front the land falls away, rolls over lush pasture, then tumbles into the sea. Sheep graze by the hundred, birds play in the sky. Believe it or not, despite the grandeur, this is a B&B, a family home with children and dogs pottering about. The informality is infectious, you feel immediately at home. First you bounce up a four-mile drive, then you step into a vast hall, where sofas wait in front of the fire and big art hangs on the walls. An oak staircase sweeps you up to fabulous country-house rooms (three have the view). You get warm colours, antique furniture, sofas if there's room, excellent bathrooms. Elsewhere: a panelled library for guests to use with a selection of whiskies 'on the house'; a family room with games galore (digital and hard copy); a vast kitchen garden and magnificent coastal paths. Breakfast is a feast. There's a farm shop and café, so stop for lunch. Good restaurants wait in Tobermory.

Price	£130–£210.
Rooms	5: 3 doubles, 1 four-poster, all en suite. 1 double with separate bath.
Meals	Restaurants 5 miles.
Closed	Castle closed Christmas & New Year.
Directions	North to Tobermory on A848. Straight over roundabout (not right for town). Over x-roads after half a mile and straight ahead for four miles to castle.

Tom & Marjorie Nelson
Tobermory, Isle of Mull PA75 6QE
Tel   +44 (0)1688 302321
Email   enquiries@glengormcastle.co.uk
Web   www.glengormcastle.co.uk

Tiroran House

The setting is magnificent with 17 acres of lush gardens rolling down to Loch Scridian and the Ross of Mull rising beyond. Otters and dolphins pass by, as do red deer, who try to raid the garden. As for this extremely welcoming 1850 shooting lodge, you'll be hard pressed to find a more comfortable island base. There are fires in the drawing rooms, fresh flowers everywhere, games to be played, books to be read. Big country-house bedrooms hit the spot perfectly: crisp linen on pretty beds, beautiful fabrics and the odd chaise longue, watery views and silence guaranteed. You eat in a smart dining room, either at the front in the vine-shaded conservatory or at the back amid gilt mirrors. And the food is exceptional with much from the island or waters around it, perhaps venison and pork terrine, home grown vine leaf parcels, traditional Scottish Cranachan. You're bang in the middle of Mull with loads to do. Seek out Tobermory, the prettiest town in the Hebrides; Calgary and its magical beach; day trips to Iona with its famous monastery; boat trips to Fingal's Cave. Come back for afternoon tea; it's as good as the Ritz.

Price	£155–£210.
Rooms	10: 5 doubles, 5 twins/doubles.
Meals	Dinner, 4 courses, £46.50.
Closed	November to mid-March.
Directions	From Craignure or Fishnish car ferries, A849 for Bunessan & Iona car ferry. Right onto B8035 for Gruline. After 4 miles left at converted church. House 1 mile further.

Laurence & Katie Mackay
Isle of Mull PA69 6ES

Tel	+44 (0)1681 705232
Email	info@tiroran.com
Web	www.tiroran.com

Knockinaam Lodge

Lawns run down to the Irish sea, roe deer come to eat the roses, sunsets turn the sky red. This exceptional 1869 shooting lodge is nothing short of glorious: a Michelin star in the dining room, 150 malts in the bar and a level of service you rarely find in such far-flung corners of the realm. There's history, too. Churchill once stayed and you can sleep in his elegant room, where his books wait to be read and you need steps to climb into an ancient bath! Elsewhere, immaculate country-house interiors abound: gorgeous bedrooms, the very best bathrooms, an immaculate morning room where the scent of flowers mingles with the smell of burnt wood. Outside: cliff walks, nesting peregrine falcons, a rock pool where David keeps lobsters for the pot. In storms, waves crash all around. Trees stand guard high on the hill, their branches buffeted by the wind, while bluebells carpet the hills in spring. John Buchan knew the house and described it in *The Thirty-Nine Steps* as the house to which Hannay fled. Remote, beguiling, utterly spoiling – grand old Knockinaam is simply unmissable.

Price	Half-board £90–£220 p.p. Singles from £170.
Rooms	10: 4 doubles, 5 twins/doubles, 1 family suite.
Meals	Lunch, by arrangement, £30–£40. Dinner, 5 courses, included; non-residents, £58.
Closed	Never.
Directions	From A77 or A75 pick up signs to Portpatrick. West from Lochans on A77, then left after 2 miles, signed. Follow signs for 3 miles to hotel.

David & Sian Ibbotson
Portpatrick,
Stranraer DG9 9AD

Tel	+44 (0)1776 810471
Email	reservations@knockinaamlodge.com
Web	www.knockinaamlodge.com

Cavens

The Solway firth is a magical spot; overlooked by many, those who come have this patch of heaven to themselves. You swoop down from Dumfries through glorious country, then crest a hill and there it is, vast tracts of tidal sands with a huge sky above. It's a magnet for birdlife, the rich pickings of low tide too tempting to refuse. As for this 1752 shooting lodge, it stands in 20 acres of sweeping lawns, native woodlands and sprawling fields. Inside, elegant interiors come as standard. Two lovely sitting rooms are decked out with busts and oils, golden sofas, smouldering fires, a baby grand piano; in summer, you slip onto the terrace for afternoon tea. Country-house bedrooms have garden views, period furniture, bowls of fruit. One is smaller, others big with room for sofas. One has a stunning bathroom, another has an en suite sunroom. Back downstairs you feast on Angus' delicious food in the smart yellow restaurant, perhaps scallops with lime and Vermouth, Galloway pork in a mustard sauce, lemon panna cotta. There are gardens aplenty and golf at spectacular Southerness. Dogs are very welcome.

Price	£100–£190. Singles from £80. Half-board from £85 p.p.
Rooms	5: 4 doubles, 1 twin.
Meals	Dinner: à la carte about £35; set menu £25. Packed lunch available.
Closed	Never.
Directions	From Dumfries A710 to Kirkbean (12 miles). Cavens signed in village on left.

Jane & Angus Fordyce
Kirkbean,
Dumfries DG2 8AA

Tel	+44 (0)1387 880234
Email	enquiries@cavens.com
Web	www.cavens.com

Trigony House Hotel

A small, welcoming, family-run hotel: Adam and Jan are doing their own thing without fuss. Expect delicious home-cooked food, comfortable bedrooms and a lovely garden which you may roam – look out for rare red squirrels. The house dates back to 1700, a shooting lodge for the local castle. Inside: Japanese oak panelling in the hall, a wood-burner in the sitting room and an open fire in the dining room; doors open onto the terrace for al fresco dinners in summer. Adam cooks extremely good rustic fare, perhaps crab tart, local venison, rhubarb and hazelnut crumble; there's a small, organic kitchen garden that provides much for the table in summer. Bedrooms vary in size and style, some with pretty fabrics, golden throws and summer colours: many are dog-friendly too. One has its own conservatory/sitting room which opens onto a private lawn, but even the simpler rooms have flat-screen TVs with DVDs; there's a film library downstairs. Falconry, riding and fishing can be arranged, even vintage car hire. Fill up with a cooked breakfast – one of the best – then head west into the hills for fabulous countryside.

Price	£105–£125. Suite £155. Singles from £80. Half-board from £75 p.p.
Rooms	9: 4 twins/doubles, 4 doubles, 1 suite.
Meals	Lunch from £5. Dinner, 3 courses, £30.
Closed	24–26 December.
Directions	North from Dumfries on A76; through Closeburn; signed left after 1 mile.

Adam & Jan Moore
Closeburn,
Thornhill DG3 5EZ

Tel	+44 (0)1848 331211
Email	info@trigonyhotel.co.uk
Web	www.countryhousehotelscotland.com

21212

21212 is the new jewel in Edinburgh's crown. Paul left his Michelin star down south, bought this Georgian townhouse, spent a small fortune converting it into a 21st-century pleasure dome, then opened for business and won back his star. The house stands at the top of a hill with long views north towards the Firth of Forth. It's bang in the centre of town with Arthur's Seat and Princes Street both close by. Inside, contemporary splendour waits. High ceilings and vast windows come as standard, but wander at will and find a chic first-floor drawing room, cherubs on the wall, busts and statues all over the place, even a private dining pod made of white leather. Stunning bedrooms have enormous beds, cool colours, fat sofas and iPod docks. Those at the front have the view, all have robes in magnificent bathrooms. As for the restaurant: the kitchen is on display behind a wall of glass and the food it produces is heavenly, perhaps fillet of beef with apricots and thyme, Gloucestershire Old Spot with white asparagus, saffron-poached pineapple baked in a caramelised lemon curd. Out of this world.

Price	£195–£325.
Rooms	4 doubles.
Meals	Lunch from £28. Dinner from £68.
Closed	10 days in January & 10 days in summer.
Directions	A720 ring road, then A702/A7 into town. Right at T-junc. at Balmoral Hotel, then immediately left with flow. Right at second r'bout and 1st right. On right.

Paul Kitching & Katie O'Brien
3 Royal Terrace,
Edinburgh EH7 5AB

Tel	+44 (0)131 523 1030
Email	reservations@21212restaurant.co.uk
Web	www.21212restaurant.co.uk

23 Mayfield

Edinburgh – the most beautiful city in Scotland and therefore in Britain. Those who come to gaze on its glory will enjoy the spoiling B&B hotel that stands in the shadow of Arthur's Seat. Built in 1868, it was home to a coffee merchant and comes with plaster-moulded ceilings and a fine stained-glass window on the landing. There's an airy dining room for excellent breakfasts (toasted muffins with hand-picked mushrooms, peat-smoked haddock with poached eggs), then a sitting room with chesterfield sofas where you can browse a collection of guide books or surf the net on the house computer. Super bedrooms have excellent prices. Some come with high ceilings and shuttered windows, most with travertine marble bathrooms, all have period colours, panelled walls and good beds with excellent linen. You get iPod docks, Bose technology and classical CDs, and the family room comes with a Nintendo Wii. There's good art throughout; a history of Scotland is framed on the landing. A short bus ride zips you into town, there's off-street parking and loads of local eateries. You can hire bikes, too. *Minimum two nights at weekends.*

Price	£90–£175. Singles from £80.
Rooms	9: 4 twins/doubles, 1 triple, 3 four-posters, 1 family room.
Meals	Restaurants within half a mile.
Closed	24–26 December.
Directions	A720 bypass, then north onto A722 for Edinburgh. Right onto A721 at T-junction with traffic lights. Over x-roads with main flow, under railway bridge, on right.

Ross Birnie
23 Mayfield Gardens,
Edinburgh EH9 2BX

Tel	+44 (0)131 667 5806
Email	info@23mayfield.co.uk
Web	www.23mayfield.co.uk

94DR

Close to Holyrood and Arthur's Seat, this super-friendly design B&B is not only popular for its contemporary style, but for Paul and John, who treat guests like friends and who make sure they see the best of their city. A traditional Victorian exterior gives no hint of the cool interiors that await within. You find original floor tiles and ornate ceilings intact, but other than that it's a clean sweep: deep charcoal downstairs; pure white above. There's a sitting room with iPads in case you want to book a restaurant, an honesty bar, an espresso machine and lots of handy guide books. Upstairs, stylish, well-priced bedrooms wait. Some are big with claw-foot baths, others smaller with walk-in power showers. All come with comfy beds, bath robes, beautiful linen and contemporary Scottish art. The family suite (two rooms) has bunk beds and a PlayStation for kids. Delicious breakfasts are served in a conservatory overlooking the back garden, a memorable feast orchestrated by Paul, with lively conversation that travels the world. Majestic Edinburgh is yours to explore. *Minimum two nights at weekends.*

Price	£100–£145. Suites £125–£160. Singles from £80.
Rooms	6: 3 doubles, 2 suites, 1 family suite.
Meals	Restaurants within 0.5 miles.
Closed	2–15 January.
Directions	Sent on booking.

John MacEwan & Paul Lightfoot
94 Dalkeith Road,
Edinburgh EH16 5AF

Tel	+44 (0)131 662 9265
Email	stay@94dr.com
Web	www.94dr.com

The Peat Inn

The Peat Inn has been around for 300 years. It's a Scottish institution, a national treasure, and when it changes hands (very rarely), people take note. Geoffrey and Katherine took it on five years ago and have already made their mark: a Michelin star landed here in 2010. It is divided in two: restaurant and rooms, though the latter are suites, not rooms. You get wonderful beds dressed in crisp white linen, pretty colours that soak up the light, decanters of sherry, bowls of fruit, sofas from which to watch the telly. Not that you'll have time for that. You'll be over in the restaurant digging into some of the best food in Scotland. The scene is suitably theatrical: three rooms beautifully lit, tables spaced out generously. As for the food, ambrosial delights await: wild leek soup with a poached duck egg, roast rump of lamb with a red pepper compote, pavé of chocolate with pistachio. You can eat à la carte, try the menu du jour or feast on a six-course tasting menu (the cheese course is a soufflé!); all are brilliantly priced. As for the staff, you won't find better. St Andrews is close.

Price	£185–£195.
Rooms	8 suites.
Meals	Lunch from £19. Dinner: menu du jour £40; à la carte £55–£58. 6-course tasting menu £65 (or £115 with wine flights).
Closed	Rooms & restaurant closed Sun & Mon; also 24–26 Dec & 1 week in Jan.
Directions	From Edinburgh A90 north, then A92 for Dundee. Right onto A91 and into Cupar. There, B940 for Crail to inn.

Geoffrey & Katherine Smeddle
Peat Inn,
Cupar KY15 5LH

Tel	+44 (0)1334 840206
Email	stay@thepeatinn.co.uk
Web	www.thepeatinn.co.uk

15 Glasgow

This is a seriously smart Glasgow address – bang in the middle of town, yet beautifully insulated from it. The house, a Victorian gem, stands on an attractive square with communal gardens running through. Inside, the feel is distinctly contemporary, though you still get a pair of Corinthian pillars and the original mosaic entrance hall. Shane and Laura spent a year renovating; while technically you're in a B&B, these interiors are as good as any boutique hotel. Downstairs there's a vast sitting room with a couple of sofas in front of a fire; bedrooms upstairs are no less generous. Those at the back are large, the suites at the front are enormous. All come with huge beds, crisp white linen, handmade bedheads and robes in seriously fancy bathrooms. Suites have a few added extras: big sofas, beautiful windows, one has a double-ended bath overlooking the square. Breakfast is brought to you whenever you want. As for Glasgow, you'll find great restaurants close to home. Try Crab Shakk for serious seafood, then head to Ben Nevis for a wee dram; folk musicians play most nights.

Price	£120. Suites £150.
Rooms	5: 2 doubles, 1 twin/double, 2 suites.
Meals	Restaurants on your doorstep.
Closed	Never.
Directions	West into Glasgow on M8. Exit at junc. 18 for Charring X (outside lane), then double back at lights. 1st left, 1st left, 1st left (really). Follow square round to house.

Shane & Laura McKenzie
15 Woodside Place,
Glasgow G3 7QL
Tel   +44 (0)141 332 1263
Email   info@15glasgow.com
Web   www.15glasgow.com

The Lime Tree

The Lime Tree — a hotel/art gallery — is a Mackintosh manse. It dates to 1850, while the tree itself, sublime on the front lawn, was planted in 1700, the year the town was settled. Inside you find a small, stylish world — stripped floors in the hall, bold colours on the walls, open fires scattered around, beautiful windows for views of Loch Linnhe. David — a mountain guide who also paints — has a fabulous map room, but if you want to do more than walk, you've come to the right place; climbing, cragging, mountain biking, kayaking and diving can all be arranged. Airy bedrooms are lovely — oatmeal carpets, crisp white linen, good art and flat-screen TVs. You get neat little bathrooms, white walls to soak up the light and those at the front have watery views. Downstairs, drift through to the gallery and see what's on (when the Royal Geographical Society came, they had a full-scale copy of Ernest Shackleton's boat on the front lawn). There's a rustic bistro, too, the best place to eat in town, perhaps homemade soups, slow-cooked lamb, sticky toffee pudding. Ben Nevis is close.

Price	£80–£110. Singles from £60.
Rooms	9: 3 doubles, 1 twin, 5 family rooms.
Meals	Dinner £27.95–£29.95.
Closed	Rarely.
Directions	North to Fort William on A82. Hotel on right at 1st roundabout in town.

David Wilson
Achintore Road,
Fort William PH33 6RQ

Tel	+44 (0)1397 701806
Email	info@limetreefortwilliam.co.uk
Web	www.limetreefortwilliam.co.uk

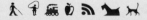

Kilcamb Lodge Hotel & Restaurant

A stupendous setting, with Loch Sunart at the end of the garden and Glas Bheinn rising beyond. As for Kilcamb, it has all the ingredients of the perfect country house: a smart drawing room with a roaring fire; an elegant dining room for excellent food; super-comfy bedrooms that don't shy from colour; views that feed the soul. The feel here is shipwreck-chic. There's a 12-acre garden with half a mile of shore, so stroll up to the water's edge and look for dolphins, otters and seals. Ducks and geese fly by, and if you're lucky you may see eagles. Back inside you'll find stained-glass windows on the landing, a ship's bell in the bar, flowers in the bedrooms. Dress up at eight for a three-course dinner and feast on scallops with cauliflower tempura, lamb with caramelised shallots, banana bavarois with rum and raisin ice cream. Bedrooms come in two styles: contemporary or traditional. Expect big beds, padded headboards, smart white towels and shiny bathrooms. Kind staff go the extra mile. Ardnamurchan Point – the most westerly point in mainland Britain – it at the end of the road. *Minimum two nights at weekends in May*

Price	Half-board £110–£180 p.p.
Rooms	10: 7 doubles, 3 suites.
Meals	Lunch from £8.50. Dinner included; non-residents, £49.50.
Closed	January. Limited opening Nov & Feb.
Directions	From Fort William A82 south for 10 miles to Corran ferry, then A861 to Strontian. Hotel west of village on left, signed. A830 & A861 from Fort William takes an hour longer.

David & Sally Ruthven-Fox
Strontian,
Acharacle PH36 4HY

Tel	+44 (0)1967 402257
Email	enquiries@kilcamblodge.co.uk
Web	www.kilcamblodge.co.uk

Doune

You arrive by boat – there's no road in – a ferry across to Knoydart, the last great wilderness in Britain. You'll find mountains, sea and beach – a thrilling landscape of boundless peace and ever-changing light. Guillemots race across the water, dolphins and seals come to play, the Sound of Sleat shoots across to Skye. As for Doune, it's a tiny community of happily shipwrecked souls, who rescued this land from ruin; Martin, Jane and Liz look after you with instinctive generosity. The dining room is the hub, pine-clad from top to toe, with a stove to keep you warm and a couple of fiddles for the odd ceilidh. The food is delicious – crab from the bay, roast lamb from the hill, chocolate tart with homemade ice cream. Bedrooms along the veranda are delightfully simple – pine clad with mezzanine bunks for children, hooks for clothes, armchairs for watching the weather; compact shower rooms sparkle. The walking is magnificent, boat trips can be arranged, the night sky will astound you. There's a lodge for groups, too. A very special place, miss it at your peril. *Boat pick-up Tues & Sat. Minimum stay three nights.*

Price	Full-board £80 p.p. (£480 per week). Lodge: full-board from £65 p.p. (£390 per week). Discounts for children.
Rooms	4 + 1: 2 doubles, 1 twin, all en suite (all with mezzanine beds for children). 1 single with separate shower. Catered lodge for 12 with shared washroom.
Meals	All meals included (packed lunches). Dinner, £30, for non-residents.
Closed	October-Easter.
Directions	Park in Mallaig; the boat will collect you at an agreed time.

Martin & Jane Davies
Knoydart,
Mallaig PH41 4PL

Tel	+44 (0)1687 462667
Email	martin@doune-knoydart.co.uk
Web	www.doune-knoydart.co.uk

Grants at Craigellachie

An old factor's house on the banks of Loch Duich with the Five Sisters of Kintail flaunting their beauty to the south; three are munros, views from the top are spectacular. This is a great base for Highland adventures with lots to do: Skye, Ben Nevis and Loch Ness are all within reach, while Dornie Castle (the one on the water you see on TV) is on the other side of the loch. After a morning dashing about, come home to this homespun restaurant with rooms. It's a tiny operation and Tony and Liz do everything themselves: cook, clean, polish and shine, chat to guests after delicious breakfasts, point you in the right direction. There are four rooms, two in the main house (small but sweet, warm colours, fine for a night), then two out back, decidedly swanky – neutral colours, lovely linen, robes in fancy bathrooms. One is a suite (with a small kitchen), both have a decked terrace. As for Tony's award-winning food, don't expect to go hungry. You might have hand-dived scallops with a vermouth cream, Rassay pork with a calvados jus, chocolate tart with a cappuccino sauce. *Wine tasting and food & wine-matching courses.*

Price	Half-board £80–£99.50 p.p. Suite £105–£120 p.p.
Rooms	4: 1 twin, 2 doubles, 1 suite.
Meals	Dinner included; non-residents, about £35. Not Sun or Mon.
Closed	December to mid-February.
Directions	A87 north from Invergarry to Shiel Bridge. Left in village for Glenleg. First right down to Loch Duich. On left in village.

Tony & Liz Taylor
Ratagan, Glenshiel,
Kyle IV40 8HP

Tel	+44 (0)1599 511331
Email	info@housebytheloch.co.uk
Web	www.housebytheloch.co.uk

Ullinish Country Lodge

This sparkling Georgian farmhouse stands on the magical west coast under a vast sky. Mighty views stretch across Loch Harport to the Cuillin mountains beyond. Samuel Johnson stayed on his famous tour, though you can bet your bottom dollar he didn't eat as well as you will. Pam and Brian came to add to Skye's gastronomic reputation and have done just that, serving up some of the best food on the island. Inside, warm interiors come with tartan carpets in the hall and leather sofas in front of the sitting-room fire. Bedrooms upstairs have huge mahogany beds, stately colours, silky crowns and watery views. You'll find claw-foot baths and flat-screen TVs, too. As for dinner, expect the best, perhaps Isle of Skye langoustine, fillet of Mallaig skate, then banana soufflé with warm chocolate sauce. Outside, the tidal island of Oronsay waits. Dolphins and whales pass by, sea eagles patrol the skies, there are standing stones and iron age remains. Finally, the famous Talisker distillery at Carbost stands on the far side of the loch, so drop in for a tour and a wee dram.

Price	£130–£170. Singles from £90. Half-board from £90–£125 p.p.
Rooms	6: 5 doubles, 1 twin.
Meals	Dinner, 4 courses, £49.50.
Closed	24 December to end of January.
Directions	North from Skye bridge on A87, then A863 for Dunvegan. Thro' Struan and signed left after 250m. House on right after 1 mile.

Brian & Pam Howard
Ullinish, Struan,
Isle of Skye IV56 8FD
Tel   +44 (0)1470 572214
Email   enquiries@ullinish-country-lodge.co.uk
Web   www.theisleofskye.co.uk

Greshornish House

On its own private peninsular, hidden away from the rest of Skye, this 18th-century country house stands in ten acres of peace directly above the sea. Outside, free-range chickens nip across the croquet lawn, while down at the loch seals and otters splash about in the water. As for the house, it's a great island base and Neil and Rosemary look after guests with infectious charm. Step inside and find a sofa'd bar that doubles as reception, an open fire crackling in the drawing room and a grand piano in the billiard room, where walls of books surround you. Upstairs, lovely big bedrooms have a smart homely feel. Two at the front have the view, all have warm colours, fresh flowers, usually a sofa. One is enormous, another has a claw-foot bath, two have fancy showers. Back downstairs, seriously tasty food waits in the dining room (candlelit tables, claret-red walls), so work up an appetite on one of Skye's mountains, then return for a feast, perhaps oak-smoked salmon, tomato and fennel soup, delicious guinea fowl in a bordelaise sauce, chocolate and hazelnut terrine. Wonderful. *Minimum stay two nights.*

Price	£130–£185. Singles from £95.
Rooms	6: 2 four-posters, 2 twins/doubles, 1 double, 1 family room.
Meals	Dinner £38–£45. Packed lunch £10.
Closed	November–March.
Directions	A87 through Portree, then west on A850 for Dunvegan. Signed right after 10 miles (1 mile west of Edinbane). 2.5 miles down single track road to hotel.

Neil & Rosemary Colquhoun
Edinbane, Portree,
Isle of Skye IV51 9PN

Tel	+44 (0)1470 582266
Email	info@greshornishhouse.com
Web	www.greshornishhouse.com

The Glenview

Small is beautiful at The Glenview. This delicious little restaurant with rooms started life in 1890 as a croft. Once the village shop, it has recently fallen into excellent hands. Simon and Kirsty are young and full of life, love Skye, have refurbished brilliantly. You find daffodils in the flower beds, logs in the porch, painted floorboards and maps on the wall. The style – a warm, rustic simplicity – fits the mood perfectly. The dining room doubles as an art gallery, you can roast away in front of the wood-burner in the sitting room, there are games to be played, books to be read, tales to be told. Rooms above the shop are excellent: warm and cosy (though not small) with smart carpets, fresh flowers and blond wood furniture. Then there's the food. Breakfasts promise seasonal fruits and organic Skye bacon, and Simon cooks a mean dinner – hand-dived scallops, roast Highland beef, chocolate fudge cake with homemade vanilla ice cream – so work up an appetite during the day. There's loads to see: the Old Man of Storr, the Kilt Rock waterfall, even dinosaur footprints on Staffin beach. A real treat.

Price	£85–£110. Singles from £75.
Rooms	5: 4 doubles, 1 twin.
Meals	Dinner £29–£35.
Closed	Sundays & Mondays. January & December.
Directions	North from Portree on A855. Signed on left in dip in village.

Simon & Kirsty Faulds
Culnacnoc,
Isle of Skye IV51 9JH

Tel	+44 (0)1470 562248
Email	enquiries@glenviewskye.co.uk
Web	www.glenviewskye.co.uk

Viewfield House Hotel

This old ancestral pile stands high above Portree Bay with fine views tumbling down to the Sound of Rassay below. Twenty acres of mature gardens and woodland wrap around you, with croquet on the lawn, paths that weave through pretty gardens and a hill to climb for 360° views of sea, ridge and peak. As for this Victorian factor's house, expect a few aristocratic fixtures and fittings: hunting trophies in the hall, cases filled with curios, a grand piano and open fire in the drawing room, Sanderson wallpaper in the dining room. Family oils hang on the walls, you'll find wood carvings from distant lands and a flurry of antiques, all of which blend grandeur with touches of humour. Upstairs is a warren of bedrooms. Most are big, some are vast, all come in country-house style with traditional fabrics, crisply laundered sheets and sea views from those at the front. Dive into Skye — wildlife, mountains, sea lochs and castles all wait. Suppers are on tap — salads, salmon, spotted dick; alternatively, dine out on Skye's natural larder. There's Highland porridge for breakfast, too.

Price	£110-£150. Singles £58-£75.
Rooms	11: 3 doubles, 3 twins/doubles, 2 twins, 2 singles, all en suite. 1 double with separate bath.
Meals	Supper £20-£25. Packed lunch £6.
Closed	Mid-October to Easter.
Directions	On A87, coming from south, driveway entrance on left just before the Portree filling station.

Hugh Macdonald
Viewfield Road, Portree,
Isle of Skye IV51 9EU

Tel	+44 (0)1478 612217
Email	info@viewfieldhouse.com
Web	www.viewfieldhouse.com

The Torridon

You're in the middle of nowhere, but you wouldn't be anywhere else. Mountains rise, red deer roam, sea eagles and otters patrol high and low. This 1887 shooting lodge was built for the Earl of Lovelace and stands in 58 acres that roll down to the shores of Upper Loch Torridon. Inside, sparkling interiors thrill: a huge fire in the panelled hall, a zodiac ceiling in the drawing room, 350 malts in the pitch pine bar. Huge windows pull in the view, while canny walkers pour off the hills to recover in luxury. Fabulous bedrooms are hard to fault, some big, others bigger. A super-smart contemporary style runs throughout: cool colours, padded headboards, exquisite linen, magnificent bathrooms; one has a shower in a turret. Outside, cattle graze in the fields, while the two-acre kitchen garden is a work of art in itself. It provides much for the table, so feast on fresh food sublimely cooked… pan-roasted monkfish, Highland beef with a red wine jus, apple tart tatin with butterscotch ice cream. You can scale Liathach or take to the sea in a kayak. Fantastic.

Price	£220–£455. Half-board from £160 p.p. Boathouse (self-catering) £875–£1,350 per week.
Rooms	18 + 1: 10 doubles, 2 twins, 2 four-posters, 4 suites. 1 boathouse for 4.
Meals	Lunch from £5.95. Dinner, 5 courses, £50.
Closed	January.
Directions	A9 to Inverness, A835 to Garve, A832 to Kinlochewe, A896 to Annat (not Torridon). Signed on south shore.

Daniel & Rohaise Rose-Bristow
Torridon,
Achnasheen IV22 2EY

Tel	+44 (0)1445 791242
Email	info@thetorridon.com
Web	www.thetorridon.com

Mackay's Rooms

This is the north-west corner of Britain and it's utterly magical: huge skies, sandy beaches, aquamarine seas, cliffs and caves. You drive – or cycle – for mile upon mile with mountains soaring into the heavens and ridges sliding into the sea. If you like big, remote landscapes, you'll love it here; what's more, you'll pretty much have it to yourself. Mackay's – they have the shop, the bunkhouse and the garage, too – is the only place to stay in town, its earthy colours mixing with stone walls, open fires and stripped floors to great effect. Bedrooms (some big, others smaller) are extremely comfy. They come with big wooden beds and crisp white linen, while Fiona, a textiles graduate, has a fine eye for fabrics and upholstery. You also get excellent bathrooms, iPod docks, flat-screen TVs and DVD players. Breakfast sets you up for the day – grilled grapefruit, whisky porridge, venison sausages, local eggs – so head east to the beach, west for great golf or catch the ferry across to Cape Wrath and scan the sea for whales. There's surfing for the brave and the beautiful.

Price	£135–£165. Singles from £110. Cottages £700–£1,400 per week.
Rooms	7 + 4: 6 doubles, 1 twin. 4 self-catering cottages for 2-6.
Meals	Lunch from £5. Dinner, 3 courses, £25–£30.
Closed	October-Easter. Cottages open all year.
Directions	A838 north from Rhiconich. After 19 miles enter Durness village. Mackay's is on right-hand side opposite memorial.

Fiona Mackay
Durine, Durness,
Lairg IV27 4PN

Tel	+44 (0)1971 511202
Email	stay@visitdurness.com
Web	www.visitdurness.com

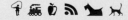

Culdearn House

Grantown is a great base for Highland flings. You can fish the Spey, jump on the whisky trail, check out a raft of castles, you can even ski in Aviemore. Loch Ness is close, as is Royal Deeside, there's golf everywhere and the walking is divine; in short, expect to be busy. As for Culdrean, it stands in a row of five identical houses that were built in 1860 by Lord Seafield, one for each of his daughters. These days it's a small, intimate hotel where William and Sonia look after guests with much kindness. There's an open fire and facing sofas in the pretty sitting room, panelled windows and a marble fireplace in the dining room, then a batch of smart homely bedrooms that offer the sort of comfort you'd want after a day in the hills. You get decanters of sherry, super beds, pretty furniture, excellent bathrooms. Back downstairs, William looks after a tempting wine list and 60 malts, while Sonia whisks up delicious four-course dinners... game terrine with poached pear marmalade, elderflower sorbet or mushroom soup, local lamb in a plum and port jus, dark chocolate torte. A treat.

Price	£130–£150. Singles from £65. Half-board £100–£135 p.p.
Rooms	6: 4 doubles, 1 twin/double, 1 twin.
Meals	Dinner, 4 courses, £38.50.
Closed	Never.
Directions	North into Grantown from A95. Left at 30 mph sign & house directly ahead.

Sonia & William Marshall
Woodlands Terrace,
Grantown on Spey PH26 3JU

Tel	+44 (0)1479 872106
Email	enquiries@culdearn.com
Web	www.culdearn.com

Dalmunzie House

Dalmunzie is quite some sight, an ancient hunting lodge lost to the world in one of Scotland's most dramatic landscapes. You're cradled by mountains in a vast valley; it's as good a spot as any to escape the world. Surprisingly, you're not that remote – Perth is a mere 30 miles south – but the sense of solitude is quite magnificent, as is the view. As for the hotel, you potter up a one-mile drive to find a small enclave of friendly Australians; Brianna searched high and low before striking gold at Dalmunzie. Interiors are just the ticket: warm, cosy and quietly grand. You find sofas in front of open fires, a smart restaurant for delicious food, a snug bar for a good malt, a breakfast room with a big view. Country-house bedrooms have colour and style. Some are grand, others simpler, several have ancient claw-foot baths. There's loads to do: fantastic walking, Royal Deeside, the Highland games at Braemar. As for the tricky golf course, it was laid out by Alister MacKenzie, who later designed Augusta National; the twelfth hole there is all but identical to the seventh here.

Price	£140–£240. Half board £85–£145 p.p.
Rooms	17: 3 tower rooms, 5 four-posters, 7 doubles, 1 twin, 1 family room.
Meals	Lunch from £4.50. Packed lunch £10. Dinner, 4 courses, £45.
Closed	December.
Directions	North from Blairgowrie on A93. Hotel signed left in Glenshee up one-mile drive.

Brianna Poole
Spittal O'Glenshee,
Blairgowrie PH10 7QG

Tel	+44 (0)1250 885224
Email	reservations@dalmunzie.com
Web	www.dalmunzie.com

Killiecrankie House Hotel

No Highland fling would be complete without a night at Killiecrankie. Henrietta runs the place with great charm and has spent the last five years pouring in love and money; now it shines. Outside, gardens galore: one for roses, another for vegetables and a fine herbaceous border. Further afield, you'll find much to please your eyes: Loch Tummel, Rannoch Moor and magnificent Glenshee, over which you tumble for the Highland Games at Braemar. Return to the indisputable comforts of a smart country hotel: tartan in the dining room, 52 malts at the bar, views at breakfast of red squirrels climbing garden trees. There's a snug sitting room where a fire burns in winter; in summer doors open onto the garden. Delightful bedrooms come in different shapes and sizes. All are smart with pretty linen, warm colours, chic fabrics and lovely views. Dinner is predictably delicious, perhaps pea and mint soup, Highland venison, sticky toffee pudding. There's porridge with cream and brown sugar for breakfast. Castles, hills and distilleries wait. A great wee place with staff who care.

Price	Half-board £115–£140 p.p.
Rooms	10: 3 doubles, 5 twins/doubles, 2 singles.
Meals	Lunch from £4.50. Dinner included; non-residents, £42.
Closed	January & February.
Directions	A9 north of Pitlochry, then B8079, signed Killiecrankie. Straight ahead for 2 miles. Hotel on right, signed.

Henrietta Fergusson
Killiecrankie,
Pitlochry PH16 5LG

Tel	+44 (0)1796 473220
Email	enquiries@killiecrankiehotel.co.uk
Web	www.killiecrankiehotel.co.uk

Craigatin House & Courtyard

Pitlochry – gateway to the Highlands – is a vibrant town. Castles and mountains, lochs and forests, skiing at Glenshee, a famous theatre festival: it's got it all. This handsome old doctor's house – now an attractive boutique B&B – is perfectly situated to explore. It stands peacefully in two acres of manicured gardens on the northern shores of town; good restaurants are a short stroll. The formality of a smart stone exterior gives way to warmly contemporary interiors, where beautiful windows flood rooms with light. There are shutters in the breakfast room, which overflows into an enormous conservatory where flames leap in a wood-burner and walls of glass open to the garden. Big uncluttered bedrooms – some in the main house, others in converted stables – are super value for money. Expect Farrow & Ball colours, comfy beds, crisp white linen, padded bedheads and pretty shower rooms. Breakfast offers the full cooked works and tempting alternatives: creamy omelettes with smoked haddock, apple pancakes with grilled bacon and maple syrup. You're on the Whisky Trail, too. *Minimum two nights at weekends.*

Price	£85–£95. Suite £112. Singles from £75.
Rooms	14: 11 doubles, 2 twins, 1 suite.
Meals	Restaurants within walking distance.
Closed	Christmas.
Directions	A9 north to Pitlochry. Take 1st turn-off for town, up main street, past shops and signed on left.

Martin & Andrea Anderson
165 Atholl Road,
Pitlochry PH16 5QL

Tel	+44 (0)1796 472478
Email	enquiries@craigatinhouse.co.uk
Web	www.craigatinhouse.co.uk

Torrdarach House

You're high on the hill with big views south and lovely gardens to enjoy them from. It's a little like an Indian hill station, the big house sitting in blissful peace with the bustle of town a short stroll below. Struan and Louise came south from the far north and renovated completely: new bedrooms, new bathrooms, new everything. The result is this very friendly, super stylish, generously priced B&B. Inside you find an iPad in the hall instead of newspapers, then an airy sitting room that looks the right way; there are comfy sofas, lovely art, a whisky bar and binoculars to scan the hills. Delightful bedrooms come in the same happy style: neutral colours, smart fabrics, textured wallpaper, tartan bedheads. You get blond oak furniture, cute leather armchairs, jugs of iced water and flat-screen TVs; shower rooms are excellent. Downstairs, the glass-walled breakfast room overlooks the garden. Here you feast on local eggs, Wester Ross salmon and Speyside bacon; the porridge comes with a splash of whisky. Good golf, fabulous walking and the famous festival theatre all wait.

Price	£85-£95. Singles £75. Min. 2 nights at weekends.
Rooms	6: 4 doubles, 2 twins/doubles.
Meals	Pubs/restaurants 200 yds.
Closed	December-February.
Directions	North to Pitlochry on A9. In town, up high street, past shops, then 1st right into Larchwood Road. Up hill, keep left, then right into Golf Course Road. On right.

Struan & Louise Lothian
Golf Course Road,
Pitlochry PH16 5AU
Tel   +44 (0)1796 472136
Email   info@torrdarach.co.uk
Web   www.torrdarach.co.uk

Royal Hotel

The Royal is lovely – softly grand, intimate and welcoming, a country house in the middle of town. Queen Victoria once stayed, hence the name. It stands on the river Earn – its eponymous loch glistens five miles up stream – but you're brilliantly placed to strike out in all directions: Loch Tay, Pitlochry, The Trossachs and Perth are close. Those who linger fare rather well. You get a wall of books in an elegant sitting room where two fires burn; newspapers hang on poles, logs tumble from wicker baskets, sofas and armchairs are impeccably upholstered. There's a grandfather clock in the hall, rugs to cover stripped floors in a country-house bar, then walls festooned with beautiful art. You can eat all over the place, in the bar, in the conservatory or at smartly dressed tables in the elegant dining room, perhaps asparagus spears with a poached egg, breast of duck with cabbage and bacon, rhubarb sponge with vanilla ice cream. Smart homely rooms have padded bedheads, crisp linen, mahogany dressers, gilt-framed mirrors. Bathrooms come with fluffy robes, one four poster has a log fire.

Price	£140. Four-poster £180. Singles from £85. Half-board £90–£110 p.p. Self-catering from £320 (low season 2 nights).
Rooms	11 + 1: 5 doubles, 3 twins, 3 four posters. Self-catering townhouse for 4.
Meals	Bar meals from £6.95. Dinner, 3 courses, £27.75.
Closed	Occasionally.
Directions	A9 north of Dunblane, A822 thro' Braco, left onto B827. Left for town centre, over bridge, hotel on square.

Teresa Milsom
Melville Square, Comrie,
Crieff PH6 2DN

Tel	+44 (0)1764 679200
Email	reception@royalhotel.co.uk
Web	www.royalhotel.co.uk

Barley Bree

A few miles north of Gleneagles, a super little restaurant with rooms that delivers what so many people want: stylish interiors, super food, excellent prices, a warm welcome. This is a small family-run affair. Fabrice is French and cooks sublimely, Alison, a Scot, looks after the wine. Their stage is Barley Bree — whisky soup to you and me — an 18th-century coaching inn that has recently had a facelift. Now a band of happy locals come for fabulous Scottish food cooked with predictable French flair, perhaps rabbit terrine with a wild garlic salad, fillet of halibut with spring onion mash, and cardamom cheesecake with chocolate ice cream. The restaurant, nicely rustic, has a fire that burns on both sides, while in summer you decant onto a terrace for lunch in the sun. Upstairs, six lovely rooms come in neutral colours. You get crisp linen and comfy beds, then underfloor heating in excellent little shower rooms. One room is big and has a claw-foot bath, all have a wee dram of whisky on the house. Head down to Gleneagles for a game of golf; the Ryder Cup comes through in 2014. *Ask about wedding receptions.*

Price	£105–£140. Singles from £70.
Rooms	6 twins/doubles.
Meals	Lunch from £5.50. Dinner, 3 courses, about £40. Not Mon or Tues.
Closed	One week in February, one week in October, Christmas & New Year.
Directions	A9 north from Dunblane, then A822 for Muthill. In village on left before church.

Fabrice & Alison Bouteloup
6 Willoughby Street, Muthill PH5 2AB

Tel	+44 (0)1764 681451
Email	info@barleybree.com
Web	www.barleybree.com

Creagan House at Strathyre

Creagan is a delight – a small, traditional restaurant with rooms run with great passion by Gordon and Cherry. At its heart is Gordon's delicious food, which draws a devoted crowd, perhaps escalope of monkfish with a five-spice sauce, local venison with a chestnut purée steamed butterscotch and pecan pudding. Food is local – meat and game from Perthshire, seafood from west-coast boats – and served on Skye pottery; some vegetables come from the garden. A snug sitting room doubles as a bar, where a good wine list and 50 malt whiskies wait; if you like a dram, you'll be in happy here. Bedrooms fit the bill: warm and comfy with smart carpets, pretty colours, flat-screen TVs, a sofa if there's room. Breakfast is a treat; where else can you sit in a baronial dining room and read about the iconography of the toast rack while waiting for your bacon and eggs? No airs and graces, just the sort of attention you only get in small owner-run places. Hens, woodpeckers and red squirrels live in the garden. There are hills to climb, boat trips on lochs, secure storage for bikes. Very dog friendly.

Price	£130–£150. Singles £75–£95.
Rooms	5: 1 four-poster, 3 doubles, 1 twin.
Meals	Dinner, 3 courses, £32.50–£37.
Closed	Wednesdays & Thursdays. February.
Directions	From Stirling A84 north through Callander to Strathyre. Hotel 0.25 miles north of village on right.

Gordon & Cherry Gunn
Callander FK18 8ND

Tel	+44 (0)1877 384638
Email	eatandstay@creaganhouse.co.uk
Web	www.creaganhouse.co.uk

Monachyle Mhor

Twenty-seven years of evolution has turned this 17th-century farmhouse into one of Scotland's coolest hotels. It's a family affair set in 2,000 acres of silence, with the Trossachs circling around you and Loch Voil shimming below. Dick farms, Melanie designs her magical rooms and Tom cooks some of the best food in Scotland. You're close to the end of the track with only the sheep and the birds to disturb you; lawns roll past a boules pitch towards the water. Step inside and find a slim restaurant behind a wall of glass, a small candlelit bar and an open fire in the sitting room. Bedrooms – most in a courtyard of converted stone outbuildings – are dreamy: big beds, crisp linen, cool colours, designer fabrics, hi-tech gadgets. Bathrooms can be out of this world: a deluge shower in a granite steam room, claw-foot baths that gaze upon the glen. Those in the main house are smaller, while suites in loft-house style are enormous. Walk, sail, fish, ride a bike through the forest. Dinner is five courses of unbridled heaven – with beef, lamb, pork and venison all off the farm. *Minimum two nights at weekends.*

Price	£195–£265. Singles from £176. Half-board from £147.50 p.p.
Rooms	14: 6 doubles, 6 twins, 1 suite, 1 family room.
Meals	Sunday lunch £32. Dinner £50.
Closed	January.
Directions	M9 junc. 11, then B824 and A84 north. Right for Balquhidder 6 miles north of Callander. 5 miles west along road & Loch Voil. Hotel on right, signed.

Tom Lewis
Balquhidder,
Lochearnhead FK19 8PQ

Tel	+44 (0)1877 384622
Email	monachyle@mhor.net
Web	www.mhor.net

Windlestraw Lodge

There are few better distractions in Scotland than following the river Tweed: fishing lines glisten in the sun, lambs bleat high on the hill, ospreys glide through the afternoon sky. This is the river which brought prosperity to Scotland, its mills a source of huge wealth in Victorian days. Windlestraw, a heavenly country house, stands in evidence; it was built as a wedding gift for a mill owner and sits on the side of a hill with timeless views down the valley. Outside, a copper beech shades the lawn; inside, a dazzling refurbishment elates. You get stripped floors, painted ceilings, roaring fires, a panelled dining room. Light pours in through windows at the front, gilt mirrors hang on walls, fat sofas encourage idleness. There are binoculars with which to scan the valley, a terrace for afternoon tea, a sitting room for a quiet snooze. Country-house bedrooms are sublime. An elegant contemporary style runs throughout, those at the front have lovely views, one has the coolest of bathrooms. Add to this Alan's fabulous food and you have a very special place. There's golf at Peebles. Not to be missed.

Price	£110–£190. Singles from £95. Half-board from £100 p.p.
Rooms	6: 5 doubles, 1 twin.
Meals	Lunch by arrangement. Dinner, 4 courses, £45. Supper, 3 courses, £30. Tasting menu £60.
Closed	Rarely.
Directions	East from Peebles on A72. Into Walkerburn; house signed left on western flank of town.

Julie & Alan Reid
Galashiels Road,
Walkerburn EH43 6AA

Tel	+44 (0)1896 870636
Email	reception@windlestraw.co.uk
Web	www.windlestraw.co.uk

Ballochneck

Donnie and Fiona's magical pile stands one mile up a private drive, soundproofed by 175 acres of lush Stirlingshire country. Swans nest on the lake in spring, which doubles as a curling pond in winter (you can), while Suffolk sheep graze the fields and deer come to eat the rhododendrons. The house – still a home, albeit a grand one – dates to 1863 and was built for the Lord Provost of Glasgow. Inside you get all the aristocratic works – roaring fires, painted panelling, magical windows that bring in the view, wonderfully ornate ceilings – but Donnie and Fiona are the real stars; expect a little banter, a few good stories and a trip to the top of the house where a full-size snooker tables stands amid purple walls. Vast bedrooms at the front have huge views, beautiful beds and acres of crisp linen; one has an open fire, while a claw-foot bath next door comes with candles and views down the valley. Breakfast is a feast, and served in summer in a magnificent Victorian conservatory amid beds of lavender and wandering clematis. Stirling Castle and Loch Lomond are close. *Children over 12 welcome. Min. two nights at weekends.*

Price	£145-£160. With interconnecting twin £215.
Rooms	3: 1 double, en suite bath. 1 double with separate bathroom. 1 interconnecting twin (let to same party only).
Meals	Dinner, 4 courses, £35.
Closed	November–March.
Directions	M9 junc. 10, A84 west, B8075 south, then A811 for Buchlyvie. In village, right onto B835 for Aberfoyle. Over bridge, up to lodge house 200 yds on left. 1 mile up drive to house.

Donnie & Fiona Allan
Buchlyvie,
Stirling FK8 3PA

Tel	+44 (0)1360 850216
Email	info@ballochneck.com
Web	www.ballochneck.com

Langass Lodge

Vast skies, water everywhere, golden beaches that stretch for miles. Nothing prepares you for the epic majesty of the Uists, a place so infinitely beautiful you wonder why you've got it to yourself. As for Langass, an old shooting lodge, it makes a great base, not least because Amanda and Niall know the island inside out and can help you discover its secrets. The hotel sits in ten silent acres with paths that lead up to standing stones or down to the water. Inside, cosy interiors fit the bill perfectly: a roaring fire in the bar; watery views in the restaurant; doors onto a terrace for drinks in summer. Bedrooms — warmly traditional in the main house, nicely contemporary in the new wing — are super value for money. Expect comfy beds, crisp white linen, excellent bathrooms, lots of colour. As for the food, it's the best on the island, with game off the estate and seafood plucked fresh from the sea. There's loads to do: kayaking, walking, wild fishing, bird watching. The night sky is magnificent, as are the Northern Lights. Children and dogs and very welcome. Don't miss it.

Price	£95–£145. Family rooms £120–£160. Singles from £65.
Rooms	11: 5 doubles, 4 twins/doubles, 2 family rooms.
Meals	Lunch from £5. Dinner in bar from £12.95; in restaurant £30–£36.
Closed	Never.
Directions	South from Lochmaddy on A867. Signed left after five miles.

Amanda & Niall Leveson Gower
Langass,
North Uist HS6 5HA

Tel	+44 (0)1876 580285
Email	langasslodge@btconnect.com
Web	www.langasslodge.co.uk

Tigh Dearg

This far-flung island chain is worth every second it takes to get here. Come for huge skies, sweeping beaches, carpets of wild flowers in the machair in summer, stone circles, ancient burial chambers, white-tailed eagles and fabulous Hebridean light. It's hard to overstate the sheer wonder of these bleakly beautiful islands, five of which are connected by a causeway, so drop south to Benbecula (*Whisky Galore* was filmed here) or Eriskay (for the Prince's Strand, where Bonnie Prince Charlie landed). Up on North Uist you'll find 1,000 lochs, so climb North Lees for wonderful watery views, then tumble back down to this island sanctuary. The house is a delight, immensely welcoming, full of colour, warmly contemporary, with windows that flood the place with light. Bedrooms come with suede headboards, power showers, bathrobes and beach towels, bowls of fruit and crisp white linen. In the restaurant find homemade soup, seafood pie, sticky toffee pudding. Walk, ride, fish, canoe, then return and try the sauna. Come in November for the northern lights. St Kilda is close for day tripping.

Price	£80–£145. Suite £160.
Rooms	9: 8 twins/doubles, 1 suite.
Meals	Bar meals from £8.50. Dinner, 3 courses, £25–£30.
Closed	Never.
Directions	North into Lochmaddy. Left, signed Police Station. Hotel on left after 200 yards.

Iain MacLeod
Lochmaddy,
North Uist HS6 5AE

Tel	+44 (0)1876 500700
Email	info@tighdearghotel.co.uk
Web	www.tighdearghotel.co.uk

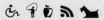

Scarista House

All you need to know is this: Harris is one of the most beautiful places in the world. Beaches of white sand that stretch for a mile or two are not uncommon. If you bump into another soul, it will be a delightful coincidence, but you should not count on it. The water is turquoise, coconuts sometimes wash up on the beach. The view from Scarista is simple and magnificent: field, ridge, beach, water, sky. Patricia and Tim are the kindest people, quietly inspiring. Their home is island heaven: coal fires, rugs on painted floors, books everywhere, old oak furniture, a first-floor drawing room and fabulous Harris light. Homely bedrooms come in country-house style. The golf club has left a set of clubs by the front door in case you wish to play (the view from the first tee is one of the best in the game). A corncrake occasionally visits the garden. There are walking sticks and Wellington boots to help you up the odd hill. Kind local staff may speak Gaelic and the food is exceptional, maybe quail with an armagnac mousse, fillet of Stornoway halibut, orange marmalade tart. A perfect place.

Price	£190–£240. Singles from £137.
Rooms	6: 4 doubles, 2 twins.
Meals	Dinner, 3 courses, £43. Packed lunch £7.50.
Closed	January & February.
Directions	From Tarbert A859 south, signed Rodel. Scarista 15 miles on left after golf course. W10 bus stops at gate.

Patricia & Tim Martin
Scarista,
Isle of Harris HS3 3HX

Tel	+44 (0)1859 550238
Email	timandpatricia@scaristahouse.com
Web	www.scaristahouse.com

Entry 307 Map 10

Wales

Ye Olde Bulls Head Inn

With 600 years of history under its belt, it's no surprise to learn that a host of luminaries have enjoyed the hospitality of Anglesey's most famous inn. Dr Johnson stayed, as did Dickens, while General Mytton took up residence when besieging Beaumaris' medieval castle. These days the past lives on – the front bar is little changed in a hundred years – but contemporary comforts abound, too. Beautiful fabrics decorate a gorgeous sitting room where you can roast away in front of the fire, while glass walls flood the brasserie with light. You can eat here informally (slow-cooked lamb, crumbed haddock and chips) or in the chic first-floor Loft Restaurant (no children under seven), where you dig into the best local food. Try crab cannelloni with vichyssoise mousse, Welsh beef with an onion purée, baked cinnamon croissant with pressed apple. Bedrooms in the main house come in country-house style. Some are lavish (regal colours, exposed beams, claw-foot baths), others simpler (warm florals, brass beds). Those in the Townhouse across the road have a contemporary feel: lots of colour, funky art, media hubs.

Price	£110-£165. Four-poster £135-£150. Suites £165-£180. Singles from £80.
Rooms	26: 7 doubles, 4 twins, 1 four-poster, 1 suite. Townhouse: 11 twins/doubles, 1 single, 1 suite.
Meals	Lunch & dinner in brasserie £5-£30. Dinner in restaurant, 3 courses, £45 (Tues-Sat evenings only).
Closed	Christmas.
Directions	A55 onto Anglesey, then A545 to Beaumaris. On left at far end of main street.

David Robertson
Castle Street,
Beaumaris LL58 8AP

Tel	+44 (0)1248 810329
Email	info@bullsheadinn.co.uk
Web	www.bullsheadinn.co.uk

Ty Mawr Country Hotel

Pretty rooms, attractive prices and delicious food make this super country house hard to resist. It's a very peaceful, tucked-away spot. You drive over the hills, drop into the village and wash up at this 16th-century stone house that glows in yellow. Outside, a sun-trapping terrace laps against a trim lawn, which in turn drops into a passing river. Gentle eccentricities abound: croquet hoops take the odd diversion, logs are piled high like giant beehives, a seat has been chiselled into a tree trunk. Inside, exposed stone walls, terracotta-tiled floors and low beamed ceilings give a warm country feel. There are fires everywhere – one in the sitting room, which overlooks the garden, another in the dining room that burns on both sides. Excellent bedrooms are all big. You get warm colours, big beds, crisp linen, good bathrooms. Some have sofas, all are dog-friendly, three overlook the garden. Back downstairs, the bar doubles as reception, and there's Welsh art on sale. Steve's cooking is the final treat: Cardigan Bay scallops, organic Welsh beef, calvados and cinnamon rice pudding. First class.

Price	£113–£128. Singles from £70. Half-board from £77.50 p.p.
Rooms	6: 4 doubles, 2 twins/doubles.
Meals	Dinner £24–£29.
Closed	Rarely.
Directions	M4 west onto A48, then B4310 exit, for National Botanic Gardens. 6 miles north to Brechfa. In village centre.

Annabel & Steve Thomas
Brechfa SA32 7RA

Tel	+44 (0)1267 202332
Email	info@wales-country-hotel.co.uk
Web	www.wales-country-hotel.co.uk

Penbontbren

You're lost in lovely hills, yet only three miles from the sea. Not that you're going to stray far. These gorgeous suites don't just have wonderful prices, they're also addictive – this is a great spot to come and do nothing at all. Richard and Huw have thought it all through. You get crockery and cutlery, kettles and fridges, you're also encouraged to bring your own wine and to nip up to the farm shop for provisions for lunch. As for the suites, they have big beds, super bathrooms, sofas and armchairs in cosy sitting areas, and doors onto semi-private terraces – perfect for lunches in summer. Potter about and find iPod docks, flat-screen TVs, robes and White Company lotions. Breakfast is served in the big house – the full Welsh works. Incredibly, this was a caravan park once, all trace of which has vanished; in its place, field and sky, birdsong and sheep. Beaches, hills, Cardigan and magical St David's all wait. Good local restaurants are on hand: lobster from the sea, lamb from the hills. A great place to unwind with discounts for longer stays. *Minimum two nights in high season.*

Price	£105–£120. Singles from £75. Cottage £700–£900 per week.
Rooms	5 + 1: 5 suites. 1 self-catering cottage for 7.
Meals	Restaurants within 3 miles.
Closed	Christmas.
Directions	Sent on booking.

Richard Morgan-Price & Huw Thomas
Glynarthen, Llandysul SA44 6PE

Tel	+44 (0)1239 810248
Email	contact@penbontbren.com
Web	www.penbontbren.com

Harbourmaster

The harbour at Aberaeron was created by an Act of Parliament in 1807. Shipbuilding flourished and the harbourmaster got his house on the quay with big views over Cardigan Bay. Step in to find that winning combination of seductive good looks, informal but attentive service and a menu overflowing with fresh local produce. The airy open-plan dining room/bar has stripped floors and a horseshoe bar for good beers and wines, with harbour views looming through the windows. Wind up the staircase to super little bedrooms that come with shuttered windows, loads of colour and quietly funky bathrooms. You get Frette linen, Welsh wool blankets and a hot water bottle on every bed in winter. There are flat-screen TVs and DVD players, watery views and tide books. Come down for supper and try fishcakes with lime mayonnaise, rack of lamb with dauphinoise potatoes, bara brith pudding or chocolate fondant. There are bikes to borrow, cycle tracks that spin off into the hills, coastal paths that lead north and south. Sunsets are fabulous, too.
Minimum two nights at weekends.

Price	£110–£195. Suites £150–£250. Singles £65. Half-board from £80 p.p.
Rooms	13: 9 doubles, 2 suites, 2 singles.
Meals	Lunch & bar meals from £9.50. Dinner from £16. Sunday lunch, 3 courses, £21.
Closed	Christmas Day.
Directions	A487 south from Aberystwyth. In Aberaeron right for the harbour. Hotel on waterfront.

Glyn & Menna Heulyn
Pen Cei,
Aberaeron SA46 0BT
Tel   +44 (0)1545 570755
Email info@harbour-master.com
Web   www.harbour-master.com

Nanteos Mansion

A fabulous old manor house lost at the end of a one-mile drive, with a small lake, a Georgian walled garden and 25 acres of ancient woodland. Outside, four pillars stand at the front door; inside, sofas wait by a wood-burner in the hall. The house dates to 1731, but stands on medieval foundations; it is most famous for the Nanteos Cup, thought to be the Holy Grail, which was carried here by monks from Glastonbury Abbey. A magnificent renovation has recently bought the house back to life – electric-shock therapy performed by interior designers. Downstairs, there's a morning room, a smart bar, then an irresistible restaurant where you dig into delicious food, perhaps mackerel with a rhubarb compote, slow-roasted pork with a toffee apple sauce, dark chocolate mousse with white chocolate ice cream. Bedrooms are dreamy: cool colours, fabulous bathrooms, lovely beds, wonderful art; the bridal suite is divine. There's loads to do: rivers to fish, mountains to climb, coastal paths to follow. Don't miss the music room (Wagner may have visited). You can self-cater in a cool mews house, too. Brilliant.

Price	£150–£220. Singles from £90. Half-board from £110 p.p.
Rooms	14 + 1: 14 twins/doubles. 1 four-bed mews house.
Meals	Lunch from £7.50. Dinner £29.95–£37.50. Sunday lunch from £19.95.
Closed	Rarely.
Directions	Leaving Aberystwyth to the south, take A4120 Devil's Bridge Road, then immediately right onto B4340. House signed left after 1 mile.

	Mark Rawlings-Lloyld Rhydyfelin, Aberystwyth SY23 4LU
Tel	+44 (0)1970 600522
Email	info@nanteos.com
Web	www.nanteos.com

Escape Boutique B&B

A super-cool boutique B&B with fabulous rooms, attractive prices and some seriously lovely bathrooms. The house stands high on the hill, away from the crowds, a short stroll from the buzz of town and its two-mile sandy beach. This is a 19th-century mill owner's villa and its fine old windows, sparkling wood floors and enormous carved fireplace bear testament to Victorian roots. Other than that it's a clean sweep of funky interiors. Sam and Gaenor scoured Europe for the eclectic collection of colourful retro furniture that fills the rooms – orange swivel chairs, iconic G-plan sofas, beautiful beds wrapped in crisp white linen. Urban Cool, Retro Red, Modern Romance... take your pick. All come with flat-screen TVs, Blu-ray DVD players and iPod docks. Bathrooms are excellent: one room has a magnificent shower for two, another has a copper bath in the room. Downstairs, there's an honesty bar and a fire in the sitting room, while delicious breakfasts are served in the attractive dining room. Excellent restaurants wait in town: try Osborne's for a little glamour or the Seahorse for great fish.

Price	£89–£140. Singles from £74. Minimum 2 nights at weekends.
Rooms	9: 8 doubles, 1 twin/double.
Meals	Restaurants within walking distance.
Closed	Christmas.
Directions	A55 junc. 19, then A470 for Llandudno. On promenade, head west hugging the coast, then left at Belmont Hotel and house on right.

Sam Nayar & Gaenor Loftus
48 Church Walks,
Llandudno LL30 2HL

Tel	+44 (0)1492 877776
Email	info@escapebandb.co.uk
Web	www.escapebandb.co.uk

Pentre Mawr Country House

The setting is beautiful, 190 acres of deep country at the end of a lane. The house isn't bad either. This is an old estate, which fell into ruin 80 years ago. It has been in Graham's family for 400 years and he and Bre have done a fine job renovating the place. Outside, a lawn runs down to fields, Doric columns flank the front door. Inside is half B&B (informal, personal, very welcoming), half hotel (smart rooms, attentive service, a menu in the restaurant). Wander about and find a couple of sitting rooms, open fires, vast flagstones, a bust of Robert Napier. Bedrooms are scattered about. Big rooms in the main house have a country-house feel and spa baths for two; stylish suites in the gardener's cottage have hot tubs on private terraces; super-cool safari lodges in the garden flaunt faux leopard-skin throws and fabulous bathrooms. There's a sun-trapping courtyard with a small pool, tennis on the grass, a kitchen garden that's being teased back to life. And Bre cooks a fine dinner, perhaps smoked salmon, rack of lamb, bread and butter pudding. *Min. two nights in hot-tub suites & at weekends.*

Price	£150. Suites £220. Lodges £200. Half-board £100–£140 p.p. (obligatory Friday & Saturday).
Rooms	8: 3 doubles. Gardener's Cottage: 2 suites. Garden: 3 canvas lodges.
Meals	Dinner, 5 courses, £35.
Closed	Christmas.
Directions	A55, then A525 south to Denbigh. Left at second roundabout to Llandyrnog, then left at mini-roundabout onto B5429. 1st left; signed left after 0.5 mile.

Graham & Bre Carrington-Sykes
Llandyrnog,
Denbigh LL16 4LA

Tel	+44 (0)1824 790732
Email	info@pentremawrcountryhouse.co.uk
Web	www.pentremawrcountryhouse.co.uk

The Hand at Llanarmon

Single-track lanes plunge you into the middle of nowhere. All around, lush valleys rise and fall, so pull on your boots and scale a mountain or find a river and jump into a canoe. Back at The Hand, a 16th-century drovers' inn, the pleasures of a traditional country local are hard to miss. A coal fire burns on the range in reception, a wood fire crackles under brass in the front bar and a wood-burner warms the lofty dining room. Expect exposed stone walls, low beamed ceilings, old pine settles and candles on the mantelpiece. There's a games room for darts and pool, a quiet sitting room for maps and books. Delicious food is popular with locals, so grab a table and enjoy seasonal menus – perhaps game broth, lamb casserole, then sticky toffee pudding. Bedrooms are just as they should be: not too fancy, cosy and warm, spotlessly clean with crisp white linen and good bathrooms. A very friendly place. Martin and Gaynor are full of quiet enthusiasm and have made their home warmly welcoming. John Ceiriog Hughes, who wrote "Bread of Heaven", lived in this valley. Special indeed.

Price	£90–£125. Singles from £52.50.
Rooms	13: 8 doubles, 4 twins, 1 suite.
Meals	Lunch from £6. Sunday lunch £20. Dinner £12–£20.
Closed	Rarely.
Directions	Leave A5 south of Chirk for B4500. Llanarmon 11 miles on.

Gaynor & Martin De Luchi
Llanarmon Dyffryn Ceiriog,
Llangollen LL20 7LD

Tel	+44 (0)1691 600666
Email	reception@thehandhotel.co.uk
Web	www.thehandhotel.co.uk

Plas Dinas Country House

This is the family home of Lord Snowdon. It dates to the 1600s and stands in 15 acres with an avenue of oak that sweeps you up to the house. Princess Margaret stayed often and much of what fills the house belongs to the family: stunning chandeliers, oils by the score, gilt-framed mirrors – an Aladdin's cave of beautiful things. There's a baby grand piano in the sitting room, where you find smart wood floors, an honesty bar and a fire that roars, but potter about the house and find masses of memorabilia framed on the walls (make sure you visit the private dining room). Bedrooms are quite something, the past mixing gracefully with modern design. Nothing is left to chance, a constant programme of refurbishment sees to that. You get four-posters, classic colours, sumptuous fabrics, a sofa if there's room. Bathrooms are excellent, some with showers, others with free-standing baths. Back downstairs Andy's cooking hits the spot, perhaps smoked salmon mousse, lamb shank with mint and rosemary, then Baileys crème brûlée. Snowdon is close, as you'd expect.

Price	£129-£275. Singles from £99. Min. 2 nights on bank holiday weekends.
Rooms	9: 4 doubles, 3 twins/doubles, 2 four-posters.
Meals	Dinner, 3 courses, £26-£30.
Closed	22 December-2 January.
Directions	South from Caernarfon on A487. Through Bontnewydd and signed right after half a mile at brow of shallow hill.

Andy & Julian Banner-Price
Bontnewydd,
Caernarfon LL54 7YF

Tel	+44 (0)1286 830214
Email	info@plasdinas.co.uk
Web	www.plasdinas.co.uk

Plas Bodegroes

Close to the end of the world and worth every second it takes to get here. Chris and Gunna are inspirational, their home a temple of cool elegance, the food possibly the best in Wales. Fronted by an avenue of 200-year-old beech trees, this Georgian manor house is wrapped in climbing roses and wildly roaming wisteria. The veranda circles the house, as do long French windows that lighten every room, so open one up, pull up a chair and listen to birdsong. Not a formal place – come to relax and be yourself. Bedrooms are wonderful, the courtyard rooms especially good, where exposed wooden ceilings give the feel of a smart Scandinavian forest hideaway. Best of all is the dining room, almost a work of art in itself, cool and crisp with exceptional art on the walls – a great place to eat Chris's ambrosial food; try sea trout wrapped in Carmarthen ham, mountain lamb with rosemary jus, baked vanilla cheesecake with passion fruit sorbet. Don't miss the Lleyn Peninsula: sandy beaches, towering cliffs and country walks all wait. Snowdon and Portmeirion are close too.

Price	£130–£180.
Rooms	10: 8 doubles, 1 twin, 1 four-poster.
Meals	Sunday lunch £22.50. Dinner £45. Not Sun or Mon evenings.
Closed	December–February & Sunday & Monday throughout year.
Directions	From Pwllheli A497 towards Nefyn. House on left after 1 mile, signed.

Chris & Gunna Chown
Efailnewydd,
Pwllheli LL53 5TH

Tel	+44 (0)1758 612363
Email	gunna@bodegroes.co.uk
Web	www.bodegroes.co.uk

Y Meirionnydd

By day you explore the mighty wonders of Snowdonia, by night you return to this lovely small hotel and recover in style. It's one of those places that delivers just what you want; it's smart without being posh, the welcome is second to none, there's great food and the bedrooms are fantastic. You're in the middle of a small country town with a terrace at the front, so sit outside in summer and watch the world pass by. Inside, soft colours and warm lighting create a mellow feel. There's a cute bar with armchairs and games, an airy breakfast room for the full Welsh works, then a smart restaurant cut into the rock, which was once the county jail; the food is somewhat better than it was then, perhaps venison pâté with hot chillies, fillet of salmon with lime and ginger, fresh fruit crumble with lashings of cream. Bedrooms upstairs are gorgeous. Some are bigger than others, but all have the same style: clean lines, cool colours, huge beds, beautiful linen. You get the odd stone wall, an armchair if there's room, then super bathrooms. There's secure storage for bikes, too.

Price	£85–£125. Singles from £59. Min. 2 nights at weekends.
Rooms	5: 3 doubles, 2 twins/doubles.
Meals	Dinner, 3 courses, £25. Not Sundays (or Wed/Thurs off season).
Closed	One week at Christmas.
Directions	In centre of town on one-way system, off A470.

Marc Russell & Nick Banda
Smithfield Square,
Dolgellau LL40 1ES

Tel	+44 (0)1341 422554
Email	info@themeirionnydd.com
Web	www.themeirionnydd.com

Ffynnon

A seriously indulging boutique B&B hidden away in the backstreets of this old market town. By day, you try valiantly to leave your luxurious room to explore the majesty of North Wales (many fail). Cycle tracks lead over forested hills, white beaches stretch for miles, there are rivers to ride, castles to visit, even Snowdon to climb. If you fail to budge, make do with luxury. The exterior of this former rectory may be a touch stern, but interiors sparkle with abandon. You find open fires, Farrow & Ball colours, fancy chandeliers and rugs on stripped floors. Breakfast is served in an elegant dining room, there's an honesty bar in the airy sitting room and doors fly open in summer to a lawned garden complete with standing stone. Bedrooms upstairs are magnificent, those at the front have views over the town. Expect laundered linen on beautiful beds, high ceilings and elegant fabrics, flat-screen TVs, DVD players and iPod docks. Faultless bathrooms are somewhat addictive, so expect to go home smelling of roses. Kids are very welcome, good restaurants wait in town, Steve and Debra couldn't be nicer. Don't miss it.

Price	£145–£200. Singles from £100.
Rooms	6: 3 doubles, 1 twin/double, 2 suites.
Meals	Restaurants within walking distance.
Closed	Christmas.
Directions	Leave A470 for Dolgellau, over bridge, into town. At T-junction, right then 1st left. Straight across Springfield Road & 2nd right into Bryn Teg. Entrance at end of road.

Debra Harris & Steve Holt
Love Lane, Brynffynnon,
Dolgellau LL40 1RR

Tel   +44 (0)1341 421774
Email   info@ffynnontownhouse.com
Web   www.ffynnontownhouse.com

Penmaenuchaf Hall

The gardens are amazing – woodlands strewn with daffodils in spring, topiary on the upper lawn, a walled garden of tumbling colour. The position high on the hill is equally sublime, with the Mawdacch estuary carving imperiously through the valley below. The house has attitude, too – built in 1865 for a Bolton cotton merchant. The smell of woodsmoke greets you at the front door. Step inside to find an open fire crackling in the half-panelled hall, where armchairs take the strain. The drawing room is even better with mullioned windows to frame the view, a grand piano and cavernous sofas, country rugs on original wood floors. Steps illuminated by fairy lights lead up to the airy conservatory/dining room, where French windows open onto to a terrace for al fresco dining in good weather. Bedrooms come in traditional country-house style with a warm contemporary feel, ornamental fireplaces, padded window seats and comfy beds. Some rooms are huge, several have balconies, all have bathrooms that are more than adequate. There are 13 miles of river to fish, while Snowdon, Bala and Portmeirion are close.

Price	£170–£260. Singles from £115.
Rooms	14: 7 doubles, 5 twins/doubles, 1 four-poster, 1 family room.
Meals	Lunch from £6. Afternoon tea from £7.90. Dinner, 3 courses, £42.50.
Closed	Rarely.
Directions	From Dolgellau A493 west for about 1.5 miles. Entrance on left.

Mark Watson & Lorraine Fielding
Penmaenpool,
Dolgellau LL40 1YB
Tel   +44 (0)1341 422129
Email   relax@penhall.co.uk
Web   www.penhall.co.uk

The Bell at Skenfrith

The position here is magical: an ancient stone bridge, a magnificent valley, glorious hills rising behind, cows grazing in lush fields. It's a perfect spot, not least because providence has blessed it with this sublime inn, where crisply designed interiors ooze country chic. In summer doors fly open and life spills onto a stone terrace, where views of hill and wood are interrupted only by the odd chef pottering off to a productive and organic kitchen garden. Back inside, airy rooms come with slate floors, open fires and plump-cushioned armchairs in the locals' bar, but the emphasis is firmly on the food, with a very happy kitchen turning out delicious fare, perhaps seared scallops with cauliflower purée, heather-roasted venison with chestnut gnocchi, marmalade soufflé with whisky ice cream. Country-house bedrooms are as good as you'd expect: uncluttered and elegant, brimming with light, some beamed, others overlooking the river, all with fabulous bathrooms. Idyllic circular walks sweep you through blissful country. Don't miss it. *Minimum two nights at weekends.*

Price	£110–£170. Four-posters £195–£220. Singles from £75.
Rooms	11: 6 doubles, 2 twins, 3 four-posters.
Meals	Lunch from £18. Sunday lunch from £22. Dinner, 3 courses, around £35.
Closed	Last week in January & 1st week in February.
Directions	From Monmouth B4233 to Rockfield; B4347 north for 5 miles; right on B4521; Skenfrith 1 mile.

William & Janet Hutchings
Skenfrith,
Abergavenny NP7 8UH

Tel	+44 (0)1600 750235
Email	enquiries@skenfrith.co.uk
Web	www.skenfrith.co.uk

Penally Abbey

A fabulous position up on the hill with a ridge of sycamore and ash towering above and huge views of Carmarthen Bay to the front. Caldy Island lies to the east, the road ends at the village green, a quick stride across the golf course leads to the beach. Up at the house, a fine arched window by the grand piano frames the view perfectly, so sink into a chesterfield in front of the fire and gaze out to sea. The house dates to 1790 and was once an abbey; you'll also find St Deiniol's, a ruined 13th-century church that's lit up at night. Sprawling lawns are yours to roam, bluebells carpet the wood in May. Bedrooms are all different: grand four-posters and wild flock wallpaper in the main house; a simpler cottage feel in the coach house; warm contemporary luxury in St Deiniol's Lodge. Steve's gentle, unflappable manner is infectious and hugely relaxing; don't expect to feel rushed. Eileen cooks in the French style, much of it picked up in the kitchen of a château many years ago; her Tenby sea bass is exquisite. The Pembrokeshire coastal path passes by outside – don't miss it. *Minimum two nights at weekends.*

Price	£148–£225. Singles from £138. Half-board from £97 p.p.
Rooms	17: Coach house: 4 doubles. Lodge: 5 twins/doubles. Main house: 6 doubles, 1 twin, all en suite. 1 double with separate bath.
Meals	Lunch by arrangement. Dinner, 3 courses, £36.50.
Closed	Never.
Directions	From Tenby A4139 for Pembroke. Right into Penally after 1.5 miles. Hotel signed above village green. Train station 5-min walk.

Steve & Elleen Warren
Penally,
Tenby SA70 7PY
Tel   +44 (0)1834 843033
Email info@penally-abbey.com
Web   www.penally-abbey.com

Stackpole Inn

This friendly inn is hard to fault. It sits in a quiet village drenched in honeysuckle with a fine garden at the front, a perfect spot for a drop of Welsh ale in summer. Wander further afield and you come to the sea at Barafundle Bay – a Pembrokeshire glory – where you can pick up the coastal path and follow it west past Stackpole Head to St Gorvan's Chapel. Stride back up to the inn and find interiors worthy of a country pub. There are smart red carpets, whitewashed walls, a hard-working wood-burner and obligatory beamed ceilings. Locals and visitors mingle in harmony, there are four hand pumps at the slate bar and tasty rustic cooking in the restaurant, perhaps deep-fried whitebait, rack of lamb, fresh raspberry brûlée. Super bedrooms are tremendous value for money and quietly positioned in a converted outbuilding. Two have sofabeds, two have velux windows for star gazing. All come in seaside colours with tongue-and-groove panelling, stripped floors, comfy beds, crisp linen and excellent bathrooms. Don't miss Pembroke Castle or the beach at Freshwater West.

Price	£90. Singles from £60.
Rooms	4: 2 twins/doubles, 2 family rooms.
Meals	Lunch from £5. Dinner, 3 courses, £25–£30 (not Sun Oct-Mar). Sunday lunch, 3 courses, £17.95.
Closed	Rarely.
Directions	B4319 south of Pembroke for 3 miles, then left for Stackpole. Through Stackpole Cheriton, up hill, right at T-junction. On right.

Gary & Becky Evans
Stackpole,
Pembroke SA71 5DF

Tel	+44 (0)1646 672324
Email	info@stackpoleinn.co.uk
Web	www.stackpoleinn.co.uk

The Grove at Narberth

In the last couple of years the Grove has emerged as one of the loveliest places to stay in Wales – a cool country-house hotel with one foot in its Georgian past and the other in the contemporary present. It stands lost in Pembrokeshire's beautiful hills with big views to the front and a vast kitchen garden that provides much for the table. Inside, exquisitely refurbished Arts & Crafts interiors come as standard – an explosion of wood in the entrance hall, a roaring fire in the drawing-room bar, and a smart restaurant for some of the best food in Wales, perhaps home-smoked salmon, local beef, pecan pie with roasted figs. Gorgeous bedrooms are split between the main house and converted outbuildings. All are divine, some are just bigger than others. Expect beautiful fabrics, cool wallpaper, crisp white linen and super-comfy beds. Bathrooms are equally spoiling with robes and heated floors. There's a parterre garden for lunch in summer and Wellington boots for those who want to walk; the coastal path is close. Don't miss Narberth, a pretty country town full of lovely shops. *Minimum two nights at weekends.*

Price	£150–£210. Suites £220–£290. Singles from £140. Half-board from £120 p.p.
Rooms	20: 17 doubles, 3 suites.
Meals	Lunch from £15. Dinner, 3 courses, £45.
Closed	Never.
Directions	M4, then A48 & A40 west towards Haverfordwest. At A470 roundabout, take 1st exit to Narberth. Through town, down hill, then follow brown signs to hotel.

Neil Kedward & Zoe Agar
Molleston,
Narberth SA67 8BX

Tel   +44 (0)1834 860915
Email   info@thegrove-narberth.co.uk
Web   www.thegrove-narberth.co.uk

Entry 324   Map 1

Crug Glas

If you've never been to St David's, know this: it is one of the most magical places in Britain. It sits in Pembroke's national park, has an imperious 12th-century cathedral, and is surrounded by magnificent coastline that's dotted with cliffs and vast sandy beaches. As for Janet's country retreat, it's part chic hotel, part farmhouse B&B: stylish but personal, a great place to stay. The house dates from 1120 and sits in 600 acres of arable and grazing land (they run cattle, grow cereals). Outside, you find lawns and a small copse sprinkled with bluebells, then field and sky, and that's about it. Inside, there's an honesty bar in the sitting room and a Welsh dresser in the dining room, where Janet serves delicious food: homemade soups, home-reared beef, ginger sponge with vanilla ice cream. Bedrooms are the big surprise: a vast four-poster, a copper bath, old armoires, beautiful fabrics. All have robes in fancy bathrooms, while one room occupies much of the top floor. Two beautiful suites in an old barn have exposed timbers and underfloor heating. The coast is close.

Price	£115–£150. Suites £170–£185. Singles from £90.
Rooms	7: 3 doubles, 1 twin/double, 1 suite. Barn: 2 suites.
Meals	Sunday lunch, £22, by arrangement. Dinner, 3 courses, £25–£30.
Closed	24-27 December.
Directions	South from Fishguard on A487. Through Croes goch, then signed right after 2 miles.

Janet & Perkin Evans
Solva,
Haverfordwest SA62 6XX
Tel   +44 (0)1348 831302
Email   janet@crugglas.plus.com
Web   www.crug-glas.co.uk

Cnapan Restaurant & Hotel

Cnapan is a way of life – a family affair with two generations at work in harmony. Judith excels in the kitchen, Michael looks after the bar and son Oliver has returned to the fold to assist them both. It is a very friendly place that ticks to its own beat with locals popping in to book tables and guests chatting in the bar before dinner. As for the house, it's warm, cosy and traditionally home-spun – whitewashed stone walls and old pine settles in the dining room; comfy sofas and a wood-burner in the sitting room; a tiny telly in the bar for the odd game of rugby (the game of cnapan, rugby's precursor, originated in the town). There are maps for walkers, bird books, flower books, the daily papers, too. Spill into the garden in summer for pre-dinner drinks under the weeping willow, then slip back in for Judith's delicious food, perhaps spicy seafood chowder, roast duck with a clementine sauce, honey ice cream. Comfy bedrooms, warmly simple with modest bathrooms, are good value for money. You're in the Pembrokeshire National Park; beaches and cliff-top coastal walks beckon. *Minimum two nights at weekends.*

Price	£90. Singles from £60.
Rooms	5: 1 double, 3 twins, 1 family room. Extra bath available.
Meals	Dinner £25–£30. Not Tuesday evening Easter to October.
Closed	Christmas, January & February.
Directions	From Cardigan A487 to Newport. 1st pink house on right, 300yds into Newport.

Michael, Judith & Oliver Cooper
East Street,
Newport SA42 0SY

Tel	+44 (0)1239 820575
Email	enquiry@cnapan.co.uk
Web	www.cnapan.co.uk

Llys Meddyg

This fabulous restaurant with rooms has a bit of everything: cool rooms that pack a designer punch, super food in a sparkling restaurant, a cellar bar for drinks before dinner, a fabulous garden for summer treats. It's a very friendly place with charming staff on hand to help, and it draws in a local crowd who come for the seriously good food, perhaps mussel and saffron soup, rib of Welsh beef with hand-cut chips, cherry soufflé with pistachio ice cream. You eat in style with a fire burning at one end of the restaurant and good art hanging on the walls. Excellent bedrooms are split between the main house (decidedly funky) and the mews behind (away from the road). All have the same fresh style: Farrow & Ball colours, good art, oak beds, fancy bathrooms with fluffy robes. Best of all is the back garden with a mountain-fed stream pouring past. In summer, a café/bistro opens up out here — coffee and cake or steak and chips — with doors that open onto the garden. Don't miss Pembrokeshire's fabulous coastal path for its windswept cliffs, sandy beaches and secluded coves.

Price	£100–£180. Singles from £85.
Rooms	9: 4 doubles, 4 twins/doubles, 1 suite.
Meals	Lunch from £7. Dinner £33.
Closed	Rarely.
Directions	East from Fishguard on A487. On left in Newport towards eastern edge of town.

Louise & Edward Sykes
East Street,
Newport SA42 0SY

Tel	+44 (0)1239 820008
Email	info@llysmeddyg.com
Web	www.llysmeddyg.com

Gliffaes Hotel

A charming country house that stands above the river Usk as it pours through the valley below. In summer, doors in the sitting-room bar open onto a large terrace, where you can sit in the sun and take in the view – red kite circling above the water, sheep grazing majestic hills. You're in 35 acres of formal lawns and mature woodland – expect nothing but peace. Inside, interiors pack a punch. Afternoon tea is laid out in a sitting room of panelled walls and family portraits, while logs crackle in a grand fireplace. This is a fishing hotel, one of the best, and fishermen often gather in the bar for tall tales and a quick drink at the end of the day. Eventually, they spin through to the restaurant and dig into seasonal food (the hotel is part of the Slow Food Movement) – perhaps goats cheese soufflé, lemon sole, plum and cherry crumble. Bedrooms above all come in country-house style with smart fabrics and carpets, all mod cons, a sofa if there's room; others are in the coach house annexe. Several have river views, a couple have small balconies, one has a claw-foot bath that overlooks the front lawn.

Price	£108–£255. Singles from £96. Half-board from £90 p.p. Minimum 2 nights at weekends.
Rooms	23: 5 doubles, 14 twins/doubles, 4 singles.
Meals	Light lunches from £5. Sunday lunch £22–£29. Dinner, 3 courses, £40.
Closed	January.
Directions	From Crickhowell, A40 west for 2.5 miles. Signed left and on left after 1 mile.

James & Susie Suter
Gliffaes Road,
Crickhowell NP8 1RH

Tel	+44 (0)1874 730371
Email	calls@gliffaeshotel.com
Web	www.gliffaeshotel.com

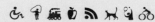

Peterstone Court

Sheep graze in fields to the front, a swimming pool shimmers by an 11th-century church, a sun-trapping dining terrace overlooks the river Usk, you can walk straight into sublime country. The house dates back to 1750 and is just as good. You'll find a panelled sitting room with an open fire, a cute little spa in the vaulted cellars, a brasserie/bar that overlooks the garden with stunning views across the river to the mountains beyond. Bedrooms mix country-house style with contemporary colours. Rooms in the old stables reach over two floors and have a smart-rustic feel. Those in the main house have grander dimensions, some with high-ceilings and four-poster beds, others with leather headboards and cavernous sofas; all have fine views. Downstairs, much of the food in the restaurant is reared on the hotel's farm eight miles up the road (free-range chicken, Aylesbury duck, mountain lamb, succulent pork), so dig into pressed ham hock with homemade piccalilli, roast duck with a shallot and thyme tart, rhubarb and ginger mousse. Brecon is close, mountains wait. *Minimum two nights at weekends.*

Price	£110-£220. Singles from £90. Half-board from £85 p.p.
Rooms	12: 3 doubles, 5 twins/doubles, 2 family rooms, 2 suites.
Meals	Lunch from £5.50. Dinner, 3 courses, £25-£30.
Closed	One week in January.
Directions	A40 west from Abergavenny for Brecon. Peterstone Court signed on left, two miles east of Brecon.

Sean Gerrard & Glyn & Jessica Bridgeman
Llanhamlach, Brecon LD3 7YB

Tel	+44 (0)1874 665387
Email	info@peterstone-court.com
Web	www.peterstone-court.com

Entry 329   Map 2

The Felin Fach Griffin

It's quirky, homespun, utterly intoxicating and thrives on a mix of relaxed informality and colourful style. The timber-framed bar resembles the sitting room of a small hip country house, with sofas in front of a fire that burns on both sides and backgammon waiting to be played. Painted stone walls throughout come in blocks of colour. An open-plan feel sweeps you through to the restaurant, where stock pots simmer on an Aga; try hake fillet with pernod cream, pheasant rillette, Eve's pudding with cinnamon custard, all of it delicious. Bedrooms above are warmly simple with comfy beds wrapped in crisp linen, making this a must for those in search of a welcoming billet close to the mountains. There are framed photographs on the walls, the odd piece of mahogany furniture, good books, no TVs (unless you ask). Breakfast is served in the dining room; wallow with the papers and make your toast on the Aga. A road passes outside, quietly at night, lanes lead into the hills, and a small organic kitchen garden provides much for the table. The Beacons are close, so walk, ride, bike, canoe – or head to Hay for books galore.

Price	£115–£155. Singles from £80. Half-board from £82.50 p.p.
Rooms	7: 3 doubles, 2 twins/doubles, 2 four-posters.
Meals	Lunch from £18.50. Dinner £27.50. Sunday lunch, 3 courses, £23.50.
Closed	Christmas Day & Christmas Eve (night). 4 days in Jan.
Directions	From Brecon A470 north to Felin Fach (4.5 miles). On left.

Charles & Edmund Inkin, Julie Bell
Felin Fach,
Brecon LD3 0UB
Tel   +44 (0)1874 620111
Email   enquiries@felinfachgriffin.co.uk
Web   www.felinfachgriffin.co.uk

The Lake Country House & Spa

Deep in the silence of Wales, a country house intent on pampering you rotten. Fifty acres of lawns, lakes and ancient woodland sweep you clean of city cobwebs, and if that's not enough a spa has been added, with an indoor pool, treatment rooms and a tennis court by the lake. Sit in a hot tub and watch guests fish for their supper, try your luck on the nine-hole golf course, saddle up nearby and take to the hills. Come home to afternoon tea in the drawing room, where an archipelago of rugs warms a brightly polished wooden floor and chandeliers hang from the ceiling. The hotel opened over a hundred years ago and the leather-bound fishing logs go back to 1894. A feel of the 1920s lingers. Fires come to life in front of your eyes, grand pianos and grandfather clocks sing their songs, snooker balls crash about in the distance. Dress for a delicious dinner – the atmosphere deserves it – then retire to cosseting bedrooms. Most are suites: those in the house are warmly traditional, those in the lodge are softly contemporary. The London train takes four hours and stops in the village. Resident geese waddle. Marvellous.

Price	£195. Suites £240-£260. Singles from £145. Half-board from £122.50 p.p.
Rooms	30: 6 twins/doubles, 12 suites. Lodge: 12 suites.
Meals	Lunch, 3 courses, £22.50. Dinner, 4 courses, £38.50.
Closed	Never.
Directions	From Builth Wells A483 west for 7 miles to Garth. Signed from village.

Jean-Pierre Mifsud
Llangammarch Wells LD4 4BS
Tel   +44 (0)1591 620202
Email   info@lakecountryhouse.co.uk
Web   www.lakecountryhouse.co.uk

Milebrook House Hotel

An old-school country hotel with three acres of fabulous gardens that run down to the river Teme. You'll find Wales on one bank and England on the other, so bring your wellies and wade across; the walking is magnificent. The house, once home to writer Wilfred Thesiger, is run in informal style by three generations of the Marsden family with Beryl and Rodney leading the way. Step inside and enter a world that's rooted in a delightful past: clocks tick, cats snooze, fires crackle, the odd champagne cork escapes its bondage. Beautiful art hangs on the walls, the sitting room is stuffed with books, the bar comes in country-house style and there's food to reckon with in the wonderful dining room – perhaps Cornish scallops with a pea purée, rack of Welsh lamb with dauphinoise potatoes, ginger crème brûlée with poached rhubarb. A kitchen garden supplies much for the table, you can fish for trout, spot deer in the woods, play croquet on the lawn. Red kite, moorhens, kingfishers and herons live in the valley. Homely bedrooms are more than comfortable, so don't delay. *Minimum stay two nights at weekends.*

Price	£115–£127.50. Singles from £74. Half-board (min. 2 nights) from £80 p.p. Children over 8 welcome.
Rooms	10: 5 doubles, 4 twins, 1 family room.
Meals	Lunch, 2 courses, £14.95 (not Mon). Dinner, 3 courses, £32.95.
Closed	Never.
Directions	From Ludlow A49 north, then left at Bromfield on A4113 towards Knighton for 10 miles. Hotel on right.

Rodney, Beryl & Joanne Marsden
Stanage, Knighton LD7 1LT
Tel   +44 (0)1547 528632
Email   hotel@milebrookhouse.co.uk
Web   www.milebrookhouse.co.uk

Lake Vyrnwy Hotel & Spa

Wedged into the mountains of mid-Wales, Lake Vyrnwy shimmers under forest and sky, lost to the world and without great need of it. The position here is faultless, a tonic for the soul, a great spot to shake off the city. The hotel sits high on the hill with stupendous views of lake and mountain stretching five miles north; the sofa in the drawing room (grand piano, roaring fire) must qualify as one of the loveliest places to sit in Wales. The view follows you around wherever you go – even into the spa where the spa pool and sauna look the right way (there are treatment rooms, too). Bedrooms, most with lake views, have a country-house feel. Some are seriously grand, others snug in the eaves, many have balconies, in one you can soak in a claw-foot bath while gazing down the lake. Elsewhere, a terraced bar, a country pub, and walls of glass in a super restaurant, so come for smoked salmon, local lamb, baked chocolate cheesecake. Outside, pheasants roam, sheep graze on mountain pastures, there's a tennis court if you want to play and fish to coax from the lake.

Price	£131–£236. Singles from £106. Half-board from £96 p.p.
Rooms	52: 42 twins/doubles, 7 four-posters, 1 suite, 2 singles.
Meals	Lunch & bar meals from £8.50. Dinner, 5 courses, £39.95.
Closed	Rarely.
Directions	A490 from Welshpool; B4393 to Lake Vyrnwy. Brown signs from A5 at Shrewsbury as well.

The Bisiker Family
Llanwddyn,
Oswestry SY10 0LY

Tel	+44 (0)1691 870692
Email	info@lakevyrnwyhotel.co.uk
Web	www.lakevyrnwy.com

Fairyhill

The Gower Peninsula has legions of fans who come for its glorious heathland, its rugged coastline and some of the best beaches in the country. Fairyhill is bang in the middle of it all, a sublime country house wrapped up in 24 acres of blissful silence. There's a terrace for lunch, a stream-fed lake, an ancient orchard, a walled garden with vegetable beds and herbs. Inside, country-house interiors come fully loaded with warmth and colour. You'll find an open fire in the bar, a grand piano in the sitting room and super local food in the restaurant, where as much as possible comes from Gower. So tuck into confit of duck and pistachio terrine, local sea bass with scallops and green beans, then apple and tarragon tart with ice cream. Most bedrooms are big and fancy, a couple are small, but sweet. Some have painted beams, others have golden wallpaper, all have robes in excellent bathrooms. Mattresses are Vi-Spring, but if that's not enough there's a treatment room, so book a massage. There's croquet on the lawn in summer, while duck eggs come courtesy of resident Muscovys. *Minimum stay two nights on Saturdays.*

Price	£180–£280. Singles from £160. Half-board from £125 p.p.
Rooms	8: 3 doubles, 5 twins/doubles.
Meals	Lunch from £20. Dinner £35–£45.
Closed	First 3 weeks in January.
Directions	M4 junc. 47, A483 south, then A484 west to Gowerton and B4295 for Llanrhidian. Through Oldwalls, 1 mile up on left.

Andrew Hetherington & Paul Davies
Reynoldston,
Swansea SA3 1BS

Tel	+44 (0)1792 390139
Email	postbox@fairyhill.net
Web	www.fairyhill.net

Quick reference indices

Wheelchair–accessible
At least one bedroom and bathroom accessible for wheelchair users.

Event hire
The whole building can be hired for an event.

Weddings
You can get married at
these places.

Quick reference indices

Quick reference indices

Scotland

Wales

Singles
Single room OR rooms let
to single guests for half the
double room rate, or under.

Channel Islands

England

Music
Places where there is a sound system in all bedrooms.

Quick reference indices

For many years Alastair Sawday Publishing has been 'greening' the business in different ways. Our aim is to reduce our environmental footprint as far as possible and with almost everything we do we have environmental implications in mind. In recognition of our efforts we won a Business Commitment to the Environment Award in 2005, a Queen's Award for Enterprise in the Sustainable Development category in 2006, and the Independent Publishers Guild Environmental Award in 2008.

The buildings

Beautiful as they were, our old offices leaked heat, used electricity to heat water and rooms, flooded spaces with light to illuminate one person, and were not ours to alter.

So in 2005 we created our own eco offices by converting some old barns to create a low-emissions building. Heating and

Photo left: Tom Germain
Photo right: Jackie King

lighting the building, which houses over 30 employees, now produces only 0.28 tonnes of carbon dioxide per year – a reduction of 35%. Not bad when you compare this with the six tonnes emitted by the average UK household. We achieved this through a variety of innovative and energy-saving building techniques, some of which are described below.

Insulation By laying insulating board 90mm thick immediately under the roof tiles and on the floor, and lining the inside of the building with plastic sheeting, we are now insulated even for Arctic weather, and almost totally air-tight.

Heating We installed a wood pellet boiler from Austria in order to be largely fossil-fuel free. The heat is conveyed by water to all corners of the building via an underfloor system.

Water We installed a 6,000-litre tank to collect rainwater from the roofs. This is pumped back, via an ultra-violet filter, to lavatories, shower and basins. There are also two solar thermal panels on the roof providing heat to the one hot-water cylinder.

Lighting We have a mix of low-energy lighting – task lighting and up lighting – and have installed three sun pipes.

Electricity Our electricity has long come from the Good Energy Company and is 100% renewable.

Materials Virtually all materials are non-toxic or natural, and our carpets are made from (80%) Herdwick sheep wool from National Trust farms in the Lake District.

Doors and windows Outside doors and new windows are wooden, double-glazed and beautifully constructed in Norway. Old windows have been double-glazed.

More greenery

Besides having a building we are proud of, and which is pretty impressive visually, too, we work in a number of other ways to reduce the company's overall environmental footprint.

- office travel is logged as part of a carbon sequestration programme, and money for compensatory tree planting donated to SCAD in India for a tree-planting and development project

- we avoid flying and take the train for business trips wherever possible
- car sharing and the use of a company pool car are part of company policy, with recycled cooking oil used in one car and LPG in the other
- organic and Fair Trade basic provisions are used in the staff kitchen and organic and/or local food is provided by the company at all in-house events
- green cleaning products are used throughout
- kitchen waste is composted on our allotment
- the allotment is part of a community garden – alongside which we keep a small family of pigs and hens

However, becoming 'green' is a journey and, although we began long before most companies, we realise we still have a long way to go.

Photo: Cavendish Hotel, entry 67

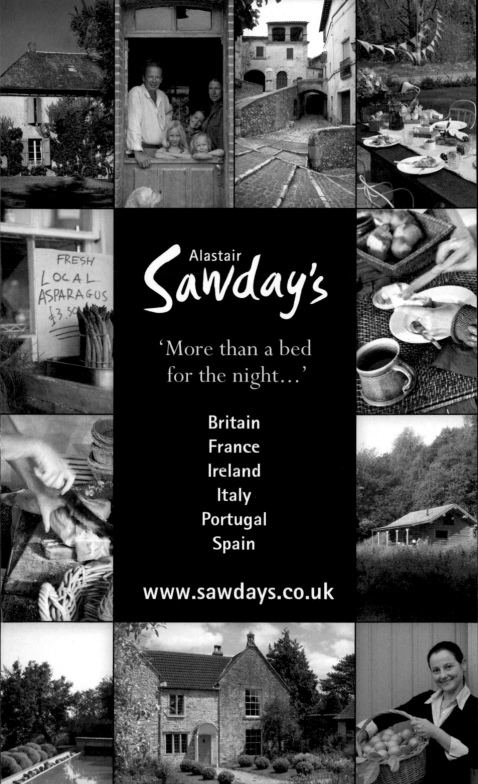

We have indexed places under their MAIN postal town. See maps for clear positioning.

① Cambridgeshire   Hotel ②

③ **The Old Bridge Hotel**

④ A smart hotel, the best in town, one which inspired the founders of Hotel du Vin. A battalion of devoted locals come for the food (delicious), the wines (exceptional) and the hugely comfortable interiors. Ladies lunch, business men chatter, kind staff weave through the throng. You can eat wherever you want: in the muralled restaurant; from a sofa in the lounge; or sitting in a winged armchair in front of the fire in the bar. You feast on anything from homemade soups to rack of lamb (starters are available all day), while breakfast is served in a panelled morning room with Buddha in the fireplace. Beautiful bedrooms are scattered about. Expect warm colours, fine fabrics, padded bedheads, crisp linen. One has a mirrored four-poster, several have vast bathrooms, others overlook the river Ouse, all have spoiling extras: Bose iPod docks, Bang & Olufsen TVs, power showers and bathrobes. Finally, John, a Master of Wine, has an irresistible wine shop opposite reception, so expect to take something home with you. The A14 may pass to the back, but it doesn't matter a jot.

Price	£140–£230. Singles from £89. Half-board £95–£125 p.p.	⑤
Rooms	24: 13 doubles, 1 twin, 7 singles, 3 four-posters.	⑥
Meals	Lunch & dinner £5–£35.	⑦
Closed	Never.	⑧
Directions	A1, then A14 into Huntingdon. Hotel on southwest flank of one-way system that circles town.	⑨

Nina Beamond
1 High Street,
Huntingdon PE29 3TQ
Tel   +44 (0)1480 424300
Email   oldbridge@huntsbridge.co.uk
Web   www.huntsbridge.com

⑪ Entry 14   Map 3   ⑩